TALES FROM THE PUMP ROOM

TALES FROM THE PUMP ROOM

*Nine Hundred Years of Bath:
the Place, its People and its Gossip*

by

THOMAS HINDE

LONDON
VICTOR GOLLANCZ LTD
1988

First published in Great Britain 1988
by Victor Gollancz Ltd,
14 Henrietta Street, London WC2E 8QJ

© Thomas Hinde 1987

British Library Cataloguing in Publication Data
Hinde, Thomas
 Tales from the Pump Room: nine hundred
 years of Bath, the place, its people and
 its gossip.
 1. Bath (Avon)—Social life and customs
 Rn: Sir Thomas Willes Chitty   I. Title
 942.3'98   DA690.B3

ISBN 0-575-03965-5
ISBN 0-575-04193-5 Pbk

Typeset in Great Britain by Centracet
and printed and bound in Great Britain by
Biddles Ltd, Guildford and King's Lynn

CONTENTS

ILLUSTRATIONS

First section of plates

A *View of the Parade at Bath c.* 1781.
Front of the Pump Room in the City of Bath. Engraving *c.*
1765.
Richard Beau Nash *c.* 1761.
Miss Murray.
Her Royal Highness, Princess Amelia.
A view of the Theatre Royal, Bath, as it appeared at the royal
dramatic fête in honour of His Majesty's birthday, 28th April
1824.
The Grand Pump Room, 1841.

Second section of plates

Prior Park, Bath.
The Upper Rooms (the Grand Ball Room) referred to in Jane
Austen's novel *Persuasion*.
Hester Lynch Piozzi, formerly Mrs Thrale, friend of Dr
Johnson, by George Dance, 1793.
Louisa, Countess Craven.
"A Peep at the Fancy". Theatre Royal, 23rd April 1824.
A View of King's Bath *c.* 1800.
Portrait of the actress Mrs Siddons by Gainsborough.

AUTHOR'S INTRODUCTION

No city in Britain has a history like Bath's. Others have exploited their mineral waters – Bristol, Buxton and Tunbridge Wells for example – and many have been holiday resorts, but none of them was ever the country's alternative capital – a kind of English Simla. For almost one hundred years in the eighteenth century, Bath was a place to which a large part of society came annually, and just about everybody who was anybody visited at least once.

Strictly speaking, Bath has had two great periods, the first being in Roman times. The remains of Roman Bath can today be seen more clearly than ever before: its great bathing complex, which makes the eighteenth-century baths look like the work of savages, and its nearby temple to the goddess Minerva. All of these lie some ten to twenty feet below the modern city, and much more could certainly be uncovered. Bath was a Roman spa for several hundred years, between the first and fourth centuries AD.

The city's second great period can be dated more precisely: 1705 to about 1790. In 1705 Richard 'Beau' Nash arrived in Bath, and it was Nash more than anyone who made the place both fashionable and safe. Around 1790 sea bathing became popular and seaside holidays began to replace visits to inland spas. Bath's subsequent decline was not immediate, indeed today's Pump Room was opened only in 1795, but from then onwards the best that was hoped for the city was that it would retain something of its past prestige and prosperity.

If one excepts war, gossip is probably the most important bond uniting the members of any community. For a community mainly concerned with amusing itself, which had too much time in which there was too little to do, gossip was not just socially valuable but an essential defence against boredom. At each of the social events which so precisely punctuated a Bath day, from early-morning dip in the waters to evening ball at the Assembly Rooms, its visitors and residents gossiped. But the Pump Room, where they gathered after bathing and before breakfasting, acquired a particular reputation as a place where rumour flourished and scandal was spread.

Bath's eighteenth-century Pump Room is the imaginary setting for the telling of my own tales of Bath which form the first two parts of this book: those of the time, and those of earlier times – about which so little was then known. For tales of later times I have necessarily moved forward and put myself, as it were, in the second Pump Room.

Much of Bath's talk was necessarily trivial, as Mrs Montagu confirmed when she wrote that during the morning all that could be heard was 'How d'ye do', and during the afternoon, 'What is trumps?' But much of it concerned the personalities and escapades of the time. I believe it was Brigid Brophy who once remarked 'Sex and the eighteenth century are the only two worthwhile subjects of conversation'. For anyone who shares this view Bath is essential. Just as Bath was a product of the eighteenth century, so the eighteenth century without Bath would be like a painting with a large hole in the canvas.

Apart from knowing so little of the Roman and mediaeval history of their city, the fashionable of eighteenth-century Bath were as prone as other tellers of tales to fantasy, inaccuracy and embroidery. My aim has been to take the most interesting, amusing or scandalous personalities and events which they talked about and tell the – often equally astonishing – truth which lay behind them. For the reader who wishes to follow up the subject, I have described principal sources at the back of the book.

TALES FROM THE PUMP ROOM

PART ONE

Tales of the Past

Prince Bladud

Visitors to the Pump Room, from the time it first opened in 1706, have looked across the King's Bath to a niche in the far wall which holds the small seated statue of King Bladud. For at least the next century and a half many of them believed that Bladud, ancient King of Britain and father of King Lear, was the founder of Bath. In 1741 a number of the city's leading citizens appended to an account of the legend: 'We, whose names are hereunder written, natives of the city of Bath, having perused the above tradition, do think it very truthfully and faithfully related . . .' As late as 1864 the story was retold in a guide to Bath as if it was genuine history.

The earliest place it can be found is in the writings of the twelfth-century Welsh bishop and chronicler, Geoffrey of Monmouth. He merely says that, about the time of the prophet Elias, Bladud built Kaerbadus, now Bath, and made hot baths there for the benefit of the people. He adds that Bladud 'was a very ingenious man' who taught and practised magic in his kingdom until he tried to fly with some wings he had made, but 'fell on to the temple of Apollo, in the city of Trinovantum, where he was dashed to pieces'.

Well before 1706, Geoffrey's story had been improved to make the one which eighteenth- and nineteenth-century citizens knew: Bladud, when still a prince, had contracted leprosy and been banished from the court of his father, Lud Hudibras. To survive he became a swineherd, but his swine also caught leprosy. When herding them in a remote part of Somerset, near Keynsham, he saw them wallow in some hot springs on a river bank and emerge cured. He, too, wallowed and was cured. Restored to royal favour, he spent the next eleven years in Athens studying magic, mathematics and philosophy, but returned to Britain to inherit his throne. It was then that he made the baths at Bath, a palace nearby, and a city around it which became his capital. The legend gave Bath's foundation a precise date: 863 BC.

An eighteenth-century ballad completed the story of the pigs. Bladud, it suggests, was annoyed at their privileged cure and drove them away:

> The hogs, thus banished by the Prince,
> Have lived at Bristol ever since.

Bladud's statue beside the King's Bath was erected in 1699.

Mediaeval Bath

A monastery was founded at Bath around AD 670, and a small church built there. This was enlarged or replaced about a hundred years later by a more imposing one. It stood east of the present abbey, to the south of the Orange Grove. The prestige of Bath's Saxon church reached its peak on Whit Sunday, AD 973, when the Archbishops of Canterbury and York crowned King Edgar here. For the following hundred years, and throughout the reign of William the Conquerer, Bath and its monastery flourished.

The year after William's death, however, the barons of the West Country revolted against his son, William Rufus, and destroyed the city. When Rufus had crushed the rising he gave what remained of Bath's abbey to the man who became the city's new founder: John de Villula of Tours. Bishop John bought the rest of the city for 500 pounds of silver.

At Bath he planned a new abbey church so large (354 feet long) that the present abbey (210 feet long) occupies only the site of its nave. When he died thirty-four years later the building was still unfinished. He had, however, enclosed a park and founded a priory across the river from the city which later gave its name to Bath's great house, Prior Park. And – appropriately since he was also a physician – he had revived the use of the city's thermal springs. It was in his time that the King's Bath was built – on top of the buried walls of the reservoir which the Romans had built around the sacred spring.

This is clearly the bath which the *Gesta Stephani* (1138) described: 'Streams of water, warmed without human agency, and from the very bowels of the earth, rise into a receptacle beautifully constructed, with chambered arches. These form baths in the middle of the city, warm and wholesome, and charming to the eye. Sick persons resort thither to bathe in these healing waters.' The 'arches' had been set against the remains of the chamber which the Romans had built to enclose the spring and its reservoir.

Soon afterwards (*c.* 1180) St John's Hospital was founded in the city, and by the next century – as Geoffrey of Monmouth's story of Prince Bladud confirms – Bath's baths had acquired a reputation for curing 'leprosy' – a general term for skin diseases. For four hundred years, until the Dissolution, the abbey controlled the baths. But by the fifteenth century the monks of the abbey were notoriously worldly and Bishop John's great abbey church was 'ruined to its foundations'.[1] Then, between 1499 and 1514, Bishop Oliver King began to build the church which is, in essence, today's abbey. It was the last great English church to be built before the Reformation and, because of its many Perpendicular-style windows, it is sometimes known as the Lantern of England.

Whether or not Bishop Oliver also reformed the behaviour of the abbey's monks, they quickly reverted to earlier practices. At the time of the Dissolution Thomas Cromwell's agent reported that they were 'worse than any I have found yet both in buggerie and adulterie, some of them haveying ten women some eight, and the rest fewer'. John Leland, who came to Bath during the same period, once in 1533 and once in 1542, gave a better report of the bathing facilities. The Cross Bath was 'much frequented of people diseased with lepre, pokkes, scabbes and great aches, and is temperate and pleasant'.

Doctors of earlier times

The earliest of the doctors who began to make Bath famous as a health resort was William Turner, described as 'the father of English physicke'. He was a doctor to Lord Protector Somerset in Edward VI's reign (1547–53), and Dean of Wells. During Mary's five-year reign which followed, Turner was in exile, but he was Dean of Wells again for a while under Elizabeth. As well as a doctor he was a herbalist, and in his herbal (1562) he included 'A Booke of the nature and properties as well of the bathes in England as of other Baths in Germany and Italy'. His aim in describing the baths of Bath was 'to allure thyther as manye as have nede of suche helpe as almighty God hath granted it to gyve', and he addressed his book to his neighbours of 'Bath, Bristowe, Wellis, Wynsam and Charde'. Only ten years later John Jones, another physician, published the first book specifically about Bath: *The Bathes of Bathes Ayde*, which describes them as 'wonderful and most excellent agaynst very many sicknesses'.

Best known in the following century was Dr Edward Jordon (1569–1632). He had been trained in Padua and had practised in London, where James I employed him to examine a girl who claimed to be possessed – a phenomenon which interested the king. Jordon showed that the girl was a fake. Presently he moved to Bath where he lived in comparative poverty, having speculated unsuccessfully in the manufacture of alum and 'having children not a few'. One of his sons drowned in the King's Bath. 'He had the applause of the learned, the respect of the rich, the prayers of the poor, and the love of all. But, living a studious and sedentary life, which might encourage the two grand distempers, the stone and gout', he died aged sixty-three.

This was the description of Jordon by Dr Thomas Guidott, the most prolific of the Bath doctors in the later years of the seventeenth century. Guidott wrote an introduction to the third edition of Jordon's book, *A Discourse of Naturall Bathes and Mineral Waters . . . especially of our Bathes at Bathe* (1632). Guidott's own book, *A Discourse of the Bath* (1676), gives polite descriptions of some fifteen other Bath doctors, for example, John Vincent Ostendorph:

> Of this physician I can give no other account than that he was a German, and like field-fares and wind-thrushes did change his climate for better food, which he liked so well that he married one Mrs Cavell, sister to an ingenious limner of that name; and after some years practice, died and was buried in the Abbey-Church in Bath, the 12th day of April . . . 1648.

Guidott was not always polite, and lost much of his Bath practice in 1679 because of his 'impudence, lampooning and libeling'. He was a 'person of good parts, well versed in Greek and Latin learning, and intelligent in his profession; but so much overwhelmed with self-conceit and pride as to be in a manner sometimes crazed, especially when his blood was heated by too much bibbing'. Another of his works, *The Register of Bath*, gives the case-histories of two hundred Bath cures, for example:

> George Long of Downshead in the county of Somerset, Esquire, received great benefit in the year 1692, by bathing in the Cross Bath, and drinking the waters at the King's in arthritick distempers. He lost his grey hairs, and had new hair and nails, which is attributed to the Bath, and is a singular instance.

Guidott does not mention Dr Robert Peirce, perhaps because he was still alive, perhaps because the two doctors disliked each other. Peirce, in his own book on Bath's waters, wrote, 'And here by the way it may be observed, that these waters were thus drunk long before Mr Guidott came to Bath, or ever saw it, though he arrogates to himself the drinking of them.'

Peirce came to Bath in 1653 for the good of his own health, and gradually expanded his practice by taking on work which other doctors would not do. 'I was often desired by them,' he wrote, 'to go in their stead, to patients in the country, when they were hindered by a full Bath practice here, by which means in the process of time, I had the riding practice for ten or twenty, sometimes thirty miles about.'

He became a person of importance at Bath, living in the Abbey House, adjoining the King's Bath and the abbey, and in 1663 received Charles II and his court here. On this visit the King brought with him his own doctor, Sir Alexander Frayser. Frayser was impressed by Bath's waters, and corresponded with Peirce about them. He concluded that they were little different from the waters at Bourbon to which he had previously sent patients, and instead now began to send them to Bath. Eventually he returned himself with the Duke of Louthersdale. The duke was suffering from 'more than ordinary corpulency and scorbutical distempers', Frayser from 'an old cough, and cachectick habit of body'. 'Both went off much advantaged; the Duke loosing a large span of his girt.'[2] Frayser's improvement was not permanent; he died eight years later in 1681.

Peirce describes in detail the way in which the waters were drunk before pumps were installed (as they were at Frayser's

suggestion). Previously they had gushed up through 'a pyramidal stone, hollow in the middle, artificially placed over one
of the large springs' in the King's Bath. 'The strength of the
spring was so great that it forced itself up through the cavity of
the pyramidal stone. The water discharged itself at a copper
spout, and to this spout some set their mouths and drank;
others put cups.'

Early royal visitors

'People of distinction', to use the phrase Oliver Goldsmith
employs in his biography of Beau Nash, had begun to visit
Bath long before Nash made the city famous in the early
eighteenth century. Its many prosperous doctors prove that it
had already taken a lead over rival English spas. When Queen
Elizabeth, in 1574, made a royal progress through the West
Country, she included Bath on her return journey to Hampton
Court.

From Bristol she sent ahead a group of ten courtiers of
various grades to make preparations. The city prepared too,
spending 2s. on having its walls cleaned 'against the queen's
coming', 7s. 6d. on material for a new coat of 'black frize' for
the Bellman, and 4s. 4d. on reglazing the windows of Stalles
Church and St Michael's Church.[3] The Queen arrived on
Saturday 21 August and her entertainment for the day cost
£192 2s. 5¾d.

Next day, Sunday, it cost much the same – £181 13s. 6½d.,
plus 10s. for having the 'queresterer' brought from Wells to
sing for her in St Michael's Church. She left on Monday and
was back at Hampton Court by Wednesday. There is no record
of her bathing at Bath or drinking its waters.

In the next reign, James I's Queen, Anne of Denmark, made
three visits to Bath for her dropsy. During these a lady of Bath
named Mary Permay was appointed to be her servant and
gentlewoman. The people of the city called her 'Muddy Moll'
and invented a tavern song about her which was 'soe obscenous
and fowle as it is not fytt herein to be wrytten or remembred,
neyther is the same fyttinge or decente for any modest eyes to
reade or eares to heare'.[4]

Whether or not the waters cured the Queen's dropsy is not

known, but she did have a terrifying experience which produced an important change in the city's bathing arrangements. 'As the Queen was bathing in the King's Bath, there arose from the bottom of the cistern just by the side of her Majesty a flame of fire like a candle, which had no sooner ascended to the top of the water than it spent itself upon the surface into a large circle of light, and then became extinct. This so frightened the Queen, that notwithstanding the physicians assured her the light proceded from a natural cause, yet she would bathe no more in the King's Bath, but betook herself to the New Bath, where there were no springs to cause the like phenomenon; and from thence the cistern was called the Queen's Bath. It was soon enlarged, and the citizens erecting a tower or cross in the middle of it, in honour of the Queen, finished it at the top with the figure of the Crown of England over a globe . . .'

Though Richard Warner in his history of Bath (1801) is the only authority for this incident, there is nothing intrinsically impossible about such a phenomenon, caused, like a will-o'-the-wisp, by a bubble of methane gas.

As Anne crossed Salisbury Plain on her first return from Bath she was intercepted by the Rev. George Fereby, who held a living in the area. He had taught his parishioners church music and asked permission for them to perform for the Queen. When she agreed, they emerged from a wild ravine, dressed as Druids and Ancient British shepherds and shepherdesses. She was so impressed by this ecumenical performance that she appointed Fereby to be one of her chaplains.

At the Restoration of 1660, Bath, whose citizens were frequently suspected of royalist sympathies, sent Charles II a loyal address. Three years later the king came there with his queen, Catherine of Braganza. The queen hoped that the waters would cure her sterility. 'The Queen's physicians, men of great prudence, sagacity and wisdom, as they always are, having duly weighed and considered that the cold waters of Tunbridge had not succeeded in the preceding year, concluded that it would be advisable for her to try the warm baths at Bristol. This journey was therefore fixed for the next season; and in the confidence of its proving effectual, this excursion would have afforded her much pleasure, if the most dangerous of her rivals had not been one of the first that was appointed to attend the court . . . Miss Stewart, more handsome than ever, was appointed for this excursion, and began to make magnificent preparations. The poor Queen durst say nothing against it, but all hopes of success immediately forsook her.'[5]

The royal party went to Bath, not Bristol, where they stayed with Dr Peirce at Abbey House which had a private door to the King's Bath; but the queen did not conceive, and no doubt Frances Stewart – the king's beautiful but stupid sixteen-year-old current mistress – contributed to the failure.

Charles visited Bath again in 1674, with both his earlier and still influential mistress, Barbara Villiers, Lady Castlemaine, and his most important later mistress, Louise Kérouaille, Duchess of Portsmouth. The Cross Bath was now the most fashionable, and this year a band played there to entertain the bathers. Those who were not entertained 'set up such a chorus' of complaint that, two years later, the corporation passed a by-law 'to stop the progress of vocal music'.[6]

James II's queen, Mary of Modena, like Charles II's, came to Bath to induce pregnancy. The result was not only different but produced political consequences that permanently affected English history. By this time she had had four sons, but since all of them had died English Protestants could comfort themselves that even if they had a Catholic king, at least he had no Catholic successor; for James's heir was Mary, the daughter of his previous wife, Anne Hyde. Mary was a Protestant and married to William, Prince of Orange.

The queen's Catholic advisers were of course well aware of the situation. Her chaplain, Ronchi, recommended the king and queen to drink at St Winifred's Well (a miraculous well at Sion Hill, now no longer in existence) and to go to Bath for its waters. A new royal child would, Ronchi wrote, 'be the most fitting antidote for extinguishing the heat which the Prince of Orange doth somewhat foment in the country'.

The queen arrived at Bath on 18 August 1687 and stayed there till early October. The king stayed at first for only three days, but returned for another brief visit in September. Nevertheless the queen became pregnant, and nine months later produced a son, James Stuart, who became the 'Old Pretender'.

Queen Mary had bathed in the Cross Bath. It already had a cross to give it its name, but a new one was erected in honour of the conception which it was believed to have caused. A more significant result of the queen's visit and conception, however, occurred later in the year of her new son's birth, when the Prince of Orange landed at Torbay and James II and his family fled, for ever, to France.

The battle of Lansdown Hill

The citizens of Bath who attended the ceremonial opening of the first Pump Room in 1706 would certainly have heard their parents talk about the battle of Lansdown Hill, and the older of them could even have been present. It had occurred just over sixty years earlier, in 1643, some four miles from Bath. It was one of the most dramatic battles of the English Civil War.

North of the city the ground rises steeply before levelling into the plateau which forms the top of Lansdown – where the racecourse was later to be established and William Beckford built his tower. Two miles beyond, the land drops even more steeply into the valley of a tributary of the River Boyd. It was along the top of this escarpment, on the morning of 5 July 1643, that the Parliamentarian general, Sir William Waller, drew up his troops. The position seemed impregnable and, to add to its strength, he 'raised breast-works with faggots and earth and placed cannon there'.

He had another advantage. Recently he had been reinforced from London with a troop of 500 horse, equipped with iron shields. The troop was described by the Royalists as 'the regiment of lobsters', but the shields gave such effective protection that the swords of the Royalist cavalry were useless.

During the manoeuvrings of the previous weeks, Waller had used Bath as his base and this, too, had been an advantage. The Royalists had no comparable base and, in order to find provisions in a countryside which was generally hostile, they were forced to disperse into separate parties. Now, however, they were assembled four miles beyond the Lansdown escarpment, at the industrial village of Marshfield. And in spite of the armoured Parliamentarian horse, they were full of 'unreasonable contempt'[7] for the enemy.

In command at Marshfield was Sir Ralph Hopton, described by the historian the Earl of Clarendon as 'the soldiers' darling'.[8] Supporting him with the Cornish contingent was Sir Bevil Grenvile who had done so much for Charles I's cause in Cornwall, including capturing Launceston. He was a man of great courage and good temper, and of such invariable optimism that 'no accident which happened could make any impression on him'.

The first move in the battle was made by the Royalists, who advanced to Freezing Hill, the rising ground which faced Lansdown Hill; but when they saw Waller's position they retired again towards Marshfield. To tempt them to attack, Waller sent his new cavalry after them and a fierce fight followed, in which the Royalist cavalry at first seemed totally routed, and the officers could not persuade their men to regroup. The Cornish musketeers were more effective, however, and when the cavalry did reassemble (those who had not fled to Oxford), the whole Parliamentarian force was driven back to Lansdown Hill.

Again Hopton was reluctant to attempt to take the hill, but Grenvile's Cornish troops were so keen that he eventually agreed to an assault. This took the form of attacks by musketeers on the two woods which flanked the Parliamentarian defences, and a direct attack up the hill with cavalry and more musketeers. The battle now reached a climax and, according to Richard Atkyns, a Royalist cavalry officer, 'the air was so darkened by the smoke of powder, that for a quarter of an hour together (I dare say) there was no light seen'.

The centre attack at first failed but Grenvile personally led a second assault and reached the brow of the hill. In the process he and his Cornishmen had beaten off two charges of the enemy's cavalry, but during a third 'he received, after other wounds, a blow on the head with a pole-axe, with which he fell, and many of his officers about him; yet the musketeers fired so fast upon the enemy's horse, that they quitted their ground, and the two wings, who were sent to clear the woods, having done their work, and gained those parts of the hill, at the same time beat off their enemy's foot, and became possessed of the breast-works; and so made way for their whole body of horse, foot, and cannon, to ascend the hill; which they quickly did, and planted themselves on the ground they had won'.[9]

The day's fighting had been so fierce that only 600 out of the 2000 Royalist cavalry survived, though others had by now reached Oxford, where they 'according to the custom of those who run away, reported all to be lost, with many particular accidents, which they fancied very like to happen when they ran away'.[10] The Parliamentarians had suffered equally severely. They had retreated to a second line of defence, half a cannon's shot away, and although at midnight they seemed about to make a counter-attack they then fell silent. Presently a Royalist scout reported that they had 'left lighted matches in the wall'[11] and abandoned their position.

When dawn came the Royalists, in spite of their losses, could have felt well satisfied that they had taken the hill, driven the enemy from the field of battle and captured a valuable quantity of munitions, including ten barrels of powder. Later that morning, however, the citizens of Bath – who had woken to find the defeated Parliamentarians back in the town – might have heard an enormous explosion from beyond the downs to the north. A waggon containing eight of the ten captured barrels of powder had exploded. Whether this was an accident or whether the waggon had been left as a booby trap has never been discovered; but the result was devastating. Many more Royalists were killed or wounded, and Sir Ralph Hopton, who had been riding past, was left with 'hardly so much life, as not to be numbered with the dead'.[12] Now equally discouraged, the Royalists also retreated from the hill they had won, and were presently besieged in Devizes, where Hopton, recovering from his wounds, directed the defence from his bed.

Today, at the place where Sir Bevil Grenvile fell, stands a monument to him, erected in 1720 by his grandson, George, Lord Lansdown. Almost one hundred years after the battle, in 1738, John Wood the elder built a house a quarter of a mile below the monument for the Bath surgeon, Jerry Peirce (probably a descendant of Robert Peirce) – first surgeon of Bath's General Hospital when William Oliver was its first physician. Jerry Peirce can be seen with Oliver in William Hoare's painting which now hangs in the hospital boardroom and shows the two men sitting at a table interviewing patients. The house which Wood designed for Peirce, fully described by Wood in his *Essay towards a Description of Bath*, was 21 feet square and built for strength, with stone from the hill above. This, Wood says, justified its name: Lilliput Castle.

One aspect of Lilliput Castle which Wood regretted was 'the hospitality of the builder' (presumably Jerry Peirce himself). This, Wood wrote, had 'twice brought our little castle . . . to the very brink of destruction'. Each time the kitchen fire had been made so fierce that it had set the chimney alight, and 'such a pillar of flame, smoke and burning soot' had 'surmounted poor *Lilliput* as was sufficient to have . . . kindled any other structure into one universal blaze'.

After Wood's time, it was perhaps another chimney fire which destroyed the castle. Certainly it has disappeared, though part of it may have been incorporated into Battle-Fields, the house which now stands on the site.

Pepys and his family visit 'the Bath'

'I am resolved to see the Bath and it may be Bristol,' Samuel Pepys (1633–1703) wrote in his diary on 11 June 1668. That day, after a bad experience at Wilton where he had been charged the 'exorbitant' sum of 7s. 6d. for bread and beer, and losing his way on Salisbury Plain in spite of a hired guide, he had reached Chitterne where the innkeeper had made room for Pepys and his wife by turning a pedlar out of his bed. 'Up, finding our beds good but we lousy,' Pepys wrote next morning, 'which made us merry.'

Presently the party reached Somerset, which was Mrs Pepys's native county and where Pepys was amused by the Somerset accent. He made the boys of Beckington recite the Lord's Prayer for his entertainment, and then kiss Deb, Mrs Pepys's companion. Before night they came to Bath and the same evening Pepys was shown the town by his landlord, including the baths where people were still bathing. 'They are not so large as I expected,' he wrote, 'but yet pleasant and the town most of stone and clean though the streets generally narrow.' This impartial description contradicts the sordid one given by John Wood, the architect in the following century – who was anxious, no doubt, to establish the superiority of the new city he was building.

Next morning Pepys, his wife and their companions were up at four o'clock and were carried one after another to the Cross Bath. They had hoped to be finished before it grew crowded, but soon came 'much company' including 'very fine ladies'. The ones who knew each other made 'good conversation', but 'methinks it cannot be clean to go so many bodies in to the same water'. Pepys stayed in for two hours – finding it too hot for his feet near the inlet – then he and his party were wrapped in sheets and carried home. Here he went to bed, sweating for an hour.

At eleven o'clock the same morning, after being entertained by some music 'extraordinary good as ever I heard in London', they set off for Bristol, where there were tearful reunions between Deb (who was born there) and her relations. Deb's uncle feasted them on strawberries, venison cold pasty, 'and plenty of brave wine and above all Bristoll milk'. By ten o'clock that night they were back in Bath.

Next day Pepys went to church in the abbey where he noticed two men in litters brought to hear the service, and listened to 'a vain pragmatic fellow' preach a 'ridiculous sermon . . . that made me angry'. In the evening he heard 'the same idle fellow' preach again, but 'slept through most of the sermon'.

On his final day at Bath he went again to see the King's and Queen's baths which were 'full of a mixed sort of good and bad and the Cross only almost for gentry'. Before setting out for London he tipped a boy a shilling to dive for him in the King's Bath.

Queen Anne makes Bath fashionable

Although Bath had been well known and considerably visited for its healing waters during the sixteenth and seventeenth centuries, Queen Anne's visits, after she succeeded to the throne in 1702, were the immediate cause of the city's promotion to the country's summer capital. The people of England, as Oliver Goldsmith explained, wanted 'some place where they might have each other's company, and win each other's money, as they had done during the winter in town'. Previously, because the pleasures of places like Bath, Tunbridge and Scarborough had been 'merely rural' and the company there 'splenetic, rustic and vulgar', they had been forced to go abroad to game at places like Aix and The Hague. 'By the arrival of Queen Anne there for her health', Goldsmith continued, 'Bath became in some measure frequented by people of distinction.' It was three years later that Nash came to Bath to make it respectable and safe as well as a gaming resort.

Anne had first visited Bath in 1688 to avoid being in London when her step-mother, Queen Mary of Modena, was due to have the child she had conceived at Bath, James, the 'Old Pretender'. As soon as Anne returned to London she showed how she might use her absence from her step-mother's lying-in to spread suspicion about her new half-brother, who now had a superior claim to the throne. 'My dear sister,' Anne wrote to Mary, wife of the Prince of Orange, 'can't imagine the concern and vexation I have been in, that I should be so unfortunate to be out of town when the Queen was brought to bed, for I shall never now be satisfied whether the child be true or false. It may be it is our brother, but God knows . . .'

Anne returned to Bath in 1692, bringing her husband, Prince George of Denmark, and also her close friend and Lady-in-Waiting, Sarah Churchill, the future Duchess of Marlborough. At this time Anne was quarrelling with her sister Mary, now Queen Mary, and her brother-in-law, William III. The queen took offence at the attention paid by the civic authorities to her sister, and ordered her secretary-of-state to reprove them. He wrote to the Mayor of Bath:

> Sir, – The Queen has been informed that yourself and your brethren have attended the Princess with the same respect and ceremony as have been usually paid to the Royal family. Perhaps you may not have heard what occasion her Majesty has had to be displeased with the Princess; and therefore I am commanded to acquaint you, that you are not for the future to pay her Highness any such respect or ceremony, without leave from her majesty . . .

The Bath corporation, after taking legal advice, told the princess what had happened and she graciously agreed not to be offended when they ceased to give her ceremonial treatment. Sarah Churchill was not so gracious. Anne, writing to her in the way she regularly did, as if from 'Mrs Morley' to 'Mrs Freeman', said that she thought Mrs Freeman had 'looked tonight as if she had the spleen' after the Mayor had 'failed in the ceremony of going to church with me'. 'I hope these foolish things *they* do,' Anne continued, referring to the king and queen, 'will every day show more and more what *they* are, and that *they* truly deserve the name your faithful Morley has given them' – a reference to Anne's name for the king: Caliban.

When Anne became queen the corporation of Bath hurried to make amends for the slight they had done her, and at once asked her to revisit the city. She came that same year, 1702, again accompanied by Prince George who suffered from asthma, and was met at the Somerset border by a hundred young men of Bath, uniformed and armed, and two hundred young women, dressed as Amazons, who escorted her from the top of Lansdown by a specially made road to the city's West Gate.

Anne's visit to Bath 'brought such a concourse of people to the city, for the use and benefit of the hot waters, that the drinking pumps could not supply them; all the neighbouring villages were filled with people of rank and fortune that flocked to Bath for health, for pleasure, or for any other purpose; and lodgings were then so scarce, that many were obliged to pay a guinea a night for their beds'.[13]

On her return from this visit the queen passed the royal forest of Wolmer in Hampshire where, according to a story told by an old keeper to Gilbert White, who related it in *The Natural History of Selborne*: 'she came out of the great road at Lippock [Liphook] which is just by, and reposing herself on a bank smoothed for that purpose, lying about half a mile to the east of Wolmer Pond, and still called Queen's bank, saw with great complacency and satisfaction the whole herd of red deer brought by the keepers along the vale before her, consisting then of about five hundred head. A sight this, worthy the attention of the greatest sovereign.'

According to the Duchess of Marlborough, it was on one of Queen Anne's visits to Bath that she fell fatally under the influence of Abigail Hill, the Woman of the Bedchamber who was to become her next favourite and to supplant the duchess.

For the health of Prince George, who suffered from dropsy and gout as well as asthma, Anne continued to patronise Bath, and they visited the city a final time in 1708, but Prince George died soon afterwards. The Duchess of Marlborough commented bitchily on the fact that the queen asked to have a door taken down at Windsor so that the prince's body should not be shaken as it was carried out to be buried, for she remembered how Anne had taken the prince on 'long rumbling journeys to the Bath . . . when he was gasping for breath'.

PART TWO

Tales of the Great Days

THE FOUNDERS

Captain Webster, King of Bath

The tradition of electing a King of Bath is said to go back to King Edgar, who was crowned in Bath Abbey in AD 973; but the 'King of Bath' who took the first essential steps in turning the city into the country's summer capital reigned some seven hundred years later. He was a certain Captain Webster.

Little is known of Webster except that he 'had a thirst for gaming and introduced it to a great degree'. Society had begun to come to Bath in the seventeenth century for its health, but from the early 1700s it came in far larger numbers to find a summer gambling place.

Writing in 1771, F. Fleming, a Bath musician, author of *Life and Extraordinary Adventures . . . of Timothy Grinnadrake*, who knew many of the city's traditions, added that the Duke of B——t (Beaufort), whose seat was fourteen miles away at Badminton, had been Webster's immediate predecessor and had already done something to organise Bath's social life. Before Beaufort's time there had been 'neither ball-room or places of amusement. When a party was made to dance, they repaired to the Bowling-green, open and exposed to the weather.' Beaufort 'took upon himself to conduct the company to the Town Hall. Ten couples at that time was thought to be a great assembly.'

Webster, now also appointed 'Master of Ceremonies' of Bath, not only gave the city its gaming reputation, but befriended the young Richard (Beau) Nash when he arrived there in 1705. It was this friendship even more than the promotion of gaming which made Bath the place it became. Webster was 'a man of spirit and address', Flemming wrote – qualities which led directly to his death. One night soon after Nash's arrival Webster was accused of cheating at the gaming table. He and his accuser fought with swords in the Grove (now the Orange Grove). Webster was killed and Nash succeeded him.

Beau Nash

Richard Nash (1674–1761), nicknamed 'Beau' for his refined dress and manners, was for fifty-six years Master of Ceremonies at Bath and, as such, principally responsible for making it the most fashionable provincial city in England during the eighteenth century. He was a Welshman, born in Swansea, the son of a bottle manufacturer. Though he rarely mentioned his father, he once explained to the Duchess of Marlborough that it was 'not because I have any reason to be ashamed of him; but because he has some reason to be ashamed of me'. This anecdote, like many others, comes from the biography of Nash published by the poet and playwright, Oliver Goldsmith, in 1762, the year after Nash's death.

Nash's father was sufficiently hopeful about his son to spend money he could hardly afford on sending him to Jesus College, Oxford. Here, however, Nash showed more 'genius' than 'industry', and before he was seventeen became engaged to one of the girls to be found around universities of the time, of 'some beauty, some coquettry, and little fortune' who would 'lie upon the watch for every raw amorous youth, more inclined to make love than to study'.[1] Nash's tutors discovered the engagement and he was sent home to his father.

Nash next tried the army, but gave this up when he found that it paid him too little and that it required him to spend time soldiering as well as wearing a red coat. Instead he moved to London and became a law student at the Middle Temple. Again other interests distracted him. In a systematic effort to impress the rich and titled, he wore fine clothes and lived beyond his means, becoming the sort of person who would 'spend more in chair hire, than house-keeping; and prefer a bow from a lord to a dinner from a commoner'.[2]

He was successful enough for his friends to name him 'the count' and for his Inn to choose him to stage a pageant for William III. The king was so well impressed that he offered Nash a knighthood. Nash declined, unless he could be made a knight of Windsor 'and then I shall have a fortune, at least able to support my title'.[3] William did not repeat the offer, and the future 'King of Bath' remained a commoner for the rest of his life.

Though Nash in these London years promoted himself in a

calculating way, he was a likeable and generous man. In an
expense claim to his masters at the Temple he included '£10 for
making one man happy'. He had heard a poor man with a large
family say that this amount would make him happy, Nash
explained to his masters, and 'could not avoid trying the
experiment'.[4] The masters were impressed and doubled the
sum.

On another occasion a friend, who could never collect a debt
of £20 from Nash (Nash claimed he was broke, 'stripped by the
billiard room'), sent a second friend to ask Nash for a loan of
£20. Nash obliged, so enabling the second friend to pay Nash's
debt to the first. 'Perdition seize thee,' Nash cried when told
what had happened, 'thou hast been too many for me.'[5]

When genuinely poor, Nash would make money by betting
on his own outrageous behaviour. On one occasion he won £50
by standing outside York Minster dressed only in a blanket.
'Penance . . . for keeping bad company,'[6] he told the Dean,
who recognised him. Another time he rode through a village
naked, mounted on a cow.

A visit to friends on a warship led to a less contrived
adventure. On board he fell into a drunken stupor, and, when
he woke, discovered himself at sea, on his way to the Mediterranean. Here his ship was in action, his friend was killed by his
side and he himself wounded in the leg. At Bath, Nash would
often tell this story, which he gradually improved. In Wiltshire's
Assembly Room one day a 'lady of distinction' said she believed
none of it. 'If I may not be believed,' Nash told her, 'your
ladyship may, if you please . . . feel the ball in my leg'.[7]

To support his life of pleasure and gaming, Nash courted a
certain Miss Verdun, daughter of a *nouveau-riche* Londoner. The
father approved of Nash and pressed the girl to marry him. But
when Nash discovered that she was in love with someone else
he not only withdrew but brought the girl and her lover
together and gave her the money which she would have had
from her father, so shaming him into forgiving her. Her
marriage was not a success, and within six months she had
eloped with her own footman. This was the story which
inspired the young architect, John Vanbrugh, to write *The
Relapse* (1696), and establish himself as a dramatist.

Nash was more successful with other young ladies. When
friends concluded that his extravagant way of life could not

possibly be supported by gaming and accused him of robbery or purse-snatching he produced love letters from twenty girls, including a recent one which enclosed a £50 note.

By 1705 Nash was tired of London and that summer he visited Bath. It was the move which made him famous and, for many years, rich. In his first season of gaming there he made £1000, and it was this which so impressed Captain Webster that Webster made him his gentleman-in-waiting. Soon afterwards, when Webster was killed, the corporation appointed Nash to succeed him as Master of Ceremonies and the citizens elected him 'King'.

Nash was lucky. His own passion – gaming – was the passion of the English upper classes of the time, and these classes turned out to be looking for a place in the country where they could continue to game during the summer, as they gamed in London in winter. But Nash was clever to choose Bath, already known for its waters and still better known since Queen Anne's visits of 1702 and 1703. And he was skilful in turning Bath into a place where the upper classes felt they could be fashionable and safe as well as modestly wicked.

To make Bath fashionable he forced visitors to dress well. Men's boots and ladies' white aprons he particularly disliked because of their rustic associations. If he met a man in one of Bath's public rooms wearing boots he would bow to him 'in an arch manner and tell him that he had forgotten his horse'. When he saw the Duchess of Queensberry at a ball wearing a white apron he stripped it from her and tossed it to her lady's-maids. But he was so respected that 'the good-natured duchess'[8] did not object.

To make Bath safe he ordered all balls to end punctually at 11pm, and regulated them meticulously, like everything else at Bath. 'The ball is commonly opened with a minuet,' John Wood, the architect, wrote, 'danced by two persons of the highest distinction at it, the whole assembly becoming still and quiet at the dancers first standing up, and generally shining with a real splendour, perhaps, equal to that of the most brilliant court of Europe.' After about two hours 'the country dances begin, ladies of quality, according to their rank, standing up first. About nine o'clock the gentlemen treat their partners with tea; and when that is over, the company pursue their diversion till the moment comes for the closing of the ball: then the king of the assembly, entering the ball room, orders the music to cease; and the ladies thereupon seating themselves till they grow cool, their partners compleat the ceremonies of the evening by handing them to the chairs in which they are to be convey'd to their respective lodgings.'

The Master of Ceremonies also regulated the behaviour of Bath's sedan-chair men, and encouraged the corporation to spend money on new pavements and street lights; and he persuaded a Bath citizen, Thomas Harrison, to build an Assembly Room.

Eventually (1742) 'Beau' Nash posted in the new Pump Room (built about 1705), and in Bath's other public rooms, a list of eleven rules for good behaviour, covering everything from costume to gossip. Nash would describe his pen as 'his torpedo; whenever he gripped it, it numbed his faculties';[9] his rules are curiously expressed but suggest that he was trying to soften with humour instructions which were meant seriously. For example:

'4. That no person take it ill that any one goes to another's play, or breakfast, and not theirs; —— except captious by nature . . .

'8. That the elder ladies and children be content with a second bench at the ball, as being past or not come to perfection.'

Gaming quarrels remained a danger. To prevent gamblers from doing 'what they had no mind to'[10] he tried, at first without much success, to forbid the carrying of swords. But the much-discussed torch-light duel between Taylor and Clarke (see page 99) helped to convince the people of Bath that he was right, and, after this, if he heard of a proposed duel he would arrest both parties.

Though Nash lived by gaming, his attitude to it was ambiguous; he knew the personal tragedies it caused and would often try to dissuade or reform addicts. From one young lord he won the whole of his estate and as a final stake 'his very equipage'.[11] He then returned everything, asking only the promise of £5000 if he ever needed it. Whether he ever claimed this is not known; but when he heard of people in distress he would organise collections for them, raising £200 and procuring a better living for one poor clergyman with six children whose clothes were so worn out that he called him Dr Cullender. When it grew fashionable for ladies to game, he took a particular interest in the misfortunes of Fanny Braddock, whose gaming losses drove her to commit suicide by hanging herself from the door of her bedroom cupboard (see page 101). Summing up Nash's character, Goldsmith says that he was too 'constitutionally passionate and generous' ever to make a fortune by gaming, and his decline into poverty suggests that this was true.

During the years of his success his later misfortunes seemed impossible. He would spend his time in the best company, wearing a costume which made him seem 'a beau of several generations',[12] mixing the fashions of the last age with those of the present. It always included a white hat, which he excused by saying that he had to wear it or it might be stolen. When he visited Tunbridge Wells, where he also had interests, he drove in a carriage pulled by six grey horses, surrounded by outriders, footmen and French horn players.

As a lover he was also successful, although 'his person was clumsy, too large and awkward, and his features harsh, strong and peculiarly irregular'. His statue in today's Pump Room and the painting of him in an adjoining room, with double chin and piggy eyes, confirm this description. But he would work on his own principle, that 'wit, flattery, and fine clothes' were 'enough to debauch a nunnery'. In apparent contradiction, he compared lovers of Charles II's reign (who would visit their mistresses in state and even take snuff with a flourish) and those of the last years of Anne's reign (who would be forever laughing at their own ridiculous situations) with those of Hanoverian times, who knew that 'the only way to make love now was to take no manner of notice of the lady'.[13] For many years his mistress was Fanny Murray who was also at one time mistress of the notorious fifth Earl of Sandwich, inventor of the beef sandwich.

Nash's career as Bath's greatest impresario reached its zenith in about 1739, but then, with the passing of various gaming laws, declined. These laws first forbade such games as Ace of Hearts, Faro, Basset and Hazard. New games were invented which the law did not cover but new laws were passed forbidding these as well. For a time, however, Roly Poly (roulette) and EO (Evens and Odds, another form of roulette) still seemed to be legal. Of these EO was the most popular, according to Goldsmith, and Nash made various agreements with a Mr C——k, its inventor, and a Mr A——e, its

Tunbridge Wells promoter, to bring it to Bath in return for a percentage of the profits.

Presently Nash realised that he was being cheated and took Mr A——e to court, but he lost his case and in the process revealed what had not been realised before, that he had been making his living by taking cuts from the professional gaming organisers.

As he grew older and poorer, Nash also became a bore. It was not surprising, Goldsmith wrote, that in a life of almost ninety years, 'five or six sprightly things' which he said were remembered, particularly as he took every opportunity of repeating them himself. 'His usual way, when he . . . said anything clever, was to strengthen it with an oath . . .' But his reputation for wit had been exaggerated. His stories, 'in which he always made himself the principal character', he told in a manner which 'was not displeasing' but these, too, he would repeat again and again.

The commonest concerned a rich Devonshire clergyman whom Nash once entertained lavishly at Bath. Six months later Nash tried to return the visit, as he had been pressed to do, but was told that the clergyman was away. Suspecting that this was not true, he got himself let into the parlour where he saw the man's legs hanging down the chimney. When the maid refused to light the fire, on the grounds that it smoked, Nash asked for a candle and himself lit the straw in the grate. 'This quickly unkennelled the old fox; there he stood in an old rusty night gown, blessing himself, and looking like – a – hem – egad.'

Though Goldsmith considered that few of Nash's stories were worth transcribing, Nash announced in the last years of his life that he was writing his autobiography. His friends subscribed, in the belief that he would make scandalous revelations, not realising that public characters like Nash 'were the most unlikely in the world to be made partakers of these secrets which people desired the public should not know'. They may, however, have realised that their subscriptions were a discreet form of charity, and the book indeed was never written.

From 1758 Nash lived on ten guineas a month, granted him by the Corporation of Bath. He was forced to sell the house he had built himself in St John's Court and move to a smaller one nearby in Saw Close. Since Fanny Murray had left him and he had a new mistress, Juliana Papjoy, now that he could not keep her in proper style he honourably dismissed her; however, Juliana loved him and, according to Bath's Victorian historian R. E. M. Peach, stayed to nurse him till he died. Nash's house in Saw Close is now a restaurant, politely named Popjoy's.

His funeral, on 7 February 1761, was a great affair to which the corporation subscribed £50. The procession to Bath Abbey was led by the charity boys and the charity girls singing a solemn hymn. The city music and his own band came next, sounding a dirge at proper intervals. The coffin pall was carried by six aldermen. Last came Bath's invalids, 'the lame, the emaciated and the feeble'. 'Even the tops of the houses were covered with spectators' who asked each other 'as when a real king dies . . . , where shall we find such another?'[14]

Fanny Murray and Juliana Papjoy

'A man can no more be termed a whoremonger for having one whore in his house,' Beau Nash said, 'than a cheesemonger for having one cheese.' Nash had two ladies in his house who, in a broad sense, were his whores, but not simultaneously. The first was Fanny Murray.

Fanny is often said to have been the daughter of a Bath musician but more probably came from London where she started her professional career at the age of twelve on the steps of Covent Garden Theatre. Here she was seduced by John Churchill, a grandson of the first Duke of Marlborough. For a time she lived with Churchill, but she allowed herself to be patronised by a number of other well-known figures of the eighteenth century, becoming at different times the mistress of Sir William Stanhope and Lord Chesterfield. She used to claim to have 'entertained' at Sir Francis Dashwood's Hell Fire Club, where she may have met another of her lovers, Lord Sandwich.

Sandwich was a much disliked man, blamed in particular for attacking Wilkes in the House of Lords on the suspicion that Wilkes had written the *Essay on Women*, an indecent parody of Pope's *Essay on Man*. The Wilkes original, of which only a dozen copies were printed, most if not all of which have been lost, was said to have begun, 'Awake my Sandwich . . .' but in fact probably began 'Awake my Fanny . . .'[15] When Sandwich read his version – probably a stolen proof – half their lordships shouted in horror for him to stop, the other half for him to continue.

He was a grotesquely clumsy man. When about to leave Paris after a visit his dancing master asked him for one favour: that in London he would not say who had taught him to dance. An acquaintance said that he knew it was Sandwich approaching in the distance if he saw a man walking down both sides of the street at once. It was when Sandwich said to Wilkes that he could not decide whether Wilkes would die of hanging or syphilis that Wilkes made his celebrated reply, 'That must depend on whether I embrace your Lordship's principles, or your mistress.'

For some years Sandwich was President of the Board of Admiralty; but it was not for snacks at his Admiralty desk that he devised the idea of 'sandwiching' a slice of beef between two slices of bread, but for long sessions at the gaming table, where he once played for twenty-four hours without a break.

He possessed a painting of Fanny Murray with another well-known courtesan of the time, Kitty Fisher, both naked. Fanny survived her time as Sandwich's mistress better than the singer, Martha Ray, who was shot dead one night as she emerged from Covent Garden Theatre by a rival admirer, James Hackman, an ex-army officer, but by then Vicar of Wiveton, Essex.

After living with Nash at Bath for a number of years Fanny moved back to London, where she became the respectable wife of a rich landowner, Mr David Ross. She died in 1770.

Just enough is known about Juliana Papjoy, generally described as Beau Nash's second mistress, to create romantic legend, even if some of the supposed facts do not agree with each other. Her name, for a start, is uncertain, although its modern versions – Popjoy or Pobjoy – were probably prudish Victorian modifications.

She was born at the village of Bishopstrow, near Warminster, Wiltshire, but had moved to Bath and was a dressmaker when she became 'the latest victim of Nash's unrestrained lust. During her early connection with Nash,' R. E. M. Peach continues, 'she rode about the streets of Bath on a dapple-grey horse; in her hand she carried a many-thonged whip, and hence she was known as "Lady Betty Besom".' Peach then quotes an unidentified 'Contemporary Account' which describes how Nash, after he had persuaded Juliana to 'tread the flowery paths of pleasure with him', grew poor so that 'a separation took place'.

If Juliana later returned to nurse Nash during the last five years of his life (as Peach says) the 'Contemporary Account' omits this episode and instead compliments her for not 'parading the streets for a livelihood . . . like too many of her sisterhood', but returning to the part of Wiltshire where she had been born and making her 'principal residence . . . in a large hollow tree'. Here she slept on a 'lock of straw', resolved never again to use a bed. She lived in this style, it claims, for thirty or forty years, but sixteen would have been the maximum if she was with Nash at his death in 1761 and if the *Gentleman's Magazine*'s report of her own death in April 1777 is correct.

W. Gurney Benham's late-Victorian ballad, 'Beau Nash and Juliana Pobjoy, the Bishopstrow Belle', is the most fantastic of the elaborations of Juliana's career. About her early flirtatiousness he writes:

> There was scarce a young squire in the whole of the shire
> But had found, to his sorrow and cost,
> That to set his affection in such a direction
> Was Love's labour very much lost.

According to his version, Nash carried off Juliana to Scotland where they were married 'at the Blacksmith's shop over the border'. Back at Bath he was challenged to a duel by 'a certain old flame of Julia's':

> But Mr Beau Nash soon 'settled his hash'
> With a terrible gash in his breast
> So the poor fellow got 'satisfaction' or what
> At any rate set him at rest.

Ralph Allen – Man of Bath

Ralph Allen, postmaster, quarry owner and philanthropist, played at least as important a part in creating eighteenth-century Bath as did Beau Nash. He was born in Cornwall in 1693, grandson of the postmistress at the small village of St Columb, and came to Bath at about the age of eighteen. In 1712, aged twenty, he was made its deputy postmaster.

Three years later the Jacobite rising of 1715 gave him the

chance for an act of loyalty which led to his later success. General George Wade had been sent to suppress any rising which might occur in Bath. When Allen, as postmaster, 'got intelligence of a waggon-load of arms, which was coming up from the west, for the use of the dissaffected in this part of England'[16] he reported it to Wade. In total, eleven chests of firearms, a hogshead full of swords and another of cartouches, a mortar, three cannon and a mould for making others were discovered at Bath.

From then onwards General Wade became Allen's most important supporter. The Rev. Richard Graves, Rector of Claverton near Bath, claimed that Allen soon married one of Wade's two illegitimate daughters. The story has been repeated for over two centuries but is supported by no other evidence, and in fact in 1721 Allen first married Elizabeth Buckenridge, daughter of a fairly prosperous City of London merchant. Two years earlier Wade had done Allen a more important service when he supported Allen's application to the Postmaster-General for control of a large part of the country's postal services. This consisted of the cross-country routes (carrying 'cross-road' letters) for much of the West Country, and the handling of letters which were picked up *and* dropped on routes to or away from London ('bye-way' letters) for the whole of England and South Wales. Allen was granted a contract by which he paid £6000 annually to the post office but had the right to keep any profits. It was General Wade who lent him money to secure this.

Previously the routes which Allen acquired had brought the post office only £3,700 annually, and after three years it seemed that Allen might have made a bad bargain. He was in debt by £270. But when his first seven-year contract expired he was pleased enough with his success to ask for, and be granted, another. For the rest of his life he was given successive seven-year contracts and in total during this time post office receipts for the part of the service he ran amounted to over £1,500,000.

Postal officials had been notoriously corrupt. Early in his first contract Allen toured the whole country hunting for frauds and, when he found them, tracing them 'fully and minutely through all their windings'.[17] At important towns where postal routes crossed he appointed deputies whom he could trust and established a system by which these deputies would report on each other and periodically be visited by his own surveyors.

Before the end of Allen's first contract, John Wood, the architect and the third of the great creators of eighteenth-century Bath, had begun to take an interest in the place, and it was probably Ralph Allen who encouraged Wood to submit his grandiose plans for creating a Roman Bath. Allen's support for Wood, together with Allen's stone quarries above the town at Combe Down, were his great contributions to the city's development.

The first work which Wood did for Allen was to redesign the house in which he lived – from which he ran his postal business – close to Bath Abbey. Wood added an extra storey, and gave the house the fine Palladian front which survives today, though it is now hemmed in by later buildings.

Meanwhile he was quarrying and selling his Bath stone at a price which undercut his rivals, and developing a new way to transport it downhill to barges on the river Avon. This consisted of waggons with iron wheels running on wooden tracks, with effective brakes so that one man could operate them. Allen's rail-way and its stone carriages, which followed the line of what is now Allen Road, became a local sight. Wood said that they cut his costs by twenty-five per cent. He and Allen worked together to promote the use of Bath stone not just in Bath but throughout the country.

They had opponents, who claimed that Bath stone was softer than Portland stone, and though Wood reports a satisfactory occasion on which the well-known architect, Colin Campbell, was shown blocks of each and could not tell which was which, Bath stone was rejected for the buildings of Greenwich Hospital. It was partly to demonstrate its good qualities that Allen had Wood design for him his great country house at Widcombe near Bath, to be called Prior Park. In a place of honour in its grounds he set a memorial to General Wade, in the form of a Roman figure holding a truncheon.

When Allen eventually moved to Prior Park in 1741 it was the culmination of twenty years during which his reputation, as well as his fortune, had steadily improved, until he was regarded as a paragon of honesty and benevolence. 'All who love virtue, love to speak your praise,' wrote Mary Chandler, Bath's local poet. Alexander Pope included eight lines of flattery in his poem *One Thousand Seven Hundred and Thirty Eight*, and described Allen in a letter as 'sincerer and plainer than almost any man now in this world'. The Rev. William Warburton, who became Allen's permanent house guest and married his niece, said he believed that Allen was the 'greatest private character that ever appeared in any age of the world'.

One of Allen's acts of benevolence was the founding (with Beau Nash, John Wood and Dr William Oliver) of Bath's General Hospital, to which he gave £1000 as well as all the stone. The city officially recognised him by making him an alderman, and in 1743 he was mayor. He was commonly spoken of as 'The Man of Bath'.

At Prior Park Allen entertained and befriended a wide range of the most interesting writers and artists of his time. Pope was a close friend until they quarrelled about Pope's friend, Martha Blount (see page 164). Richardson and Fielding were his friends too. Fielding dedicated *Amelia* to Allen, and in *Tom Jones* drew an easily recognised portrait of him as Squire Allworthy. He described the squire's – and no doubt Allen's – style of entertaining: 'Every person in the house was a perfect master of his time: . . . so he might, if his health required, or his inclination prompted him to temperance, or even abstinence, absent himself from any meals, or retire from them whenever he was so disposed, without even a solicitation to the contrary.'

The squire's view included 'one of the towers of an old ruined Abbey, grown over with ivy, and part of the front which remained still entire'. Allen added to his resemblance to Squire Allworthy by having built in sight of Prior Park 'a very considerable Gothic object',[18] designed for him by the Gothic specialist, Sanderson Miller. 'Sham Castle', as it was called, is a battlemented and turreted structure with no interior, so placed that someone standing in the alley in front of Allen's town house, if he turns round will see it directly ahead of him across the Avon valley high up near the crest of Bathampton Downs. After Fielding's death in 1754 Allen supported his family and left his widow and three surviving children £100 each in his will.

When Royalty came to Bath they visited Allen. Frederick, Prince of Wales, spent three hours at Prior Park in 1750. For ten days in August the following year the Allens evacuated their house and went to Weymouth so that Princess Amelia could stay there. Allen was back in September, in time to receive the

Duke of Cumberland, since the duke soon afterwards sent him a medal inscribed 'The Gift of His Royal Highness, W[illiam] D[uke] of Cumberland, To the Famous Mr Allen, 4 December 1752'. And Allen demonstrated his loyalty to the crown by lighting up Prior Park to celebrate national victories. In 1745, as Prince Charles Edward's Highlanders advanced into England, at his own expense he had raised a troop of 100 men; when the rebels retreated from Stirling the bells of Bath were rung, the town's cannon were fired and 'Mr Allen's house . . . finely illuminated, a very large bonfire made near it; and his men lately raised fired several vollies'[19] – dangerously, perhaps, since they were not yet uniformed or trained. Thirteen years later he had Prior Park again extensively illuminated, to celebrate the capture of Quebec.

For the most part Allen avoided becoming involved in party politics or making close friends of politicians. William Pitt the Elder, who was for a time one of Bath's Members of Parliament, was an exception. It was Pitt, a keen landscape gardener, who had written to Sanderson Miller to ask him to design Sham Castle. In 1763, however, when peace was made with France by George III's ministers against Pitt's violent opposition, Allen took the king's side. With sixteen other members of the Bath Council, he sent a loyal address to the king congratulating him on an 'adequate' peace. Allen had commercial reasons for joining the sending of this message: the war had been putting the stone he was sending by sea from Bristol to London at risk from French privateers. And one of Pitt's principal political opponents, his brother-in-law George Grenville, was the First Lord of the Treasury, with power to end Allen's postal contract whenever he chose.

Pitt took offence at the word 'adequate', and he and Allen exchanged pained letters; for once Allen was less than generally admired in Bath, and because of the important part he had played in organising the loyal address a caricature was circulated in the city captioned 'The Knights of Bathe, or the One-Headed Corporation'. It showed Allen with a Cornish chough perched on his wig. But Allen and Pitt's respect for each other survived. In his will Allen left Pitt £1000, and described him as 'the best of friends as well as the most upright and able of ministers', and Pitt wrote to Allen's widow, 'I fear not all the examples of his virtues will have power to raise up to the world his likeness again.'

Four years earlier Allen had been affected in another way by the succession of George III to his grandfather, George II. The young king's ministers had at once cancelled Allen's postal contract, so that a new one could be negotiated. During the negotiations the two new Postmasters-General discovered that Allen had failed for the last twenty-seven years to submit annual accounts of his receipts, distributions and profits. They knew, however, that without Allen the country's postal service would collapse and granted him a new contract on condition that within a year he produced such statements. Allen duly sent them a 'narrative', which covered the whole period of his contracts, starting in 1720, and the Postmasters were satisfied.

Allen's two marriages were happy but had left him without an heir. When he died, therefore, in 1764, he left Prior Park to Gertrude Tucker, the niece who had lived with him as a child and married the Rev. William Warburton, now Bishop of Gloucester. The Warburtons moved out of the house in 1769, and in 1829 it became a Catholic theological college. Six years later it was severely damaged in a fire, and the college closed in 1856; but in 1878 the house was bought back by the Catholic Church and became the Catholic public school it remains today.

The two John Woods

The year in which Beau Nash first came to Bath was also probably the year of birth of the architect, John Wood (1705–1754). But Nash had been Bath's Master of Ceremonies for over twenty years before Wood, the man who set the architectural tone for the splendid city it was to become, arrived to live there.

Not much is known about Wood's early life. His father and brother may have worked as builders at Bath, but he only tells us that as a young man he was a road surveyor in Yorkshire. He also worked in Yorkshire for Lord Bingley, and it was either then or a little later in London that he became an enthusiast for Palladian architecture, the style recently imported from Italy by Lord Burlington.

This enthusiasm led him, around 1725, to devise his grandiose plans for turning Bath into a Roman city. 'I proposed', he wrote, 'to make a second place of assembly, to be called the Royal Forum of Bath; another place no less magnificent for the exhibition of sports, to be called the Grand Circus; and a third place of equal state with either of the former, for the practice of medicinal exercises, to be called the Imperial Gymnasium of the City.' The plans were not accepted by the landowners whose land would be required. Wood, still only twenty, was an unproved architect and of unimpressive, chinless appearance.

Soon, however, he found patrons who would commission him. The earliest of these was the Duke of Chandos, for whom he transformed St John's Hospital into a lodging house. But the palace-like façades which Wood was soon building at Bath sometimes hid less magnificent interiors. Chandos received many complaints from his tenant at St John's, Mrs Anne Phillips; the walls were frail, the floorboards so thin they could not be planed, and the roof leaked so badly that it had to be replaced after two years. The many water closets which Chandos had ordered had been made with wooden pipes and the whole system had to be abandoned. Presently Mrs Phillips reported a more remarkable development. On part of Chandos's land Wood was building without permission a house for himself. Chandos told Wood to move it at once to 'somewhere else less offensive'. He was perhaps tolerant because he was capable of such behaviour himself. Some years later the Bath Council fined him £80 for seizing a piece of land which didn't belong to him for stairs to his new lodging house. And far from dismissing Wood, he became a godfather to one of his daughters.

But it was Ralph Allen, Bath's postmaster, who became Wood's most important patron. For Allen, Wood built a town house close to the abbey, with its elegant Palladian front; and Wood became supervisor of Allen's stone quarries at Combe Down. Without Allen's stone Wood's fine buildings in Bath would not have been possible.

According to Wood, London opponents maliciously compared Bath stone 'to *Cheshire* cheese, liable to breed maggots that would soon devour it', and then refused to use it at Greenwich Hospital. Prior Park, which Wood designed for Allen at Widcombe, was meant to show Bath stone 'in much greater variety of uses than it had ever appeared in any other structure. With this in view several designs were formed, wherein the orders of architecture were to shine forth in all their glory.' Even the pigeons were to be magnificently housed. Above the stable gatehouse 'their particular cells are all made with wrought free stone: so that if a beautiful habitation is really an allurement to this species of bird, as some pretend, Mr Allen's pigeons will, in all probability, never desert their place of abode'. In the house's basement 'an apartment was reserved for water closets, if such conveniences should be wanting within the body of the house'.

Wood's map of Bath, published in 1736 by the bookseller, James Leake, shows how commercial Wood's motives were. Around the outside, among recommendations of Bath as a resort, is an advertisement for his new 'Deal Yard . . . in which persons may be supplied with the best Norway goods'. They were also given directions about how to choose their material.

Wood's finest achievement at Bath was Queen's Square, begun in 1729, two years after he came to live in the city, and finished seven years later. He and his family moved into number twenty-four. He also built Dame Lindsey's Assembly Rooms, not far from Harrison's, also in the lower part of the town (they were demolished in the early nineteenth century) and the Parades by the River Avon. And he found time to write his *Essay Towards a Description of Bath*. This was at first meant to describe Bath's ancient history (he was also planning a work on Stonehenge), but developed into a curious mixture of legend, architectural description and gossip. It was originally published in 1742, then in an enlarged form in 1749, and despite its disorganisation tells us many things about eighteenth-century Bath which we would not otherwise know.

Five years later he died, and his uncompleted work as an architect was triumphantly completed by his son, also named John (1728–1782). John the elder had already designed the Circus and laid the foundation stone. John the younger completed it, and among other things built the Royal Crescent and the new (surviving) Assembly Rooms.

Like his father, he became known outside Bath, and at Liverpool was elected a member of the Ugly Face Club which described him in its minute book in architectural terms: 'A stone coloured complexion, a dimple in his attick story. The

pillasters of his face fluted, tortoise-eye'd, a prominent nose.
Wild grin, and face altogether resembling a badger.'

General Wade, Member for Bath

> If you saw these roads before they were made,
> You would hold up your hands and bless General Wade.

So wrote Sir Walter Scott. The roads he referred to were those
of Scotland, dramatically improved by General (later Field
Marshal) George Wade (1673–1748) between 1726 and 1737.
Apart from these roads, and certain military successes, Wade's
achievements were at Bath where, along with Beau Nash,
Ralph Allen and John Wood the elder, he was one of the
creators of the eighteenth-century city.

Wade – a soldier since he was seventeen, and said to have
been the grandson of a Cromwellian major – first came to Bath
in 1715 when he was sent to forestall a Jacobite rising. It was
then, according to Richard Graves, that the young Ralph Allen
passed to Wade the information about arms which were being
sent to the city that enabled Wade to capture a small arsenal of
them and earned for Allen Wade's lasting gratitude and support.

In 1722 Wade was elected one of Bath's Members of Parliament, and about five years later showed his gratitude to the city
council (who were the electors) by paying for the mayor and
aldermen to have their portraits painted. Johan Van Diest was
given the commission, and eight of his portraits, including
Ralph Allen's, still hang at the Guildhall.

In 1733 Wade again gave money to the city council, though
it was not used as he originally intended. By this time,
according to John Wood, the Pump Room was so overcrowded
in the season that not more than a third of those who wanted to
drink the waters could do so. 'But what is worse . . . there is
no place belonging to it for the invalids to retire into, when the
waters begin to operate.' Wood was commissioned to design an
additional storey for the Pump Room, and General Wade, when
shown the plans, gave 500 guineas.

According to Wood, this plan was blocked by the mayor of
Bath who refused to put the proposal to his brethren because it
would take away custom from Shaylor's coffee house which his

son was managing. It seems likely enough that nearby coffee houses were being profitably patronised by Pump Room drinkers who needed to relieve themselves when the waters began to operate. But the Pump Room project was abandoned and Wade agreed to let his money be used 'for the public good . . . provided that the General first approves'.[20] It was eventually given to St Michael's Church, on condition that the church reserved a pew or seat for the corporation.

The suggestion that Wade would rather have had his money spent on the Pump Room than on a church fits his character. According to Bishop Thomas Newton, Wade, though a man of good understanding, 'had no great regard for revealed religion, and when the prophecies were urged as a proof of revelation, constantly derided them'.

He was also a regular gambler, even if he 'played with the caution which characterised his military tactics'.[21] Once when playing, he missed his fine snuff box. Among his party one gentleman refused to be searched except in another room. There he explained to Wade that he was so poor that he had been reduced to living on left-over food which waiters gave him, and had not wanted half a chicken to be publicly discovered in his pocket. Wade gave him £100, and later found the snuff box in his own pocket.

Wade's other important contribution to Bath was to create 'Wade's Passage'. Previously houses had stood close against the north side of the abbey, so that people who wanted to go between the Abbey Churchyard and the High Street would regularly walk through the Abbey itself. Wade bought and demolished these houses, some to make a site for his own house, and others to clear a passage alongside the abbey. His own house, probably designed for him by Lord Burlington, still stands, now Number 14, Abbey Churchyard. In 1980, when it had been restored, the house was commended by the Civic Trust, although what the Trust in fact commended was the house's back door. In Wade's time the building had faced the other way and extended across Cheap Street.

Before Wade came to Bath he had fought under Marlborough, and played a brave part in the capture of Minorca. And in 1719 he had been second-in-command to Lord Cobham (maker of Stowe's Gardens) at the successful capture of Vigo in north-west Spain. But it was not till 1724 that he was appointed

Commander-in-Chief of forces in Scotland, and made the roads for which he became famous. His five hundred road-making soldiers, whom he called his 'Highwaymen', built forty bridges, including the (first) Tay Bridge.

When Prince Charles Edward was planning the 1745 rebellion, Wade was called back from the Netherlands to take charge of the country's defences. At Bath the corporation drank 'success to Field-Marshal Wade, our representative in Parliament, against the rebels in Scotland', and a new verse was composed for the National Anthem.

> Lord grant that General Wade
> May, by Thy mighty aid,
> Victory bring!
> May he sedition hush
> And, like a torrent, rush,
> Rebellious Scotch to crush,
> God save the King!

In October Wade set out from London to take command of a northern army, and moved with it from Doncaster to Newcastle, only to discover that Prince Charles Edward's army, using Wade's new roads, had entered England on the other side of the Cheviots and was already past him on its way south. Since there was no road from Newcastle to Carlisle, Wade had no way to reach it. Ironically, when this road was eventually built it was called General Wade's road.

Meanwhile there was panic in the country and a run on the London banks, which they frustrated by paying out in sixpences. Wade, disgraced, was replaced by the Duke of Cumberland, butcher of Culloden. Though he was re-elected Member for Bath in 1747, Wade died the next year.

He had never married, but had four illegitimate children, two sons as well as two daughters. The Captain Wade who in 1769 became Beau Nash's third successor as Bath's Master of Ceremonies after Samuel Derrick was Wade's nephew. Wade left £500 for the erection of a monument to himself. In front of this in Westminster Abbey its sculptor, Roubiliac, used to stand and weep because his best work had been placed so high up that it could not be properly seen. Goldsmith was not so impressed, observing that neither Wade nor two other generals whom Roubiliac had commemorated were 'quite worthy of the elaborate mural medleys compiled in their memory'.

2

THE BATH EXPERIENCE

The journey to Bath

Early visitors to Bath came on horseback, or in private coaches. Public coaches first appeared in the second half of the seventeenth century. In 1667 the famous Flying Machine was advertised. It would run three times a week in each direction and do the journey in three days.

FLYING MACHINE

All those desirous to pass from London to Bath, or any other place on their road, let them repair to the 'Bell Savage' on Ludgate Hill in London, and the 'White Lion' at Bath, at both which places they may be received in a stage coach every Monday, Wednesday, and Friday, which performs the whole journey in three days (if God permits), and sets forth at five o'clock in the morning.

Passengers to pay one pound five shillings each who are allowed to carry fourteen pounds weight – for all above to pay three-halfpence per pound.

Early in the next century two rival companies were offering the same service, and from 1716 there was a daily coach. Gradually the journey time was reduced, but by 1770 coaches still took thirty-eight hours. Then John Palmer, proprietor of the Bath Theatre, made a revolutionary proposal: that the mail should be carried by coach instead of by post-boys on horseback, that mail coaches should carry, besides mail, a driver and a guard, four passengers, and that the time should be cut to sixteen hours. The first mail coach set off from Bristol for London via Bath on 2 August 1784 (see page 159) and many Bath visitors now began to travel with the mail.

The distance from London to Bath was 105¾ miles, reckoned from Hyde Park Corner, as it generally was in the eighteenth century, since this was where the country began. But in practice coaches picked up their passengers from various London inns where they had usually spent the night in order to start in the early morning. Originally they made two night-stops on the way, often at Maidenhead and Marlborough, but as the coaches grew faster they made only a single stop, usually at Newbury.

Early in the journey they would pass close to the house (in fact a pair) rented by a man who had many Bath connections: Samuel Richardson, novelist and printer. Richardson generally called his place in the country North End, but it had changed its name to The Grange when Burne Jones came to live there in the next century, before becoming 111 and 113 North End Road, Fulham. Here Richardson would entertain the literary celebrities of the time, or sitting in its garden would read a new chapter of *Clarissa* (which he partly wrote at North End) to his circle of admiring young ladies. He gave up North End in 1754 when his landlord wanted to raise the rent from £25 to £40 a year.

A far grander establishment to which to be invited in the early eighteenth century lay a little further down the Bath Road at Chiswick, and belonged to another man with Bath connections: the Earl of Burlington. Burlington had designed General Wade's house in the Abbey Courtyard. His better-known buildings were Burlington House, Piccadilly, now the Royal Academy, and his Chiswick villa. It was Burlington who introduced Palladian architecture from Italy to England and his villa at Chiswick was inspired by Palladio's Villa Rotunda at Vicenza. Two of England's most notable gardeners were connected with Chiswick House; the first, William Kent, Burlington's protégé who had been with him in Italy, was a key figure in transforming gardening fashion in England from French and Dutch formalism, to the native naturalism of Capability Brown. The second, Joseph Paxton, was at Chiswick when the house had passed to the Dukes of Devonshire. Paxton designed the Crystal Palace for the Great Exhibition of 1851 (burnt down in the 1930s) and the great glasshouse at Chatsworth, Derbyshire, dynamited by the ninth duke after the First World War.

A few miles west of Chiswick, just before Brentford, the Bath Road passed Syon House, the property of the phenomenally rich Percy (Northumberland) family. Here Elizabeth Percy and her third husband, the Duke of Somerset, had given Princess Anne (the future queen) refuge when she was quarrelling with her brother-in-law and sister, King William III and

Queen Mary. This was the Duke of Somerset, known as the Proud Duke, who deducted £20,000 from the inheritance of one of his daughters when he awoke from his siesta to find that instead of standing watch over him she had sat down.

In the mid-eighteenth century the house passed to Sir Hugh Smithson, for whom the Northumberland title was revived. About the duke's properties and wealth Horace Walpole wrote that he was building at Northumberland House, Syon, Stanstead, Alnwick Castle and Wentworth: 'They lived by the etiquette of the old peerage, they have Swiss porters, the countess has her pipers – in short they will soon have no estate' – a wildly mistaken forecast. About the countess he wrote that she was a jovial heap of contradictions. The duke was a regular visitor to Bath, where he bought number 11 Laura Place while it was being built.

Still on the first stage of an early-eighteenth-century journey, the travellers crossed Hounslow Heath, an expanse of uncultivated land with low scrub in which highwaymen would lie hidden. Often they were old soldiers, and it was demobilised soldiers who, after the peace of 1697, captured an earlier Duke of Northumberland among other upper-class travellers, during a hold-up in which they stopped thirty or forty coaches and took 'a great booty in guineas, watches and jewellery'.[22]

To suppress highwaymen the 'Bow Street Runners' were recruited, a body of men wearing scarlet waistcoats and therefore known as Robin Redbreasts. John Townsend was their best-known officer, the man who said about a new place of execution that 'though it would take twelve criminals at a time, it would really only hang ten comfortably'.

Beyond Hounslow, at the little village of Colnbrook, there was evidence as late as the 1930s of one of Nash's legendary and, if true, remarkable achievements: the installing of pumps alongside the Bath Road so that it could be watered in summer to keep down the dust of carriage wheels. Here Cecil Roberts (*And so to Bath* – 1940) saw two surviving iron pumps, locked and disused but in 'excellent preservation'.

At Slough, close behind the Crown Inn, travellers of later days could see the giant telescope of William Herschel, Britain's leading astronomer, once a Bath Pump Room musician. Five miles on they reached Maidenhead. Here the Crown Hotel was commonly made a first-night stop to postpone passing Maidenhead Thickets, a notoriously dangerous stretch of road which lay just beyond the town, until next morning when, with luck, the highwaymen would be asleep.

Twenty miles then brought them to the suburbs of Newbury, where, at Speenhamland, later abbreviated to Speen, The Pelican was the best known of all the Bath Road's coaching inns. About it, the actor James Quin, who retired to Bath, wrote:

> The famous inn at Speenhamland
> That stands below the hill
> May well be called *The Pelican*
> From its enormous bill.

A couple of miles south of Newbury stood Sandleford Priory, where in the 1770s and 1780s the widowed Mrs Elizabeth Montagu, the celebrated Bluestocking, was spending her late husband's money improving her property. Here travellers might have caught glimpses of James Wyatt, her architect, or Capability Brown, her garden designer, or of her head gardener, a boxer and reformed alcoholic, eating grass in an attempt to 'atone for past offences'.[23] Mrs Montagu was a frequent visitor to Bath.

West of Newbury, just south of the road, also in the 1770s they might have called on Lady Craven, another literary lady, who was greatly admired by Horace Walpole. At the first night of her second play he saw her sitting 'in the middle of the front row of the stage-box, much dressed with a profusion of white bugles and plumes, to receive the public homage due to her sex and loveliness'. They were less likely to have met Lord Craven. When his wife published her memoirs, entitled *The Beautiful Lady Craven*, she wrote: 'his life was one continued ramble: to hunt in Leicester – to drive the Oxford stage-coach – to see a new play in London – to visit Lord Craven his uncle at Coombe Abbey, or Admiral Craven at Benham, were his continual occupations. He had a dislike to remain longer than three weeks at a time at any place: which when I had observed, he kissed my hand, and replied, "Till I lived with you, my love, I never stayed three *days* in one place".'

After bearing Craven six children in twelve years, her marriage ended disastrously when Craven discovered her in a private room at a ball, sitting on the French ambassador's knee 'in such a state, as clearly proved that a few moments would have brought on an amorous conflict'.[24]

The parson who held the living at Benham (pronounced and sometimes written Beenham or Benham Vallance) from 1733 to 1752 was the learned but eccentric Thomas Stackhouse (1677–1752). For a time in his youth he was minister of the English church in Amsterdam, then lived in London where he sent his bishop a letter (subsequently published) about 'the miseries and great hardships of the inferior clergy in and about London'.[25]

Eleven years later the living at Benham helped to dispel his poverty and enabled him to continue his *New History of the Holy Bible from the Beginning of the World to the Establishment of Christianity*. He worked at this in the garden of a roadside inn known as Jack's Booth (after a fifteenth-century Newbury clothier), where he became a familiar sight to coach travellers. Drink was now his problem and on Sundays he would ask publicly from the pulpit to be forgiven his indulgences. He grew so slovenly in his dress that his bishop, during a Visitation, asked, 'Who is that shabby dirty old man?' Stackhouse replied for himself that he was Thomas Stackhouse who had written 'the History of the Bible', which was more than the Bishop would ever do.

Between Hungerford and Marlborough travellers reached a notoriously bad stretch of road known as Feather-bed-lane. It was here that the author of an anonymous poem, *A journey to Bath and Bristol*, published about 1737, had the sort of accident which must have been common.

> The Long worn Axle to the Coach, alack,
> Gave here a dismal, unexpected crack.

Soon after it had left London, at Turnham Green, his coach had picked up 'A courtly Female called *Sempronia* fair'. Together they had already had one accident, when the coach overturned on Hounslow Heath.

> Confusion great o'ertakes the Females fair
> All comic postures here presented are,
> On sweet *Sempronia* 'twas my lot to fall
> Her Cloaths were up, the sight exposed to all.

At Newbury where they spent the night he was still luckier:

The Toils of Day now o'er, the Night is Crown'd
With pleasing Mirth, the vinous Glass goes round
I kiss't and toy'd and by young Cupid led,
I lit the fair *Sempronia* to bed.

As they rode on to Marlborough, leaving their broken coach behind to be repaired, he reflected,

'Oh pitty! pitty! That so soft a Bum
Shou'd thus be subject to a Martyrdom.'

From Marlborough the repaired coach took them on to Bath.

Here Bully, sharper, trav'lling Whore you find,
The Town a perfect snare for all design'd. . .
'Tis Noise and Nonsense are their Dear delight
And Stupid pleasures crown the Drunken Night.

And to such delights he regretfully leaves the fair Sempronia.

On their ride to Marlborough the author and Sempronia would have passed along the northern edge of Savernake Forest, where the same family had been hereditary wardens since at least the twelfth century, probably since the Conquest. From the Bath Road the Grand Avenue led south through the forest for 3¼ miles, almost but not quite directly to the fine red-brick house which was another of Lord Burlington's creations, built by him in the 1720s for his relation, the Earl of Ailesbury.

Ailesbury had no children and, in 1754, he left Tottenham to his nephew, Thomas Brudenell Bruce, hoping that he would take more interest in it than his three elder brothers who would inherit other great estates. Though Bruce was often away at court, he did indeed take an interest in Tottenham and Savernake, spending much time and effort in having the grounds of the house laid out in the fashionable natural style. When he entertained George III here, Fanny Burney reported that he spent the sum of £300 on a new bed for the king.

Though Devizes was not on the direct route to Bath, it was a place where some travellers spent a night, as Fanny Burney did with the Thrales in 1780. Here, at its best inn, The Bear, they discovered that the landlord's wife, Mrs Lawrence, was 'something above her station . . . While we were at cards before supper, we were much surprised by the sound of a pianoforte. I jumped up, and ran to listen whence it proceeded. I found it came from the next room, where the overture to the "Buona Figliuola" was performing. The playing was very decent. . .'

Back at the card table, Fanny soon heard singing, and eventually met the two charming Lawrence daughters, thirteen and sixteen years old respectively. 'We were extremely pleased with them, and surprised that they could have been born and bred at Devizes.' The last member of the family made a still greater impression. 'This was their brother, a most lovely boy of ten years of age, who seems to be not merely the wonder of their family, but of the times, for his astonishing skill in drawing. They protest he has never had any instruction, yet showed us some of his productions that were really beautiful. Those that were copies were delightful – those of his own composition amazing, though far inferior. I was equally struck with the boy and his works.' Thomas Lawrence had already been noticed by Sir Joshua Reynolds and the Bath painter, William Hoare, and eventually became President of the Royal Academy.

A few miles north-west of Devizes, beside the main Bath Road, lay Bowood, where travellers from the mid-1760s would have seen the magnificent lake which Capability Brown had created for the second Earl of Shelburne. Closer to Bath, at Corsham, they could have admired Lord Methuen's house where Brown had demonstrated his versatility by designing a picture gallery with a splendidly ornate plaster ceiling which Methuen had had to add as a condition of inheriting the pictures of his uncle, Paul Methuen, a negotiator of the port wine treaty with Portugal.

A short distance to the south of the Bath Road (or an easy excursion from Bath, for that matter) would have brought them to Longleat, the great house of the Thynne family, which for forty-two years in the first half of the eighteenth century had been without an owner-occupier after the second Marquis of Weymouth had gone to live in the nearby village of Horning-sham. (He is said to have killed his wife's lover in a duel in a Longleat attic passage.) The third Marquis, who succeeded him in 1756, might in his early days have proved an unreliable host, since he was commonly so broke that the bailiffs were constantly in the house. He regularly sat up gaming till six in the morning and did not rise till midday. At the age of twenty-four he was so gouty that he was refused a ticket to George III's coronation because he could not walk in the procession. But he, too, employed Capability Brown to redesign the house's neglected grounds and to create the fine series of lakes which survives today.

The daily routine

The visitor to Bath during its great period – the first eighty or ninety years of the eighteenth century – had his day precisely ordered. Pleasures, like subjects of conversation, were taken in turn and savoured; there was no hopping from one to another according to fancy. First came bathing.

Bath had five baths from which to choose, all of them roofless and open to the weather. Largest – but far from large, since it measured only 60 feet by 40 feet – was the King's Bath. At its centre where the water was hottest stood the so-called 'kitchen', an octagonal tower with seats for bathers. Here there was also a fountain which drew water for drinking directly from the spring below. Next to the King's Bath, but smaller and cooler, was the Queen's Bath. No one knew at this time that the King's Bath (which survives) was built on top of a Roman stone-walled reservoir, which had become filled with debris; or that the Queen's Bath, demolished in the late nineteenth century, lay above a circular Roman bath, or that nearby, but entirely buried and built over, was the Great Roman Bath, far larger than either.

Some one hundred yards to the west lay three more baths, all of them also smaller than the King's Bath, though one of them, the Hot Bath, was nearly as hot. Near the Hot Bath was the Cross Bath and the Lepers' Bath.

Of these five, the Cross Bath was most favoured by the better classes in the seventeenth century when Charles II brought his mistresses, the Countess of Castlemaine and the Duchess of Portsmouth; and James II his queen, Mary of Modena; but gradually the King's Bath became more fashionable for men and the Queen's for women. The Lepers' Bath, Goldsmith laconically observes, was 'not so much frequented as the rest'.

A lady would be brought to her chosen bath at some time between six and nine o'clock in the morning, in her sedan chair which would be 'hermetically closed' if she was 'old, ugly or prudish', but 'artistically penetrable' when she was 'finely formed'.[26] Some chairs were specially made 'with very short poles, for the purpose of carrying the people straight out of their beds, in their bathing costume',[27] in which, presumably, they had slept. Alternatively, a lady was dressed for bathing when she arrived. Her costume was of fine linen, stained yellow by the waters, and resembled a voluminous smock, with sleeves like a parson's gown. On her head she wore a three-cornered 'chip' hat, in which she fixed a handkerchief to wipe the sweat from her face. At the bath she met the gentlemen who came separately and, for bathing, wore canvas drawers and jackets.

When she lowered herself into the water she would be given by her attendant – if she was sufficiently distinguished this might be a daughter of one of Bath's chief citizens – a little floating wooden dish, which she tied to her waist with a ribbon. In this she might float another handkerchief, as well as a nosegay, and – in Defoe's time, about 1724 – a snuff box and some beauty spots, 'though the bath occasioning a little perspiration, the patches do not stick so kindly as they should'. Meanwhile her bathing costume had quickly filled up with water, 'so that your shape is not seen'.[28] She then walked about in the bath, either on her own or, if inexperienced, with the help of a guide.

While bathing 'the ladies and gentlemen keep some distance, and each to their proper side,' Defoe wrote about the Cross Bath, 'but frequently mingle here too, as in the King's and Queen's Bath, though not so often; and the place being but narrow, they converse freely, and talk, rally, make vows and sometimes loves'. And Philip Thicknesse, in his *The Valetudinarian's Bath Guide*, considered that he could not decently repeat what he had seen happening during bathing hours, let alone what he had been told. But on the whole in Nash's time (1705–61) bathers behaved properly. When a gentleman who was watching his wife in the King's Bath became 'so charmed with her increase of beauty' that he paid her familiar compliments, Nash 'instantly took him by the heels, and, as an act of gallantry, hurled him over the rails into the water'.[29] The result was a duel in which Nash was slightly wounded in the arm.

Though the bathers generally behaved themselves, the baths during bathing hours were an entertaining sight, filled with the fashionable awash to their necks, their heads wreathed in steam, while bands serenaded them from the waterside. In the *New Bath Guide* (1766) Christopher Anstey described the King's Bath as seen from the windows of the Pump Room which stood immediately beside and above it.

> Oh twas pretty to see them all put on their flannels,
> and then take the water like so many spaniels:
> and though all the while it grew hotter and hotter
> they swam, just as if they were hunting an otter.

As soon as the bathers emerged, according to Philip Thicknesse, whatever their sex they were 'stripped quite naked by an old woman' who took off their wet clothes and put on dry ones, before being carried back to their lodgings. Here they either dressed formally or in contrived *déshabille* to suggest that they had come directly from bathing, then returned to the Pump Room for the second part of the medical treatment: the drinking of the waters.

Perhaps it was because the Pump Room provided the first chance each day for proper conversation that it acquired a special reputation for gossip. Lydia, in Smollett's novel *Humphrey Clinker*, describes the daily gathering there. 'The noise of the music playing in the gallery, the heat and flavour of such a crowd, and the hum and buzz of their conversation, gave one the headache and vertigo the first day; but afterwards all these things became familiar and even agreeable.'

A coloured fan of the period gives a more decorous picture of the 1706 Pump Room and its patrons. Five musicians led by a trumpeter play in a semi-circular balcony which they have reached by a ladder, two pumpers stand at the handles of an old-fashioned village pump ready to serve the waters, while elegant men in wigs and frock coats make polite conversation with elegant ladies in floor-length dresses and little black hats. Rowlandson's caricature in *The Comforts of Bath* (1798), also showing the old Pump Room, and is less decorous if more credible. The statue of Nash looks down from its niche in the wall on men with grotesquely swollen faces and legs, who stagger on sticks or sit in wheelchairs, while an equally swollen woman tosses back her glass of water at the serving counter.

Three glasses was the normal eighteenth-century dose, though far grosser quantities were taken in earlier times and again in the nineteenth century. According to Dickens' Sam

Above: A View of the Parade at Bath c. 1781.

Below: Front of the Pump Room in the City of Bath.
Engraving *c.* 1765.

Above: Richard Beau Nash *c.* 1761.

Opposite above: Miss Murray.

Opposite below: Her Royal Highness, Princess Amelia.

Eng.d by Ridley from an original miniature

Above: A view of the Theatre Royal, Bath, as it appeared at the royal dramatic fête in honour of His Majesty's birthday, 28th April 1824.

Below: The Grand Pump Room, 1841.

Weller, who accompanied Mr Pickwick there, it had 'a wery strong flavour o' warm flat irons'.

The fixed points in the rest of the visitor's day were a public breakfast at a coffee house or one of the assembly rooms, a service at 11am at the abbey, dinner in the afternoon at about 4pm, a second visit to the Pump Room and then, finally, a play or, on Tuesdays and Fridays, a public ball. The visitor fed well. For breakfast he had 'buttered rolls, or Bath buns, not to be equalled elsewhere, with the best of chocolate, tea or coffee'. 'Our butter', John Wood added, 'cannot be exceeded; the herbage in the neighbourhood being sweet; the housewifry neat and clean.'

A visitor's bun might be a Sally Lunn, a sort of brioche supposedly named after a Huguenot woman who had brought the secret recipe from France. For dinner the mutton was celebrated: 'and that which is really fed upon the downs', Wood wrote, 'has a flavour beyond comparison . . . And we have fish in great plenty, as fresh and as good as even the greatest epicure can desire.' Bath's 'cook-maids' were so skilful that gentlemen who hired them for the season would often take them home to 'the most distant quarters of the kingdom'.

The church service was a social as well as a religious occasion. The abbey would be as crowded as St Paul's and there was much passing of *billets-doux*. Most of the congregation came, as one preacher told them, 'more out of custome and formality than in devotion to the Sacred Deity'. According to the anonymous *A Step to Bath* (1700), 'The Ladies were the only saints several came there to adore.'

But even such regular daily events left much time to be filled. 'Thus we have the tedious morning fairly over,' Goldsmith wrote, in his account of a Bath day, which he largely copied from John Wood's, though adding a few comments of his own. Where Wood reported factually that there were lectures on the arts and sciences during the mornings costing a guinea a course, Goldsmith adds that these were taught 'in a pretty superficial manner, so as not to teize the understanding'.

Other ways in which the visitor could pass the tedious morning, or indeed the afternoon, were attending concerts, where 'such people of rank and fortune as were well skilled in music' could join with 'the common band of performers'.[30] Or he could visit the bookshops, for which Bath was famous, or stroll on the Parades, or merely gossip and read the newspapers at Bath's many coffee houses. Here he could also write letters, if he paid a five-shilling subscription for pen, ink and paper. Some coffee houses were mainly for men, since 'politics, scandal' and 'philosophy' were discussed there, together with other subjects which Lydia Melford's aunt in *Humphrey Clinker* thought unsuitable for young girls.

More energetically, the visitor with a fine equipage could display it by driving around a circle on the town common known as Hyde Park, or taking it three miles up the London Road and back. Some gentlemen might even be seen 'scaling some of those romantic precipices that over-hang the city'.[31]

Alongside these decorous amusements there was always the gaming table, that 'frequent ruin of opulent fortunes'.[32] Cards were such a passion that Elizabeth Montagu, writing to a friend, remarked on how the only question ever heard in the morning was 'How d'ye do', and in the afternoon, 'What is trumps?'

Hanoverian princes and princesses

Bath, whose citizens were often suspected of Jacobite sympathies, gave George I's accession to the throne no special welcome, but by the time his son, George II, succeeded him thirteen years later in 1727 they were sufficiently reconciled to the House of Brunswick to organise celebrations of 'the utmost magnificence'. And in November that year, to celebrate the king's birthday, an ox was 'roasted whole in the Market-place, which was put into a dish 12-foot long, and 6-foot wide, made on purpose . . . here was a great deal of money struck into the ox as it was roasting, and about 100 rich stones, etc. which made the populace so eager to the cutting of it up, that they jumpt over the gentlemen's shoulders, some whereof got into the very dish, and were over shoos in gravey; one of them being more eager than the rest, was thrust into the belly of the ox, and almost smothered, and the fat flew about in such a plentiful manner, that the gentlemen were obliged to quit the table'.[33]

Next year another ox was roasted for another Hanoverian: George II's seventeen-year-old daughter, Princess Amelia. Bath became Amelia's favourite resort and she became Bath's favourite royal person. She arrived at Bath by sedan chair, and stayed in the usual royal lodgings above the city's West Gate. The ox-roast was for her birthday, when Morris dancers performed for an hour in her honour, guns were fired and fireworks lit.

Another day she was taken by specially decorated barge down the Avon to Bristol. She was a girl of spirit, and on an often-described occasion at one of the city's twice-weekly balls, she asked Beau Nash to allow another dance after the official closing time of 11.00. Nash refused, telling 'her royal highness that the established rules of Bath . . . would admit of no altering, without an utter subversion of all his authority'.

Amelia made other visits to Bath, including two in 1734, the year that Bath's local poet, Mary Chandler, published her poem, *A Description of Bath*, and dedicated it to the princess.

> 'Deign YOU, bright Maid, to hear my artless lays;
> You'll awe the snarling critics into Praise,'

Mary wrote, hoping for good reviews.

> 'Too weak my voice; but Great AMELIA's Name
> Shall raise my numbers and defend my Fame.'

The princess came again in 1753, and invited herself to stay, not at her usual lodgings, but in Ralph Allen's new mansion, Prior Park. Allen obliged, moving with his family to Weymouth to let the princess have the entire use of his house for ten days, before she moved down into the city. During her stay at Prior Park there was a dramatic event. England at last abandoned the Julian calendar and adopted the Gregorian calendar, as the rest of Europe had done years before. It was another familiar figure at Bath, Lord Chesterfield, who persuaded Parliament to pass the necessary Act, because the Prime Minister of the time, Newcastle, was too stupid to understand it. The consequence was that 2 September 1752 was immediately followed by 14 September 1752. Many people considered that they had been deprived of this portion of their lives, hence the public cry, 'Give us back our eleven days.'

By this time Princess Amelia, aged forty-two, 'drank beer like a fast young buck of the present day,' wrote the historian R. E. M. Peach, 'and took snuff like an old woman of her own day . . . She wore a hunting cap, a laced scarlet coat, rode on horseback at a spanking pace, accompanied by her favourite groom, Spurrier'. She rose early in the morning and sat up late at night gambling. 'Her language, without being vulgar, was emphatic and not quite *"comme il faut."*' A contemporary reported that she would come regularly to the Pump Room to take a morning glass of water between 7am and 8am, then another at 8.15am. Her deafness was 'much as it was. It is not fixt; some days she hears tolerably, and others not so. She is very affable and civil, comes to the room at noon lately, and sometimes at nights, and plays at cards there, chiefly at Commerce. She takes all opportunity, when fair, of getting on horseback, and amuses herself almost every day some hours in angling in the river, in a summer-house by the riverside in the garden formerly known by the name of Harrison's Walks, which has two fire-places in it, and to secure her against cold, puts on a riding-habit, and a black velvet postillion-cap, tied under her chin.'[34]

The princess visited Bath again in November 1776, when Lady Diana Beauclerk wrote to a friend, '*Entre nous*, this is a most detestable place . . . and, to make it complete, the Princess Amelia is here, poking about it in every corner. It is impossible to stir without meeting her, and as I have no hopes of her being gracious enough to take notice of me, I am obliged to avoid her. Perhaps you think her taking notice of one would be a still better reason for avoiding her.' Amelia, who never married, remained loyal to Bath and made her final visit ten years later during her last illness.

Other royalty, meanwhile, had been to Bath. The Prince of Orange came twice, the first time for a seven-week stay to strengthen himself before his marriage to Princess Amelia's elder sister, Anne. He was so short and hunchbacked that, according to Lord Hervey, he looked behind as if he had no head, and in front as if without neck or legs, and his breath was 'more offensive than it is possible for those who have not been offended by it to imagine'. Nevertheless a London paper described the visit as 'one continued scene of affability, generosity, and humanity to all degrees of persons'. The prince was taken to see the sights of Bath, which included Ralph Allen's stone quarries and John Wood's part-finished masterpiece, Queen's Square.

He came back with his wife soon after their marriage. Princess Anne had 'a lively clean look and a very fine complexion, though she was marked a good deal by small-pox . . .' but her person was 'very ill made' with 'a great propensity to fat'. She was 'the proudest of all her proud family; and her family the proudest of all their proud nation'.[35] In honour of their visit Beau Nash erected a thirty-foot obelisk (the space in which this stands, the Orange Grove, takes its name from the prince, not from some medieval orange orchard) and Dr William Oliver, who attended the prince, composed the inscription.

In 1738 George II's son, Frederick, Prince of Wales, came to Bath and presented Nash with a large gold enamelled snuff box to add to his collection. In return, Nash erected a second obelisk, this time of seventy feet, to stand at the centre of Queen's Square, in the prince's honour. Nash 'was determined that the inscription should answer the magnificence of the pile' and wrote to Pope for a suitable one. Pope clearly did not fancy the task, and wrote back saying that he had no idea what kind of inscription to compose: 'Whether the P—— most loves poetry or prose, I protest I do not know, but this I dare venture to affirm, that you can give him as much satisfaction in either as I can.'

When a second letter from Nash persuaded Pope, he asked for his name not to be mentioned. This, Goldsmith says, showed his 'consciousness of his own importance . . . In all his letters, as well as those of Swift, there runs a strain of pride, as if the world talked of nothing but themselves. "Alas," says he in one of them, "the day after I am dead, the sun will shine as bright as the day before, and the world will be merry as usual!" Very strange, that neither an eclipse nor an earthquake should follow the loss of a poet.'

Pope's inscription read:

> In Memory of honours bestow'd
> And in gratitude for benefits conferred in
> This city
> By his Royal Highness
> Frederick, Prince of Wales,
> And his Royal Consort
> In the year 1738,
> This obelisk is erected by
> Richard Nash, Esq.

'I dare venture to say', Goldsmith added, 'there was scarce a common-council-man in the corporation of Bath, but could have done this as well.'

In 1750 when Frederick paid a second visit to Bath he was entertained by Ralph Allen at Prior Park. Next year the prince died, thus never succeeding to the throne. Allen, who rarely made deprecating remarks about other people, especially those with power or influence, wrote to a friend that although the prince seemed to understand quickly things he was told, soon afterwards he 'appeared to know nothing'.

From the mid-eighteenth century onwards there were regular royal visitors to Bath, including the Duke of Cumberland, victor of Culloden, known popularly as the Butcher. He spent a day and a half in the city, then left at five in the morning and rode eighty miles to Windsor by midday.

The hosts

The many well-known accounts of eighteenth- and early nineteenth-century Bath create a picture of the city which has one large gap: its ordinary people, the tradesmen, labourers and servants who made possible the comfortable lives of its twice-yearly flood of middle- and upper-class visitors. Even the successful shopkeeper-tradesmen whose names we know – Mr Gill, the pastry cook, for example – remain names rather than rounded characters. Most of Bath's fashionable residents or visitors seem to have noticed only each other, or at least only to have considered each other worth describing. Economic historians, in particular R. S. Neale, have tried to fill this gap, using for their sources the records of Bath's apprenticeships, of the applications of its poor for poor law relief, and of its law court hearings.

Until about 1765 it was essential for anyone who wished to be a Bath tradesman to serve an apprenticeship in the city and so become a freeman, since only a freeman of Bath could work as an artisan or set up in business there. The records of apprenticeships were therefore carefully kept. They show what an important place of manufacture Bath became during these years; there were apprenticeships in no fewer than 68 different trades. They also show, as one might expect, that the trades which flourished in Bath were precisely those which catered for its visitors' needs, providing them with houses, food, clothes, foot and head wear, and medicines. During the forty-five years from 1724 the largest numbers of apprentices were training to become shoemakers, carpenters, tailors, barbers and wigmakers, masons and bakers, in that order.

Companies of traders in Bath's various trades continually tried to prevent those who were not freemen from working in the city, while outsiders were continually trying to outwit them. Charles Knight, a tailor in the 1760s, who had been an apprentice in Batheaston, which was not considered a part of Bath, would make up clothes in Batheaston and avoid being discovered when he brought them to his customers in Bath by wearing them. Presently he worked in the city at Ladymead. From here he was driven by threats from an official of the Company of Merchant Taylors and moved to Wolcot, but after six months he returned to Ladymead. Far from growing prosperous as a result of his illegal trading, he was always excused the fines which the company imposed on him because of his poverty.

Bath's poor-law hearings record even more pathetic cases. Two-thirds of those who applied for relief were women and a high proportion of these were pregnant unmarried girls or pregnant deserted young wives. Frequently they were girls from modestly respectable families in the countryside around Bath who had been drawn by the work the city offered. Martha Abraham was typical. Her father was a tenant farmer in the village of Chew Magna. She had even visited Bath privately for her health, before returning there as a servant. First she worked for a young man in Orchard Street, then for a wine merchant, then for a soap boiler, each of whom gave her lodging as well as a wage. The wine merchant also made her pregnant. Since she was only three and a half months with the soap boiler, it was presumably when he discovered her condition that he dismissed her. Now she was destitute.

It may not be surprising to discover cases like Martha's at Bath in the eighteenth century, however much of a contrast they provide with fashionable Bath. The records of Bath's courts, however, show a more unexpected aspect of life among the working classes of the city. By an enormous margin, the largest number of cases in the years for which there are records (1777 and 1787–93) were for assault or for breaches of the peace: 3123 out of a total of 3813. From these figures Neale argues that the social conditions of Bath had produced a working population which was quite unusually quarrelsome and violent. 'Trapped as they were', he writes, 'in low-paid occupations and subjected to decisions made by men of substance such as the Mayor and the Justices of the Peace, they turned their rage upon themselves in acts of self-destruction.'

The number of riots which occurred in the city support the suggestion that the working population of Bath frequently became violent. The anti-Catholic riot which drove Fanny Burney and the Thrales from the city in 1780 (see page 178) may have been the most dramatic but was far from singular. Earlier the same year there had been a riot when Philip Thicknesse suggested in his memoirs that breathing the breath of young virgins promoted health and long life. The mob burned Thicknesse in effigy. Before that, in the early 1740s and in 1765, there had been bread riots. Afterwards, in 1784, journeymen rioted in an attempt to drive non-union tailors out of town, and in 1793 there was a similar outbreak with a similar cause. In 1800 when the price of wheat rose by fifty per cent in a fortnight the mob burned down a brewery and two hundred women assaulted vegetable sellers in the market place, forcing them to open their sacks and charge low prices.

Without doubt the poor of Bath were in part so fractious because of their bad living conditions. Around the architectural set-pieces of eighteenth-century Bath were great areas of narrow streets, densely lined with small, insanitary houses. Avon Street, south-west of Queen's Square, was typical. It had been built at about the same time as the square – 1726–32 – to provide accommodation which was better than the worst. But because it ran down to the river it was used by waggoners to water their horses. While the horses drank in the river the waggoners drank at its eleven alehouses – one in every eight houses in the street. Furthermore, some of the inhabitants kept pigs, and many of them threw into the street 'all kinds of nastiness', while the scavenger only came once a week. The result, according to a complaining resident, was that it became 'a perfect muckson from one end to the other'. And because building on the river banks had narrowed the channel, Avon Street's basements were regularly flooded by a mixture of river water and sewage. Not surprisingly, in 1831, when forty-nine people died of cholera in the city, twenty-seven of them lived in Avon Street.

Bath also had its prostitutes, and though few of their names or stories have survived, two clerical diarists noted them. In the 1780s James Woodforde gave a shilling and some good advice to two who were seventeen and fifteen years old respectively. And in the 1830s John Skinner of Camerton was 'not a little astonished to observe the streets so crowded with prostitutes, some of them apparently not above fourteen or fifteen years of age'. And like any prosperous resort, Bath had its beggars. John Wood described a refined form of their activities. When the time came for visitors to leave, it was usual to tip, not only the pumper of the pump room, the sergeants of the baths and the porters of the asssembly rooms, but also 'a set of lazy idle people, whose business is to pray for their good journey'. These would then quarrel about dividing their spoil before going to 'ease themselves of it, as soon as possible, in the gin shop or ale-house'.

Sally Lunns, Bath's breakfast buns

'Breakfast and afternoon teas and sally lunns, as usual obtainable at Sydney Gardens, Vauxhall, New Road [Bathwick], Bath and Spring Gardens, Vauxhall or the other side of the river opposite the Grove'.

So read a somewhat confusing advertisement of 1795. Despite the tradition that, from 1705 onwards, the fashionable society of Beau Nash's Bath would breakfast on teacakes known as Sally Lunns, this advertisement is the earliest printed mention of them that has been found. A year later the *Bath Chronicle* published an eleven-verse poem by one Major Drewe of Exeter, which included their supposedly secret recipe and began,

> No more I heed the Muffin's zest,
> The Yorkshire cake or bun
> Sweet muse of Poetry! teach me how
> To make a Sally Lunn.

From this time onwards Sally Lunns were an established part of the Bath legend. W. S. Gilbert, librettist of the Savoy Operas, knew about them:

> Now for the tea of our host,
> Now for the rollicking bun

Now for the muffin and toast –
Now for the gay Sally Lunn.

And Charles Dickens refers to Sally herself as 'the illustrious author of the tea cake'.

According to legend she arrived in Bath about 1680. At first she worked for a baker, selling her buns in the street, then she bought the business herself. At public breakfasts during the season Sally Lunns were served in silver dishes. The bakery became a coffee house which (inevitably) Beau Nash is said to have patronised. At one time Ralph Allen may also have used the house for his post office. There is firmer evidence that, until 1743, it belonged to the Duke of Kingston – father of the Duke who married the bigamous duchess (see page 169). Today Sally Lunns can still be eaten at the small house, not far from the abbey, where Sally is said to have baked them.

Certainly this house, which claims to be the oldest in Bath, has been a bakery for many centuries, possibly since Roman times. The remains of the Roman building which once occupied the site can be seen today in the house's tiny basement museum. So can remains of many other periods, among them a faggot oven of the sort used throughout Europe from mediaeval times till the present century. Such ovens consist of a tortoise-shaped cave, floored and roofed with brick or stone. Bundles of faggots are burned inside, the ashes raked out and the bread or buns baked by the oven's retained heat.

In the late nineteenth century the proprietor of the time, a Mr Palmer, no doubt used this oven for his public roasting service. He used to cook up to two hundred dinners a day, charging a penny for a small roast and twopence for a large one. A dinner of this sort was called 'a schooner on the rocks', because of its form. The meat, set on a grid at the centre of the pan, was the schooner while the vegetables, awash in the surrounding gravy, were the rocks.

Sally Lunns are real enough, but their inventor is now suspect. In France her sort of bun, because of its golden top and white underside, was traditionally called a 'Sol et Lune'.

Bath's chairs and chair-men

The sedan chair, invented in the French town of Sedan, was brought to England by the Duke of Buckingham, James I's flamboyant lover and minister. Though there was some public protest against men being made to act as horses, it grew popular, and – perhaps because it suited invalids and narrow streets – it became Bath's special method of transport.

Chairs were of various designs. Some were roofless, some had roofs which lifted to allow women with tall hats to enter, some had doors at the side like a carriage, some at the front between the poles. The poles also varied, some being long, some short so that they could be carried upstairs to bedrooms and the bathers taken directly from their beds to the baths. Christopher Anstey's *New Bath Guide* describes one of these operations (see pages 124–6).

The chair-men, who were necessarily strong and tall, had a reputation for extortion and threatening behaviour. John Wood, describing the chair-men of the seventeenth century, wrote that it was common for 'those turbulent people to provoke gentlemen to draw their swords upon them, and then, by defending themselves with their chair poles, the danger of murder frightened the ladies to such a degree that the public assemblies for diversion seldom ended without the utmost confusion'. When Beau Nash imposed his civilising authority on Bath he also disciplined the chair-men. But they continued to be unruly. In 1743 chair-men pelted a duke with mud when he refused to be carried and chose to walk. The corporation offered a twenty-guinea reward for the discoverer of those responsible.

Bath's sedan chairs may have been convenient, but they were not comfortable, according to Smollett's Matthew Bramble in *Humphrey Clinker*. 'At present [they] stand soaking in the open street, from morning to night, till they become so many boxes of wet leather . . . Even the close chairs, contrived for the sick, by standing in the open air, have their frize linings impregnated like so many spunges, with the moisture of the atmosphere, and those cases of cold vapour must give a charming check to the perspiration of a patient, piping hot from the Bath, with all his pores wide open.'

In Nash's time the hire of a chair cost sixpence for 500 yards or three shillings for two miles, but in 1793 the council tried to introduce a single charge irrespective of distance. When the chair-men rioted, gathering outside the Guildhall and destroying the chairs of anyone who came there to apply for a licence, the corporation withdrew its bye-law.

The new Bath chair with wheels, invented by one Arthur Dawson in 1780, led eventually to the disappearance of sedan chairs, but not for many years. There were still large numbers for hire in the mid-nineteenth century, alongside Bath chairs. These last, which had three wheels and were known as 'rumblers' because of the noise of their wheels on the streets' cobbles, increased in number till at one time there were 180. Some were still operating in the 1920s when H. V. Morton saw them:

> On wet days the chair-men sleep inside their chairs with little doors closed, sitting up behind glass panels like mummies in their sarcophagi; on fine days they sleep outside them.
> 'Your profession is not an exciting one?' I suggested to a veteran chair-man.
> He considered for some time and replied:
> 'No.'
> 'I can't think how you all make a living out of Bath chairs.'
> 'We don't. We do a little carpet-beating now and then and odd jobs. It isn't much of a life.'

By 1937 there were only six, and a final run was made by Ernest Ball in 1939, pulling a chair weighing 2 cwt, manufactured in 1830. His family had been in the chair business for two hundred years and his ancestors must have included those six-foot sedan chair-men who so alarmed timid eighteenth-century ladies.

Pulteney and the bridge

Pulteney Bridge, Bath's unique shop-lined bridge, and Pulteney Street, the magnificent 1000-foot street which leads away from the bridge and is certainly the city's, perhaps the country's finest, were named after Sir William Pulteney (1684–1764), who became Earl of Bath, but he never saw either of them. He commissioned his friend, Robert Adam, to build the bridge. It had an obvious commercial purpose: to link the city of Bath with the large estate Pulteney owned beyond the River Avon at

Bathwick, which until then was connected to the city only by ferry. But Pulteney died in 1764 and it was only built during the following five years. It is the sole Adam building in the city.

Adam also drew a plan for Bathwick itself but eventually Pulteney's daughter, Henrietta Laura, commissioned the city's architect, Thomas Baldwin, to design Pulteney Street. Henrietta Street and Laura Place which formed part of his plan were named after her. Work began in 1788.

Pulteney had no family connections with Bath, but bought his Bathwick estate in 1726 from the descendants of the Earls of Essex. By then he had been married to Anna Maria Gumley for twelve years. This much-abused lady was described by one contemporary as 'Bath's enobled droxy',[36] and by Lord Hervey, another regular visitor to Bath, in more measured but equally offensive terms. She had nothing to recommend her but her beauty, and was 'a weak woman with all the faults of a bad man, of low birth and lower mind, and the lowest manner . . . whose temper both he [Pulteney] and every other body abhored'. By 'low-birth' Hervey meant that she was the daughter (and sole heir) of a manufacturer of Isleworth. Pulteney had already inherited one fortune and she brought him another. Money interested them both, and she was said, by clever investment, to have turned a nest-egg he gave her of £10,000 into £60,000.

From an early age Pulteney was an active politician, at first a supporter of Robert Walpole, then, when Walpole became George I's Prime Minister, his most bitter enemy. It was Pulteney who formed the opposition group inside the Whig party known as the Patriots, which included such politicians as Pitt the Elder. He also founded and wrote for *The Craftsman*, which for ten years abused Walpole and the government.

Pulteney's pamphleteering led to the most dramatic episode in his life, his duel with Lord Hervey. This was the culmination of a pamphlet war during which Pulteney called Hervey 'half-man, half-woman', and each denied he was the author of the pamphlet the other complained about. They fought in what is now Green Park, London, behind Arlington Street, between 3 and 4pm on 25 March 1731. Each wounded the other but Pulteney presently had Hervey at his mercy and would have run him through the body if his foot had not slipped in the mud. The seconds took this opportunity to separate them, and Pulteney embraced Hervey, promising never to attack him personally again. Hervey, however, 'made a bow without giving him any sort of answer'.[37]

It may have been because of his quarrel with Pulteney that Hervey claimed that Pulteney's character changed dramatically during his life. He had been 'the most agreeable and coveted companion of his time'. 'It was very remarkable in Mr Pulteney,' Hervey continued, 'that he never liked the people with whom he acted chiefly in his public character, nor loved those with whom he passed his idler hours.' Hervey lists those, from Walpole onwards, whom Pulteney neither liked nor loved, then, coming to himself, says that the manner in which Pulteney broke off their friendship showed that it had had no deep roots.

Hervey claimed that it was he who suggested to George II in 1742 the way in which to eliminate Pulteney as a politician: by promoting him to the House of Lords. Pulteney may not have realised the effect this would have. He told a friend that during the crisis that year he 'lost his head' and had to leave London for a day or two. The title he took was Earl of Bath.

At once he became highly unpopular for betraying the cause of Liberty. During the next two years his most persistent critic, Charles Hanbury Williams, attacked him in 24 published poems or squibs.

> So virtuous Pulteney, who had long
> By speech, by pamphlet, and by song,
>   Held patriotism's steerage,
> Yields to ambition mixt with gain,
> A treasury gets from Harry Vane
>   And for himself a peerage,

Williams wrote in *The Country Girl*. Another of his verses was pinned to the front door of Pulteney's house in Piccadilly:

> Here, dead to fame, lives patriot Will,
>   His grave a lordly seat,
> His title proves his epitaph,
>   His robes his winding sheet.

Soon after the attacks began Pulteney met Hanbury Williams at Bath to discuss elections in Wales, and they even dined together. Since Hanbury Williams's verses were published anonymously, he, not Pulteney, must have enjoyed the irony of this convivial evening.

Two years earlier Pulteney had met the witty and beautiful Elizabeth Chudleigh, the future bigamous Duchess of Kingston, and by introducing her to court in London helped to promote the greatest private scandal of the century (see page 169).

During the last twenty-two years of his life Pulteney's political influence remained small, but not his fortune. When he died Lord Chesterfield sent his son a description of the enormous wealth he left – entirely to his brother, General Pulteney, 'though he never loved and justly despised him'. His legacies were trifling, Chesterfield continued, 'for, in truth he cared for nobody; the words *give* and *bequeath* were too shocking to him to repeat'.

The new Assembly Rooms

On 24 May 1769 John Wood the younger, in the presence of the Mayor of Bath, laid the foundation stone of Bath's new Assembly Rooms. 'A band of music attended and great ceremony was observed.'[38] The rooms were a private venture, with a capital of £14000, divided into 70 shares of which 53 had so far been bought. A little over two years later the new rooms were complete and ready for their official opening. Captain Wade, having succeeded Samuel Derrick as Master of Ceremonies, presided. Thomas Gainsborough, who had painted Wade's portrait for the new rooms, got three free tickets.

The new rooms were in the upper town and competed with the two older Assembly Rooms in the lower town. Early in the next century, however, Wiltshire's (originally Lindsey's, founded in 1728 by the notorious Mrs Lindsey who had misled Fanny Braddock), were demolished to make room for York Street. And in 1820 Harrison's, opened at Beau Nash's suggestion in 1708, were gutted by fire, though their shell was not finally demolished till 1933.

Captain Wade, unlike his immediate predecessor, Derrick, was an effective Master of Ceremonies, issuing regulations for correct behaviour and appropriate dress. Ladies who danced minuets at balls were to be 'dressed in a suit of clothes or a full-trimmed sack, with lappets and dressed hoops, such as are usually worn at St James's'. For country dancing they were not to wear hoops and those who chose to pull them off would 'be assisted by proper servants in an appartment for that purpose'.[39] Gentlemen who danced minuets were to wear 'a full-trimmed suit of clothes, or French frock, hair or wig dressed with a bag'. Henry William Bunbury's engraving of a ball in progress which hangs today in the Assembly Rooms shows the grotesque realities which such elegant costumes failed to hide.

The new Assembly Rooms were hit by bombs and burned down during the air raid of 25–26 April 1942. The rooms had become less and less successful during the nineteenth century. They were saved financially for a time in 1903 by the sale of Gainsborough's portrait of Captain Wade, but during the First World War they were occupied by the Royal Flying Corps, and after the war the ball room was used as a cinema. In 1931, however, Ernest Cook enabled them to be bought and presented to the National Trust. They were elaborately restored and in 1938 reopened by the Duchess of Kent – just three years before the German bombs fell on them.

It was not till 1963, twenty-five years after their first reopening, that the rooms, now reconstructed inside the surviving shell as nearly as possible in their eighteenth-century form, were again reopened, this time by HRH Princess Marina.

3

THE DOCTORS AND THE WATERS

Dr Radcliffe and the toad

Beau Nash, according to John Wood the elder, was not elected 'King of Bath' merely because he had been the assistant of his predecessor, Captain Webster, but because he had done the city an important service. At about this time 'the greatest physician of the age, in revenge for an affront that was put upon him by some of the inhabitants',[40] claimed to have put a toad into the baths of Bath.

The physician was Dr John Radcliffe (1650–1714), the Oxford-educated doctor who eventually left money which was used to found Oxford's Radcliffe Infirmary. Throughout his life he was in and out of favour with members of the royal family, saving William III's life during an acute attack of asthma, telling Queen Mary that she would die of smallpox because she had been given the wrong medicines (she did), refusing to attend Queen Anne when she was dying because he knew she disliked him, and because he had an attack of gout. Other patients had equally varied opinions of him. In London some would pretend to be ill so that they could enjoy his witty conversation. But after his death a contemporary who knew him, Peter Wentworth, wrote that 'he died like an ill-natured brute as he has lived'.

Just how the inhabitants of Bath had offended him is uncertain, but as part of the quarrel a scurrilous pamphlet was published entitled 'A Letter from a Citizen of Bath to his Excellency, Dr R—— at Tunbridge'. Radcliffe's use of a toad for revenge would suit the less kind estimates of his character, since at the time its spit was believed to be highly poisonous.

Fortunately for Nash, he knew of claims published in Paris in 1702 that a tarantula's bite could be cured by music, so 'finding that a fiddle was capable of dispelling the rankest poison, he immediately set up that instrument against the doctor's reptile'.[41] It was then that the citizens of Bath, who seem to have been as easily reassured as frightened, elected Nash as their king.

The diseases of Bath

An anonymous poem with the title *The Diseases of Bath* gives a daunting but believable picture of Bath's doctors, chemists, baths and the Pump Room in 1737. It begins,

> My friend! I've heard you often plight your faith,
> That few sick-folks go mended from the *Bath*.

After a few general warnings about Bath's 'unwholesome fogs', and 'rough jarring winds' which 'belch down rheumatic spasms from the surrounding hills'; about its 'trifling mayor', 'squabbling corporation', and 'sharking people'; and about its small-pox, 'scarlet rash, or quinzeys in the throat', and other chronic infectious diseases, it comes to the city's doctors. William Oliver, inventor of the famous biscuit, is not mentioned but his surgeon partner, Jerry Peirce, is. He is the only one to escape castigation.

> *Peirce* is humane, and tho' a surgeon bred,
> Is much too honest to enhance his trade:
> Deals but against his grain in blood and steel;
> And can the pain, he gives his patients, feel.
> Not of that base, amphibious Fry of Men,
> Whose bare Approach wou'd make a Wound gangrene.
> Proof against gold, friend to his species: – He
> Hates Mischief's hand, tho' It presents a fee.
> Oh! wou'd that canibal, man-mangling Brood
> Learn from thee, Peirce, not to delight in blood;
> Wou'd they some quarter to a Patient give:
> Hack the Dupe's fortune; but his Limbs reprieve!
> Or, if their Rage unglutted with his Store
> Must needs be fed on Flesh and drench'd with Gore;
> Wou'd they at once his Chest and Life invade,
> And, less inhuman, shoot him thro' the Head;

In turn the poem then deals with five others, Florifer, Harrington, Procus, Bostick and Cheyne:

Say, florid *Florifer*, if you can tell:
How many Patients you've dispatch'd to Hell?
Say *Harrington* of not inferior skill!
How many Church-yards thy Prescriptions fill?
Procus has laid his thousands on the Floor,
And modest *Bostick* his ten thousands more.
Big blustering *Cheyné*, not the last to fame,
Tho' the Muse lead up in the rear his Name,
Has sent such colonies to *Pluto's* land;
The God was forc'd to beg he'd stop his hand.

But its most vivid picture is of Stercorio, one of Bath's nineteen apothecaries:

Of stern *Stercorio* view the bloated *Mien*
Where ev'ry Poison of his shop is seen.
His raging Caustics flame upon his Nose,
With drowsy Poppies loaded are his Brows:
His cheeks puffed up with Arsinic, Gaul, and Sloth;
His rabid jaws bedevil'd with viper's Froth,
His Features plastered o'er with leaprous Scales
His bob in ringlets curl'd like Serpents' Tails. . .
His shop a nauseous, litter'd Magazine
Of all that is unwholesome and unclean:
From the low Roof on hempen Lines are hung
Dried insects, Bladders, and stale Simples strung.
Here Cobwebs dangle from a Crocodile;
There Spiders spin from the Prescription-file
Above on dusty Shelves in less'ning Rows,
Stand empty Gally-pots for idle Shews;
Beneath – in ranks, gilt-letter'd Draw'rs are seen,
Titled from damag'd Drugs contain'd within:
In this Glass-case a Skeleton is stow'd
And in that Box lies a disected Toad.
Behind the counter, lo! the Sloven sits,
Mixing a Cordial for *Sherbetta's* Fits
Round him in foul Confusion scatter'd lie
Spread Plaisters, Salves, and Med'cines, wet and dry. . .

The author then visits the baths and the Pump Room:

What sickly, crude, offensive vapours there
The Nostrils snuff up with the tainted Air!
Whole Groups of Foppish Slovens foully fine
In dirty Shirts, and Tinsel stink and shine;

Midst Crowds of Dames, who in their nightly Trim,
Just reeking from their Beds, still stew and steam:
An ill-bred, restless, wild, and cackling Host,
Noisy as Goslings spreading from the Roost. . .
By patient squeezing to the Pump I get;
There roughly thrust next to some Clown I wait;
Who, when he'as rudely swill'd his Potion up,
Leaves me the slobber'd favour of his Cup.

The vegetarian Dr Cheyne

In 1741 Dr George Cheyne (1671–1743) wrote to his patient,
the novelist Samuel Richardson, 'My case was at first worse
than any one's . . . I ever read of or saw[,] a putrified overgrown body from luxury and perpetual laziness, scorbutical all
over, a regular St Anthony's fire every two months, regularly
the gout all over six months of the year, perpetual reachings,
anxiety, giddiness, fitts and startings . . . vomits were my only
relief which I continued at least eight or nine years . . .'

Cheyne gives a fuller account of his case in his book, *The
English Malady*, and of how he came to believe that the cure for
most ills was a milk and vegetable diet. It was his vegetarian
theories which made him for some thirty years one of the best-
known doctors in the country.

He came from Aberdeen where he was 'born of healthy
parents in the prime of their day', but was 'disposed to
corpulence by the whole race of one side of my family'. As a
child he was studious and intended, like his half-brother, for
the church but instead chose medicine. Presently he came under
the influence of the Edinburgh physician, Dr Archibald Pitcairne. 'If I ever shall be able to do anything in medicine',
Cheyne wrote, 'it was by [Pitcairne] that the foundations were
laid.' Pitcairne specialised in fevers and Cheyne first made his
name by publishing a paper which vigorously defended Pitcairne's theories. It was written, he later admitted, 'with more
edge than became so grave a subject of debate'.

In 1702 he came to London where he was elected a Fellow of
the Royal Society. Since his first cousin once removed was
Bishop Burnet, author of the important sourcebook, *The
History of his own Times*, and Burnet was himself a Fellow of

the Royal Society, he probably helped in having Cheyne elected. Thirteen years later, when Burnet was dying, his case was so serious that three doctors were called: Dr Richard Mead, Sir Hans Sloane (the developer of Chelsea) and Cheyne. An account, written as if by Dr Mead's gold-headed cane, gives a picture of Cheyne at the bedside.

On the one side of me [the cane] stood Sloane; on the other Dr Cheyne, a Scotchman with an immense broad back, taking snuff incessantly out of a ponderous gold box, and thus ever and anon displaying to view his fat knuckles; a perfect Falstaff, for he was not only a good portly man and a corpulent, but was almost as witty as the knight himself, and, his humour being heightened by his northern tongue, he was exceedingly mirthful. Indeed, he was the most excellent wit of his time, a faculty he was often called upon to exercise to repel the lampoons which were made by others upon his extraordinary personal appearance.

Describing his way of life during this time in London, Cheyne wrote that he

found the bottle companions, the younger gentry and the free livers to be the most easy of access and most quickly susceptible of friendship and acquaintance, nothing being necessary for that purpose but to be able to eat lustily and swallow down as much liquor; and being naturally of a large size and cheerful temper and tolerably lively imagination, and having in my country retirement laid in stores of ideas and facts, by these qualifications I soon became caressed by them and grew daily in bulk and in friendship with these gay gentlemen . . .

In attempting to cure himself after he had suffered an apoplectic fit which forced him to hold on to his bedposts to prevent himself falling out of bed, he took medicines which nearly killed him, starting with four ounces of 'bark' (quinine) in forty-eight hours. When his headaches, giddiness and general depression increased he moved to more formidable remedies. A friend had told him about *mercurial medicines* so he took '20 grains of what is called *princes powder*, which gave me twelve *vomits* and near twice the number of stools; and I had certainly perished under the operation, but for an *over-dose* of *laudanum* after it. In two or three days more, I took 12 grains of *turbid mineral*, which had not quite so violent an effect; after that, I took 10 grains of *calomel*, twice a day, for about 10 days together.' Not surprisingly, he now felt 'lightsomer indeed, and less confused, though still very bad'. Presently he suffered 'an extreme sickness in my *stomach*, which obliged me to take frequent *vomits*, these now pumping up *oceans* of *choler*'. But he concluded that his remedies had 'opened my obstructed *liver, gall-bladder* and *porus bilarius*, and broken the cohesion of the viscid juices'. As a result his body was 'melting away like a snow-ball in summer'.

The following year (Cheyne does not give a date) he tried the Bath waters, so probably making his first contact with the city. He went on to Bristol waters, but found his appetite so improved that he was once again putting on weight. It was this which finally drove him to consult Dr Taylor of Croydon. Arriving there one day he found the doctor 'at home, at his full quart of cow's milk (which was all his dinner)'. Taylor told Cheyne how a milk diet had cured his epilepsy, and 'removed the barrenness of some great families [who] had wanted heirs'. Convinced, Cheyne hired his own milk-woman to bring him enough 'pure and unmixed milk' for his breakfast and dinner every day. He never ate supper.

The rest of Cheyne's medical history is a tale of regular lapses and equally regular resolutions to give up drink and meat and return to a milk and vegetable diet. He now began to practise at Bath every summer, and it was here that he suffered his most serious relapse. 'I swelled to such an enormous size, that, upon my last weighing, I exceeded 32 stone. My breath became so short, that, upon stepping into my chariot quickly, and with some effort, I was ready to faint away, for want of breath and my face turned black.' He was unable to walk more than one hundred paces, and even then 'was obliged to have a servant follow me with a stool to rest upon'. A horrible attack of erysipelas came next, which reached a climax when his 'whole *leg, thigh*, and *abdomen*' became '*tumified, incrusted* and burnt almost like the skin of a roasted pig: and such a quantity of ichor issued from it, as was not to be expressed'.

Cheyne survived and, in spite of what he says about his low spirits, was much liked as a doctor and known particularly for his cheeriness and wit. Ralph Allen consulted him. Fielding mentions him under his own name ('the learned Dr Cheyney') in *Tom Jones*. He was Samuel Richardson's doctor for many years (see page 166) and when Richardson printed a revised edition of Defoe's *A Tour Through the Whole Island of Great Britain*, Cheyne wrote the section on Bath's waters. Pope said about Cheyne that there was 'not an honester or truer philosopher', and George Lyttelton that he was 'so very like a child in the simplicity of heart that I love him as he loves Don Quixote for the most moral and reasoning madman in the world'.

Even Beau Nash, who had an interest in promoting Bath's waters as opposed to Cheyne's vegetable diet, and told Cheyne that he believed 'his design was to send half the world grazing, like Nebuchadnezzar', admitted that he was 'the most sensible fool he ever met in his life', and 'less of a blockhead than he used to be'. A number of examples have been preserved of the arguments they had with each other, which 'sometimes began with temper and jokes [but] were frequently heightened to clamour and quarrelling, so that the breeze of the mind was succeeded by a hurricane'.[42] Nash's habit of having supper about nine or ten in the evening of hot roast breast of mutton and potatoes, and then going to bed 'induced Dr Cheyney to tell him jestingly "that he behaved like other brutes, and lay down as soon as he had filled his belly."' '"This prescription I had from my neighbour's cow"', Nash replied, '"who is a better physician than you, and a superior judge of plants."'

After Cheyne's death in 1743 at the age of seventy-two his books continued to be admired, for example by Dr Johnson who recommended reading him in conversation and in a letter to Boswell. When Boswell said that Cheyne was 'reckoned whimsical', Johnson replied that there were few books to which some objection could not be made. He particularly admired *The English Malady*, but warned Boswell not to learn from it the 'foolish notion that melancholy is a proof of acuteness'. When Johnson needed for his dictionary an example of the use of the word 'popgun' he quoted Cheyne: 'Life is not weak enough to be destroyed by the popgun artillery of tea and coffee'.

Charles Wesley also admired Cheyne's books, saying that one of them was 'the most ingenious book I ever saw'. Cheyne's popular medical works – *Observations concerning the Nature and the Method of Treatment of Gout* (1720), *An Essay on Health and Long Life* (1724) and *The English Malady* (1733) – went into many editions. Besides his vegetarian recommendations, they contain judgements which were advanced by the standard of the times. 'Spirits', he wrote, 'have made more havoc among nations by far than gunpowder.'

The two Dr William Olivers

Dr William Oliver (1695–1764), the celebrated Bath physician and inventor of the Bath Oliver biscuit, is sometimes confused with an earlier Dr William Oliver (d. 1716) and sometimes said to have been his illegitimate son. In truth they were related, but not so intimately. The earlier Dr Oliver was the son of the rector of Launceston, Cornwall. The younger was the grandson of the rector's brother. They were thus first cousins once removed.

The earlier Dr Oliver also had connections with Bath. As a student he had gone to Leyden University in the Netherlands where he became involved with the Duke of Monmouth, and had joined Monmouth's rebellion of 1685 which ended so disastrously at Sedgemoor. When escaping with Monmouth he was given a feather which the Duke was wearing in his hat but was persuaded to remove to make himself less recognisable. This is the feather which is represented in stone above the older Dr Oliver's memorial tablet in Bath Abbey.

Dr Oliver, the tablet says, returned to England in 1688 as an officer in William III's army, because 'the miseries of his country called aloud for a deliverer' and he wanted to 'contribute his mite to so great a work'. He then became in turn doctor to the Fleet, doctor to the sick and wounded seamen at Chatham, and finally 'had the pleasure to have his old fellow sailors committed to his care' at the Royal Hospital, Greenwich. But he also apparently found time to 'practise physic many years' at Bath, and his love of the city, the tablet concludes, appears in his writings. The most important of these, published in 1707, was *Practical Dissertation on Bath Waters*. To the later editions of this he added the curious case-history given below.

The younger Dr William Oliver went to Pembroke College, Cambridge, and then, like his cousin, to Leyden University. He practised at Plymouth before coming to Bath about 1725. Here he was befriended by Ralph Allen and through Allen soon became doctor to many of the best-known citizens. With Allen, Beau Nash, and the architect John Wood the elder, he founded Bath's General Hospital. This was intended to be a hospital for the whole country, not for the inhabitants of Bath, who were considered to have enough opportunities to take the waters and were not admitted till the rules were changed in 1835.

Oliver was the hospital's first physician, and Jeremiah (Jerry) Peirce its first surgeon. The painting by the Bath painter, William Hoare, which hangs in the hospital's boardroom, shows Oliver and Peirce interviewing three patients, a man, a woman and a child, who are said by the caption to be suffering respectively from paralysis, rheumatism and leprosy. The woman certainly seems to have rheumatoid arthritis, the man to have 'dropped wrist' and perhaps to be a house painter with lead palsy, while the child is said to have psoriasis, often at that time called leprosy.

Oliver and Peirce had troubles at the hospital. During its early years they were involved in the sacking of Dr Cleland for improper conduct (see page 95), and fourteen years later they refused to attend consultations with two other doctors, William Baylies and Charles Lucas, because of their comments on the abuse of the waters and on their fellow physicians. But, on the whole, Oliver's life was free from such troubles, and he was much liked and trusted. Mary Chandler, Bath's local milliner poet, wrote about him, 'Heaven bade me live and you pre-scribed the way'. Perhaps she was prejudiced in his favour because he had given her so much help with her poem, *A Description of Bath* (1734) that 'ev'n Pope approv'd when you had tun'd my lyre'.

Pope himself wrote of Oliver, 'that delightful little man is the freest, the humblest, most entertaining creature you ever met,' and because of the stones that Oliver had given him for his grotto at Twickenham considered that he, and his Cornish friend, William Borlase, ought to have their statues 'erected in my cave, but I would much rather see their persons there'. The Countess of Huntingdon's description of Oliver as 'an invete-rate infidel til a short time before his death' is probably Methodist bigotry.

Oliver's only substantial medical work was *A Practical Essay on the Use and Abuse of Warm Bathing in Gouty Cases* (1757). Ironically, in old age he suffered severely from gout himself.

He also occasionally wrote verse, as when his friend Ralph Thicknesse, a composer, collapsed and died of a stroke at his side, regretting

> How he, who sounds celestial could combine
> Was snatched from earth in heavenly choir to shine.

When he tried less hard he could write more successfully. After the death of Beau Nash he published a 3d. pamphlet about him which Goldsmith used in his life of Nash. And he described nostalgically his own Cornish childhood:

> I remember the home and character of every dog I used to miss school to hunt with; I could go to every little thicket which was most likely to afford game; I have the memory of a tall sycamore out of which I used to cut whistles; I have the situation of the hazel which afforded the first *regale* in summer, and the Borlase's Pippen, which, like its namesake, was a high entertainment in a winter's evening, in a warm room, with a good fire.

In 1746, he bought a country house at Box, close to Bath, and called it 'Trevarnoe', in memory of his Cornish home. Here the famous Bath Oliver biscuit was invented and first made. It was intended to be plain, so that invalids could digest it, and consisted mainly of flour and water, but Oliver kept the precise recipe secret till he was dying. Then, according to legend, he gave it to his coachman, John Atkins, together with £100 and ten sacks of wheat flour. Atkins is supposed to have started a bakery in Green Street and grown rich.

The original recipe remained secret, but in 1829 Maria Eliza Randell published one for what she called 'Oliver's Biscuit':

> Mix a large spoonful of yeast in two spoonsful of new milk, put into a pound and a half of flour, and let it rise half an hour. Melt two ounces of butter and half an ounce of white sugar in as much milk as shall make the flour into a dough. Roll it out thin, cut into biscuits, prick well, and bake in a middling hot oven.

In the late nineteenth century the Bath Oliver was described as 'the only fermented biscuit in the world';[43] and by 1900, some 80,000 a day were being baked. A few years later it was

used in a Punch cartoon, which showed a waiter attending a
shabby man in a top hat sitting at a table. The caption read:

AWARDING THE BISCUIT
Dingy Bohemian: 'I WANT A BATH OLIVER.'
Immaculate Servitor: 'MY NAME IS NOT OLIVER.'

By the 1920s the recipe had certainly changed. Len Miles,
who was then working in the factory as a lad of seventeen,
remembered that it included white flour, pure bladder lard and
Australian butter and milk. To these, boiled and cooled hops
were added, together with malt. Another worker at this time
remembered (more probably) that it was the water in which the
hops had been boiled which was used to moisten the dough.

The Bath factory was hit by bombs in the German raid of
April 1942, and the biscuits were later made by Huntley and
Palmer at Reading, then by Jacob and Peak Frean at Liverpool.
In 1978 it was rumoured, falsely, that Bath Olivers might be
forbidden by a Common Market regulation against the mislead-
ing labelling of foods.

When Nabisco bought Jacob and Peak Frean and transferred
production to Bermondsey there was a serious shortage, and in
1984 Milburns, caterers to the Pump Room, began for the first
time for many years to make Bath Olivers at Bath, but they
had to make a guess at the secret recipe.

An extraordinarily sleepy person at Timsbury

Dr William Oliver the elder added this curious case-history to
the later editions of his *Practical Dissertation on Bath Waters*:

May the 13th, An. 1694. – One Samuel Chilton, of Timsbury, near Bath, a Labourer, about twenty-five years of age,
of a robust habit of body, not fat, but fleshy, and dark-brown
hair, happen'd without any visible cause, or preceding sign,
to fall into a very profound sleep; out of which no art, used
by those that were near him, could rouse him, till after a
month's time. Then he rose of himself, put on his cloaths,
and went about his business of husbandry as usual; slept,
could eat and drink as before, but spake not one word till
about a month after. All the time he slept, victuals stood by

him; his mother, fearing he would be starv'd in that sullen humour, as she thought it, put bread and cheese and small beer before him, which was spent every day.

From this time he remain'd free of any drowsiness or sleepiness, till about the 9th of April 1696, and then he fell into his sleeping fit again, just as he did before. After some days, they were prevail'd with to try what effect medicines might have on him; and accordingly one Mr Gibbs, a very able apothecary at Bath, went to him, bled, blister'd, cupp'd, and scarify'd him, and us'd all the external irritating medicines he could think on; but all to no purpose, nothing of all these making any manner of impression on him; and after the first fortnight he was never observed to open his eyes. Victuals stood by him as before, which he eat of now-and-then, as he had occasion; and sometimes they have found him fast asleep, with the pot in his hand in bed, and sometimes with his mouth full of meat. In this manner he lay for about ten weeks, and then could eat nothing at all; for his jaws seemed to be set, and his teeth clinch'd so close, that with all the art they had, they could not open his mouth, to put anything into it to support him. At last, observing a hole made in his teeth, by holding his pipe in his mouth, as most great smokers usually have, they, through a quill, poured some tent [Spanish red wine] into his throat, now-and-then. And this was all he took for six weeks and four days, and of that not above three pints or two quarts. He had made water but once, and never had a stool all that time.

August the 7th, which is seventeen weeks from the 9th April (when he began to sleep), he awaked, put on his cloaths, and walk'd about the room, not knowing he had slept above a night; nor could be persuaded he had lain so long, till going out into the fields, he found everybody busy in gathering in their harvest, and he remember'd very well, when he fell asleep, they were sowing of barley and oats, which he then saw ripe, and fit to be cut down.

There was one thing observable, that though his flesh was somewhat wasted with so long lying in bed, and fasting for above six weeks, yet a worthy gentleman, his neighbour, assur'd me, when he saw him (which was the first day of his coming abroad) he look'd brisker than ever he had seen him in his life before; and asking him, whether the bed had not made him sore, he assured him and everybody, that he neither found that, nor any other inconveniency at all; and that he had not the least remembrance of anything that pass'd or was done to him all that while. So he fell again to his husbandry, as he us'd to do, and remain'd well from that time till August the 17th, Anno 1697; when in the moring he complained of a shivering and coldness in his back, vomited once or twice, and that same day fell into his sleeping fit again.

Being then at the Bath, and hearing of it, I took horse on the 23rd, to inform myself of a matter of fact I thought so strange. When I came to the house, I was by the neighbours (for there was nobody at home at that time besides this man) brought to his bedside, where I found him asleep, as I had been told before, with a cup of beer and a piece of bread and cheese upon a stool by his bed, within his reach. I took him by the hand, felt his pulse, which was at that time very regular; I put my hand on his breast, and found his heart beat very regular too, and his breathing was very easy and free; and all the fault I found was, that I thought his pulse beat a little too strong. He was in a breathing sweat, and had an agreeable warmth all over his body. I then put my mouth to his ear, and, as loud as I could, called him by his name several times, pull'd him by his shoulders, pinch'd his nose, stopp'd his mouth and nose together, as long as I durst, for fear of choaking him, but all to no purpose; for in all this time he gave me not the least signal of his being sensible. I lifted up his eyelids, and found his eyeballs drawn up under his eyebrows, and fixed without any motion at all. Being baffled with all these tryals, I was resolv'd to see what effects Spirit of Sal Ammoniac would have, which I had brought with me to discover the cheat, if it had been one; so I held my vial under one nostril a considerable time, which being drawn from quick-lime was a very piercing spirit, and so strong I could not bear it under my own nose a moment, without making my eyes water; but he felt it not at all. Then I threw it, at several times, up that same nostril. It made his nose run and gleet, and his eyelids shiver and tremble a very little, and this was all the effect I found, though I poured up into one nostril about an half ounce bottle of this fiery spirit, which was as strong almost as fire itself. Finding no success with this neither, I crammed that nostril with powder of white hellebore, which I had by me, in order to make my farther tryals; and I can hardly think any imposter would ever be insensible of what I did. I tarry'd some time afterwards in the room, to see what effects all together might have upon him; but he never gave any token that he felt what I had done, nor discover'd any manner of uneasiness, by moving or stirring any one part of his body, that I could observe. Having made these my experiments, I left him, being pretty well satisfied he was really asleep, and no sullen counterfeit, as some people thought him.

Upon my return to Bath, and relating what I had observed, and what proofs this fellow had given me of his sleeping, a great many gentlemen went out to see him, as I had done, to satisfy their curiosity in a rarity of that nature, who found him in the same condition I had left him in the day before; only his nose was inflamed and swelled very much, and his lips and the inside of his right nostril blistered and scabby, with my spirit of Hellebore, which I had plentifully dosed him with the day before. His mother, for some time after, would suffer nobody to come near him, for fear of more experiments upon her son. About ten days after I had been with him, Mr Woolmer, an experienced apothecary at Bath, called at the house, being near Timsbury, went up into the room, finding his pulse pretty high, as I had done, took out his launcet, let him blood about fourteen ounces in the arm, tied his arm up again, nobody being in the house, and left him as he found him; and he assur'd me he never made the least motion in the world when he prick'd him, not all the while his arm was moving.

Several other experiments were made by those that went to see him every day from the Bath; but all to no purpose, as they told me on their return. I saw him myself again the latter end of September, and found him just in the same posture, lying in his bed, but removed from the house where he was before, about a furlong or more; and they told me, when they removed him by accident, carrying him down stairs, which were somewhat narrow, they struck his head against a stone, and gave him a severe knock, which broke his head, but he never moved any more at it than a dead man would. I found now his pulse was not quite so strong, nor had he any sweats, as when I saw him before. I tried him again the second time, by stopping his nose and mouth, but to no purpose. And a gentleman, then with me, ran a large pin into his arm to the very bone, unknown to me; but he gave us no manner of tokens of his being sensible of anything we did to him.

In this manner he lay till November 16, when his mother, hearing him make a noise, ran immediately up to him, and found him eating. She asked him how he did. He said, 'Very well, thank God.' She asked him again which he liked best, bread and butter, or bread and cheese? He answered, 'Bread and cheese.' Upon this, the poor woman, overjoy'd, left him, to acquaint his brother with it; and they came straight up into the chamber to discourse him, but found him as fast asleep again as ever, and all the art they had could not wake him. From this time to the end of January, or the beginning of February (for I could not learn from anybody the very day), he slept not so profoundly as before; for when they called him by his name, he seemed to hear them, and be somewhat sensible, though he could not make them any answer. His eyes were not now shut so close, and he had frequently great tremblings of his eyelids, upon which they expected when he would wake; which happen'd not till about the time just now mentioned, and then he walked perfectly well, not remembering anything that happened all this while. 'Twas observed he was very little altered in his flesh, only complained the cold pinched him more than usually, and so presently fell to husbandry, as at other times.

I have no reason to suspect this to be a cheat, because I never heard of any gain to the family by it, though so near Bath, and so many people went thither out of curiosity to see the sleeper, who, when awake, was a support to his old mother by his labour, but now a certain charge to her. Besides, there was seldom anybody in the house to attend any profits that might be made by it, he being left alone, and everybody at liberty to go up to his bedside.

Dr Oliver's detailed description suggests that his report of this case is not exaggerated. Nor does it seem likely that he was deceived by a fake, a possibility of which he was well aware but which he rejected. Doctors today suggest that the young man was an extreme case of hysteria, a condition which is frequently known to occur in people of low intelligence.

Dr Tobias Smollett and Mr Archibald Cleland

The novelist (and doctor) Tobias Smollett (1721–1771) was connected with Bath in two ways. In his novels, particularly *Humphrey Clinker*, he included descriptions of the social life of Bath which are some of the most lively to survive. He also played a vigorous part in the controversy over the sacking of Archibald Cleland from Bath's General Hospital.

Smollett was a Scot. He would have liked to go into the army, but was frustrated by his grandfather who considered it sufficient to have bought a commission for Smollett's elder brother, James. Instead Tobias chose medicine as a career, and studied it at Glasgow University.

Soon, however, he began to write, and by the time he moved to London at the age of about eighteen he already had an 'exceptionally bad'[44] play in his pocket. Having failed to get this staged, he became a naval surgeon, and in 1741 sailed with Admiral Vernon's fleet for South America. Here he was present during the disastrously mismanaged attempts to capture Cartagena. The fleet retreated to Jamaica, and all Smollett gained from the expedition was a Jamaican wife, Anne, the beautiful daughter of an English planter.

During the following years Smollett began to visit Bath, where he partly set his early novel, *Roderick Random* (1748). In it he included one of Beau Nash's cruder attempts to be witty: to a crippled lady who told Nash that she had come 'straight from London' Nash apparently said, 'Confound me, madam, then you must have been damnably warped on the way.' Smollett's quoting of this story was typical of his attitude to Bath, which became still more critical when he failed to establish himself as a doctor there.

In *Peregrine Pickle* (1751) he specifically attacked Bath's doctors and the way they conspired with London doctors to exploit visitors. There was, he wrote, 'a class of animals who live in this place, like so many ravens hovering round a carcass, and even ply for employment like scullers at Hungerford Stairs. The greatest part of them have correspondents in London, who make it their business to inquire into the history, character and distemper of every one that repairs to Bath for the benefit of the waters; and if they cannot procure interest to recommend their medical friends to these patients before they set out, they at least furnish them with a previous account of what they could collect, that their correspondents may use this intelligence for their own advantage.'

The following year he turned his attention to the waters themselves when he published his pamphlet, *An Essay on the External Use of Waters . . . with Particular Remarks upon the Present Method of Using the Mineral Waters of Bath*, and at the same time involved himself in the Cleland scandal.

This had begun soon after the opening of Bath's General Hospital, when Alexander Pope had asked Ralph Allen to give Cleland an appointment there. Allen, one of the governors, managed to have the rules bent in order to oblige Pope, and Cleland was made one of the hospital's assistant surgeons. It was a favour Allen must have come to regret.

A year later, in September 1743, Cleland was charged with making examinations, of an indecent sort, of patients of his fellow doctors without the permission of these colleagues. The patients were two whores, Mary Hook and Mary Hudson, and Cleland's supporters at the second of two meetings of the hospital governors which heard the case argued that their evidence should be disregarded. The governors nevertheless dismissed Cleland.

An abusive pamphlet war followed. Six were issued, some by Cleland's supporters, some by his enemies. Bath's leading booksellers, Leake and Frederick, published for the opposing sides. Cleland claimed that he had been investigating methods of treating fits and that he had not wanted to tell his fellow doctors what he was doing until he had useful results. What was more, he had suspected one of the women of being pregnant and had wanted to prevent her imposing on the hospital. But it was only when Smollett published his pamphlet some ten years later that the whole question of Cleland and the whores was shown to be irrelevant and the real explanation for Cleland's dismissal became clear. The final part of Smollett's pamphlet consisted of proposals which Cleland had made for reforming abuses at the hospital. It was these proposals which provoked the hospital establishment, and the charges against Cleland were only a convenient way of having him dismissed.

In defending Cleland, Smollett picked out for attack another notorious Bath character, William Warburton, Ralph Allen's protégé and future nephew-in-law, who later became Bishop of Gloucester. Warburton (in print at least) was one of the most quarrelsome people of the time, and Smollett suspected that, as a service to Allen, he had written one of the pamphlets attacking Cleland:

> At last, his [Cleland's] enemies had recourse to the pen of an author as notorious for the servile homage he yields to his patrons, as for the insolence and scurrility with which he treats all the world besides. True to these principles, this champion published an anonymous letter to Mr *Cleland*, wherein, after a chain of false reasoning, twanged off in all the arrogance of expression, some aukward attempts to ironical humour, and the most abusive low sarcasms, levelled at a lady of distinction, and, indeed, at a whole nation, on her account, he takes it for granted, that he has fully proved the truth of his unjust allegations . . .

The lady of distinction was Lady Inchiquin, who came from Scotland and was one of Cleland's defenders. The rest of Smollett's pamphlet must have made equally unpleasant reading for Ralph Allen, his fellow hospital governors and his fellow members of the Bath Corporation. Smollett maintained that bathing in mineral waters was of no greater benefit than bathing in any other sort of water, and that the baths of Bath in particular were dangerously insanitary and primitive. Here 'diseased persons of all ages, sexes and conditions' mixed in the same baths which were in addition exposed to 'wind, rain, hail and snow'.

In his last novel *Humphrey Clinker*, published the year he died, Smollett turned his attention to the city in general and its social life. His criticisms are made by Matthew Bramble, a gouty invalid, but they are clearly the author's own and suggest the resentment of an uncouth Scot among Bath's fashionable and affected visitors. 'Here we have nothing but noise, tumult, and hurry,' Bramble says; 'with the fatigue and slavery of maintaining a ceremonial, more stiff, formal and oppressive, than the etiquette of a German Elector.'

With a typical satirist's change of position, he then attacks this over-refined society for not in fact being refined at all but consisting mainly of 'Clerks and factors from the East Indies, loaded with the spoil of plundered provinces; planters, negro-drivers, and hucksters, from our American plantations, enriched they know not how; agents, commissaries, and contractors, who have fattened, in two successive wars, on the blood of the nation; usurers, brokers, and jobbers of every kind; men of low birth, and no breeding, [who] have found themselves suddenly translated into a state of affluence, unknown to former ages; and no wonder that their brains should be intoxicated with pride, vanity, and presumption. Knowing no other criterion of greatness, but the ostentation of wealth, they discharge their affluence without taste or conduct, through every channel of the most absurd extravagance; and all of them hurry to Bath, because here, without any further qualification, they can mingle with the princes and nobles of the land. Even the wives and daughters of low tradesmen, who, like shovel-nosed sharks, prey upon the blubber of those uncouth whales of fortune, are infected with the same rage of displaying their importance; and the slightest indisposition serves them for a pretext to insist upon being conveyed to Bath, where they may hobble country-dances and cotillons among lordlings, squires, counsellors and clergy.'

Bath's layout was as bad as its society. Because there was no way between the new upper town and the old lower town where the baths lay, visitors had to pass 'through the yard of an inn, where the poor trembling valetudinarian is carried in a chair, betwixt the heels of a double row of horses, wincing under the curry-combs of grooms and postillions . . .'

Even Bath's fine new buildings were built of stone so 'soft and crumbling' that any man of the strength of Bramble's servant 'would be able to push his foot through the strongest part of their walls, without any great exertion . . .' And 'The rage of building has laid hold on such a number of adventurers, that one sees new houses starting up in every out-let and every corner of Bath; contrived without judgement, executed without solidity, and stuck together, with so little regard to plan and propriety that the different lines of the new rows and buildings interfere with, and intersect one another in every angle of conjunction. They look like the wrecks of streets and squares disjointed by an earthquake.'

At first Matthew Bramble finds the waters suit his stomach, but presently he becomes as afraid of drinking them as of bathing in them because he suspects that there are regurgitations from the baths into the springs. 'In that case, what a delicate beverage is every day quaffed by the drinkers; medicated with the sweat, and dirt, and dandriff, and abominable discharges of various kinds from twenty different diseased bodies, parboiling in the kettle below.'

As for the atmosphere of a Bath ball, it is so overpowering that he drops 'senseless upon the floor'. 'Imagine to yourself,' Bramble explains, 'a high exalted essence of mingled odours, arising from putrid gums, imposthumated lungs, sour flatulencies, rank armpits, sweating feet, running sores and issues, plaisters, ointments, and embrocations, hungary-water, spirit of lavender, assafoetida drops, musk, hartshorn, and sal volatile; besides a thousand frowzy steams, which I could not analyse.'

His niece, Lydia Melford, the heroine of *Humphrey Clinker*, repeats some of her uncle's criticisms, in her own mock-innocent way. The Pump Room during its morning session is crowded like a Welsh fair, with people of 'the highest quality, and the lowest trades jostling each other, without ceremony'.

Smollett used his own experience of Bath for his general comments but borrowed the specific incidents which annoyed Bramble from Christopher Anstey's *The New Bath Guide* (1766). Just as Anstey's Lord Ringbone in his lodgings is infuriated by overhead heavy treading and fiddling, so Bramble is tormented by dancing lessons in the room above which make a 'strange kind of thumping and bouncing', and by the negro servants of a Creole gentleman who play the French horn outside his door 'with such discordant sounds, as might have discomposed the organs of an ass'.

4

GAMING AND GAMESTERS

Clarke kills Taylor

A much-reported duel between two gentlemen named Clarke and Taylor helped Beau Nash to suppress the custom of carrying swords at Bath. Clarke and Taylor were gamesters who quarrelled one night at play. 'They fought by torch-light in the grove; Taylor was run through the body, but lived seven years after, at which time his wound breaking out afresh, it caused his death. Clark from that time pretended to be a quaker, but the orthodox brethren never cordially received him; and he died at London, about eighteen years afterwards, in poverty and contrition.'

From then onwards, Goldsmith continued, implying early in Beau Nash's reign as King of Bath, swords were forbidden there, not only because they led to duels, but because they often 'tore the ladies cloaths, and frightened them, by sometimes appearing on trifling occasions'.

The Gaming Acts

Gaming was already one of Bath's two main attractions by the time Beau Nash became the city's Master of Ceremonies – his predecessor had, of course, died in a duel provoked by a gaming quarrel. Only eight years later the passion had infected the ladies of Bath, and Richard Steele, in the *Guardian* of 1713, described how they would go directly from church to the gaming tables.

By 1739 the personal tragedies which gaming was causing had become so many and notorious that an Act of Parliament was passed, aimed at forcing out of Bath characters who acted at the tables as 'decoy ducks'.[45] It specifically named four games: Ace of Hearts, Faro (or Pharaoh), Basset and Hazard, as lotteries and therefore illegal – but incidentally made an exception of playing them at 'Royal palaces, where his Majesty, his heirs or successors shall then reside'.[46]

Ace of Hearts, as the name suggests, was a card game, and so was Faro, its name derived from the King of Hearts or Pharaoh. Players bet on the order in which certain cards would appear when taken in turn from the top of a pack. Basset was similar to Faro, but Hazard was a dice game, played with two dice, in which 'as many as can stand round the largest table'[47] could play, attempting by following complicated rules to match the caster's throw. According to Charles Cotton's *The Compleat Gamester* (1674), Hazard 'speedily makes a man or undoes him. In the twinkling of an eye, either a man or a mouse.'

As soon as these games were forbidden, gamesters turned to Passage, another old dice game, but played between two people, with three dice, in which the dice thrower throws until he throws doubles totalling under ten, in which case he loses, or over ten, in which case he wins. Soon Passage was 'daily carried on to the ruin and impoverishment of many'.[48] To counter it, Parliament added a clause to the Horse Racing Act forbidding Passage and all other games played with dice except for Backgammon. When gamesters responded with Roulette, generally called Roly-Poly (which required no dice), Parliament, as from 24 June 1745, prohibited that as well.

At this stage the game called EO (Evens and Odds) was invented at Tunbridge Wells and brought, with Beau Nash's co-operation, to Bath. It was a form of Roulette and, as with Roulette, the table was circular, of no particular size. Bets on evens or odds were placed round the circumference and the ball spun at the centre. It might land either in one of twenty even niches or in one of twenty odd niches. Or it might land in one of the proprietors' two 'bar holes'. If it landed in the even bar hole they paid nothing on even bets and kept odd bets, and the reverse if it landed in the odd bar hole. They thus on average had 'an advantage of two to forty . . . in their favour'.[49]

Whatever Nash and his partners may have thought, the civil authorities at Bath considered EO illegal and tried to suppress it. On 8 January 1750 the *Bath Journal* reported, 'Last Tuesday night, Charles Store, Esq., Mayor of this city, accompanied by several of the corporation, attended by proper officers, went to a house near West-gate, kept by one R. Richards; for they had information that an EO table was kept there. When they arrived they went upstairs to a room where the table was, and found about sixteen persons playing; the gamesters, on seeing the magistrates, were put into great confusion, and immediately extinguished all candles; two of them jumped out of the window and made their escape, though one of them fell into the airy [area] and was like to have been killed. The magistrates prevented the escape of the others, procured some lights, took down their names and sent them two at a time to prison. They afterwards pulled down the table, carried it into the street, procured some faggots, and burnt it; amidst a great number of spectators, who were very merry on the occasion.'

In spite of such raids, EO continued to be played at Bath. As late as 9 April 1783 two EO tables were burnt in the city's market place.

The sad case of Fanny Braddock

Fanny Braddock was the sister of General Edward Braddock, later the commander-in-chief of British forces in North America who was ambushed and defeated and killed near Fort Dusquesne during the Seven Years War. She was an exceptionally attractive girl, described as gay, generous and 'good natured in the highest degree'.[50] It was for these reasons that her story seemed so shocking. The *Gentleman's Magazine* reported it in September 1731, the month of its tragic end. Two years later it was retold in 'Modern Amours', then by John Wood in 1749, and again in 1762 by Oliver Goldsmith in his life of Beau Nash. Of these accounts, John Wood's is most reliable because, for her last thirteen months, Fanny lived in his house. Like Goldsmith, he hides her identity under the name of Sylvia.

Fanny had inherited, by the death of her sister, a fortune sufficient 'to have maintained her in a handsome manner and every way suitable to her birth'. By the age of nineteen she was also widely courted and flattered. But, Goldsmith says, she was imprudent, and adds, 'I have seldom seen a girl courted by an hundred lovers, that found an husband in any. Before the choice is fixed, she has either lost her reputation, or her good sense.' Fanny lost her good sense when the favourite of her lovers, known as 'the good-natured man', was sent to prison for debt, and she spent the bulk of her inheritance on freeing him.

Now that she was poor (and less courted) Beau Nash advised her to move from London to Bath, where he would introduce her to the best people. Instead she came under the influence of Dame Lindsey, one of Bath's professional entertainers, who ran a gaming establishment known as De la Mains, and later built herself an assembly room. Whenever Dame Lindsey needed someone to 'make up a party for play' at her house she would send for Fanny and Fanny would come.

Dame Lindsey's house was also a brothel and as a result Fanny soon got the reputation of being 'a w——e, d——d, and common s——r'. Wood, however, believed that the worst she ever did was to allow herself to be 'decoyed to the gaming table', where at her own risk she would play for the amusement of others. When she asked him, he agreed to rent her part of his house.

Here at first she received such a distinguished succession of guests that 'her levy . . . looked more like that of a minister of state, than of a private young lady'. But she gradually grew more depressed, and took to looking at the moon through Wood's telescope, then discussing its beauty with him 'and what pleasure souls departed from the earth must have' if God chose to send them there. She also consulted a surgeon about the most painless method of committing suicide.

At the time Wood did not know this and when he went to London at the end of the summer of 1731 he left Fanny to look after his house and three younger children. Fanny did this loyally till the day before she expected him to return. That evening she seemed particularly cheerful, sat after supper with the two older children on her knees, and visited the nursery on her way to bed to look at the third asleep in its cradle.

In her bedroom Fanny's servant – a gentlewoman deserted by her husband, whom Fanny called Nash after Beau Nash – put Fanny to bed as usual. As usual she locked Fanny in, then pushed the key under the door so that Fanny could wake when she chose, open her own door and call Nash by ringing a handbell.

But in the morning no call came and it was not till two o'clock in the afternoon that Nash asked one of Wood's workmen to use a ladder to climb to Fanny's window. Here he lifted the window sash, pushed back the shutter 'and there discovered an object, in the furthest corner of the room, that made him descend the ladder with the utmost precipitation'. What he had seen was Fanny, hanging 'dead, cold, and stiff' from her bedroom cupboard door.

The previous night she had soon got out of bed and prepared for suicide, dressing herself entirely in white like a bride, and laying out suitable books, including *Orlando Furioso* open at the pages which told the story of Olympia's betrayal and ruin. She then tied a silk girdle in a noose round her neck, lengthened it with a gold thread girdle and led this, knotted, over the top of her cupboard door. Everything prepared, she stood on a tall stool, locked the cupboard door and kicked away the stool. The girdle broke.

Though a workman in the house heard her fall – 'the very bruises she received on her forehead were sufficient to kill her' – he assumed she was suffering from insomnia, and did nothing. Presently Fanny repeated her attempt with a stronger girdle, this time successfully. When she was found her body had so stretched that 'her ankle-bones touched the floor', and her hand was tightly clutched round the cupboard key, showing that she had used all her strength to heave downwards on it and help suffocate herself.

Wood heard the news of Fanny's death while still on his way home and was so shocked that, as he galloped on towards Bath, every bush 'looked like an infernal spirit; every large stone and clod of dirt that lay in the road appeared like a hobgoblin; and stone walls resembled nothing but swarms of dreadful spectres. The rustling of the trees, and the sound of the horses' feet filled my ears with nothing but the groans and howlings of people in the utmost distress.'

Wood sold Fanny's effects and the amount raised was enough to satisfy her other creditors, since people were willing to pay good prices in order to buy 'every trifle' which she had possessed, in order to 'preserve the memory of the poor deceased lady'. But rightly, Wood adds, it should have been his, since she owed him £52 3s. 4d. in rent.

The plot of Goldsmith's first play is clearly based on Fanny's story. Staged eight years after he published his account of her tragedy, it concerned a foolish young woman who spent the bulk of her fortune on rescuing her lover from prison where he had been sent for debt. Goldsmith even used Wood's phrase,

The Good Natur'd Man as the title, but he made his play a comedy and gave it a happy ending.

Poor Jenners

(Parts of a letter from Mr *** in Tunbridge to Lord —— in London, found among Beau Nash's papers, which, according to Goldsmith, Nash was preparing for the press as a warning to gamblers)

'What I foresaw has arrived, poor *Jenners*, after losing all his fortune, has shot himself through the head. His losses to *Bland* were considerable, and his playing soon after with *Spedding* contributed to hasten his ruin. No man was ever more enamoured of play, or understood it less. At whatever game he ventured his money, he was most usually the dupe, and still foolishly attributed to his bad luck, those misfortunes that entirely proceeded from his want of judgment.

'After finding that he had brought on himself irreparable indigence and contempt, his temper, formerly so sprightly, began to grow gloomy and unequal; he grew more fond of solitude, and more liable to take offence at supposed injuries; in short, for a week before he shot himself, his friends were of opinion, that he meditated some such horrid design. He was found in his chamber fallen on the floor, the bullet having glanced on the bone, and lodged behind his right eye.

'You remember, my Lord, what a charming fellow this deluded man was once. How benevolent, just, temperate, and every way virtuous; the only faults of his mind arose from motives of humanity; he was too easy, credulous, and good-natured, and unable to resist temptation, when recommended by the voice of friendship . . .

'The great error lies in imagining every fellow with a laced coat to be a gentleman. The address and transient behaviour of a man of breeding are easily acquired, and none are better qualified than gamesters in this respect. At first, their complaisance, civility, and apparent honour is pleasing, but upon examination, few of them will be found to have their minds sufficiently stored with any of the more refined accomplishments, which truly characterize the man of breeding . . . A sharper, when he plays, generally handles and deals the cards aukwardly like a bungler; he advances his bets by degrees, and keeps his antagonist in spirits by small advantages and alternate success at the beginning; to shew all his force at once, would but fright the bird he intends to decoy; he talks of honour and virtue, and his being a gentleman, and that he knows great men, and mentions his coal mines, and his estate in the country; he is totally divested of that masculine confidence, which is the attendant of real fortune; he turns, yields, assents, smiles, as he hopes will be most pleasing to his destined prey.'

5

DISCOVERIES

Minerva's head

Just as visitors to the Pump Room for the first twenty years
after its opening in 1706 would have seen none of the fine
buildings of Bath (apart from Bath Abbey) which now make it
the city we admire (since they had not yet been built), so they
would have seen virtually none of the remains of Roman Bath
because these had not yet been discovered.

True, the more observant might have noticed, incorporated
into the upper parts of the city walls, various blocks of Roman
stone, some carved, some with barely legible inscriptions. Henry
VIII's travelling antiquarian, John Leland, had seen these when
he visited the city at about the time of the dissolution of the
monasteries, and soon after the Pump Room's opening his notes
were published for the first time (1710–12). And eighteenth-
century visitors were no doubt vaguely aware, as Bath's citizens
had been since mediaeval times, that there had been a Roman city
there. At the end of the third century AD the Roman writer
Solinus had compiled a book of imperial curiosities, including in
his section on Britain a description of a place with hot springs,
where 'Minerva presides, and in her temple the perpetual fire
never whitens to ash, but as the flame fades, turns into rocky
lumps'. This was correctly thought to refer to Bath, where the
rocky lumps would have been the cinders of Somerset coal. But
they thought so little of the Roman stones which they could see
that they let most of them disappear when the city expanded and
the walls were demolished; and they had no idea where the
Roman temple had stood, let alone that its remains were largely
below Stall Street.

In 1727, however, just about the time that John Wood the
elder came to Bath and began to work for Lord Chandos on his
lodging house, some two years before he began his masterpiece,
Queen's Square, a sensational discovery was made. That
summer the corporation ordered the laying of a large new sewer

below Stall Street as part of a plan to give the city a better drainage system. For this a trench had to be dug some fifteen to twenty feet deep. In the earth and rubble at the trench's bottom, on 12 July, a workman found a life-size gilded bronze head. It had no body and the helmet it had clearly been wearing was also missing, but there was no doubt that this was the head of the goddess Minerva; it could have formed part of her principal statue in the temple which Solinus described.

Minerva's head was not the only find made by the sewer diggers that summer. At one point, at a depth of sixteen feet, they reached what we now know to be the west end of the Roman bathing complex, finding a flat tiled floor and below it box tiles for hot-air underfloor heating (hypocaust). But antiquarianism was not yet the general fashion and all of it was reburied. It was almost another thirty years before any sign of the Roman baths were found again, this time at their opposite, eastern end.

The Large Roman Bath and the Great Roman Bath

John Wood the elder, whose architecture set the tone for eighteenth-century Bath, and who would have liked to have made it into a new Roman city, complete with Royal Forum, Grand Circus and Imperial Gymnasium, died knowing nothing of the great series of Roman baths over which he walked daily in and around the abbey churchyard. Like his contemporaries, he believed that there had been Roman baths at Bath as well as a temple, a belief that the Stall Street finds of 1727 confirmed. But when, in 1738, he discovered remains including mosaics and a hypocaust while building Bath's General Hospital he believed that these were part of the Roman praetorium (governor's palace), although they were in fact merely part of a Roman town house.

In 1755, the year after he died, the first of the great discoveries was made which have since turned Bath into the most interesting Roman town in the country. This was the Large Bath (to be distinguished from the much larger Great Bath). By then it, like the rest of the bathing complex, had been buried for some 1200 to 1300 years.

The Large Bath was found when Abbey House, which

adjoined the King's Bath to the west and had a garden which
adjoined the abbey to the east, was knocked down to make
space to build the private Duke of Kingston Baths. It lay some
ten or twelve feet below ground level. In reaching it the
excavators had to dig through a Saxon burial ground which had
apparently been unknown to the builders of the Abbey House.

Dr Charles Lucas, who in the same year wrote the earliest
description of the bath, as well as of a nearby smaller semi-
circular bath, and who had had the help of John Wood the
younger in draining the whole excavation so that he could
measure and draw it, did not realise that both baths had been
fed by the same spring which fed the King's and Queen's Baths
some 130 feet further west; nor was he even sure that they were
Roman though he guessed they were. 'They serve to prove', he
wrote, 'what I asserted upon the authority of SOLINUS, long
before I knew of them; that we once had regular, rational and
elegant baths in Britain, upon the Roman plan, which we
rejected and changed for the present rude barbarous Gothic
baths, that reproach us for want of sense and elegance, in these
matters.'

A few years later some adjoining bathing rooms were found,
also the edge of the Great Bath. Though enough of this was
uncovered to allow guesses to be made at its shape and size,
nothing was done to excavate the rest.

6

RESIDENTS

Mary Chandler, poet of Bath

Mary Chandler (1687–1745), Bath's milliner poet, was the daughter of a Presbyterian minister from Malmesbury. She suffered an accident as a child which left her with a permanent deformity of the spine, but this did not harm her temper. 'She had something extremely agreeable and pleasing in her face,' Theophilus Cibber wrote, in his *Lives of the Poets*, 'and no one could enter into any intimacy of conversation with her, but he immediately lost every disgust towards her, that the first appearance of her person tended to excite.'

When she was eighteen she started a millinery business in the abbey churchyard, directly opposite the Pump Room, specialising in Bath lace, a material which was made in the West Country at places like Honiton, but got its name because so much was sold (and worn) in Bath. Also its patterns were invented there. It came in various forms and was expensive. Edging pieces cost 1s. 6d. each, and 'fine broad lace' three guineas a yard.

The great event in Mary's social life was her introduction to George II's daughter, Princess Amelia, during her visit to Bath in 1728, and she dedicated her *A Description of Bath* (1734) to the princess.

Writing poetry did not come easily to her, and she was helped in revising the poem by Dr William Oliver, inventor of the biscuit. Today it is remembered less as poetry than for what it says about the best-known citizens of Bath in her time. These included the doctor himself and Ralph Allen of Prior Park. About Allen's tramway for transporting stone from his quarries on Combe Down to barges on the Avon she wrote:

> Hence is seen
> The new-made road and wonderful machine,
> Self moving downward from the mountain height
> A rock its burden of a mountain's weight.

To her astonishment, when she was fifty-four an unknown old gentleman came into her shop, bought a pair of gloves and proposed marriage. Describing the incident she wrote,

> . . . when the wondrous message he declared
> I never in my life was half so scared.

She considered the offer for a night, then rejected it, explaining that 'to suppose a man can be a lover at sixty is to expect May fruits in December'.

Her business prospered and she bought another house in the Orange Grove, but after forty years put both houses up for sale and announced a sale of stock which included 'a large and well chosen parcel of Bath Lace'.[50] Her two nieces, the advertisement said, were planning to open a shop in Cheapside, London. Only the abbey churchyard house was sold and Mary moved into the other.

Towards the end of her life she suffered from a condition which today would be diagnosed as anorexia nervosa. She had come under the influence of 'the late ingenious Dr Cheyne' (see page 82) and taken to his vegetable diet, 'indeed the utmost extremes of it, living frequently on bread and water'. She believed that 'the perpetual free use of animal food, and rich wines, tends to excite and inflame the passions', and to prevent 'the conquest of herself, and subjecting her own heart more intirely to the command of her reason and principles'. But the result was that she was 'so weak as not to be able to support the attack of her last disorder'.[51] She left unfinished her poem *The Being and Attributes of God*.

Mr Gill, pastry cook

The cooks of eighteenth-century Bath were famous, but none so famous as Mr Gill. 'From the bookseller's shop,' wrote Smollett's Lydia Melford, 'we make a tour through the milliners and toymen; and commonly stop at Mr Gill's, the pastry cook, to take a jelly, a tart, or a small bason of vermicelli.' In 1766 Christopher Anstey made Gill more famous by including a fourteen-verse song in his praise in *The New Bath Guide*.

Of all the cooks the world can boast,
    However great their skill,
To bake, or fry, to boil, or roast,
    There's none like Master GILL . . .
O taste this soup, for which the fair,
    When hungry, cold and chill,
Forsake the Circus and the Square
    To eat with Master GILL . . .
My humble verse that fate will meet,
    Nor shall I take it ill;
But grant, ye gods! that I may eat
    That fowl when drest by GILL . . .
He who would fortify his mind,
    His belly first should fill   (*Forte*)
Roast beef 'gainst terrors best you'll find;
    '*The Greeks knew this*,' says GILL.
Your spirits and your blood to stir,
    Old Galen gives a pill;
But I the forc'd-meat ball prefer,
    Prepar'd by master GILL.
While he so well can broil and bake,
    I'll promise and fulfil,
No other physic e'er to take
    Than what's prescrib'd by GILL.
Your Bard has liv'd at Bath so long,   (*Piano*)
    He dreads to see your bill –
Instead of cash accept this song,   (*Pianissimo*)
    My worthy Master GILL.

From Smollett's reference and Anstey's poem it can be deduced that Gill's business was flourishing in the 1760s, but his precise dates are unknown and the site of his shop is lost.

James Leake, bookseller

The two best-known Bath bookshop-libraries in the mid-eighteenth century were William Frederick's at 18 The Parades, and James Leake's at 5 The Walks. Visitors paid them a subscription for the season, and in return could borrow books or read at the shop. No doubt both men treated their customers with deference; James Leake's obsequiousness is described in a letter from the young Earl of Orrery, who visited Bath in the early 1730s, soon after he had inherited his title.

Orrery went first to the Pump Room where 'as soon as the circling whisper had taken the air that the Earl of Orrery was present, all eyes were fixed on me . . . Some months ago I should have been as little regarded as my own natural shyness could desire. But now I had seats, salutes and innumerable civilities offered to me from every quarter.' Not enjoying this, Orrery fled to 'the asylum of all polite literature . . . the palatinate of Mr Leake the bookseller'.

'This Leake', he continued, 'is a most extraordinary person. He is the prince of all the coxcomical fraternity of booksellers: and, not having any learning himself, he seems resolved to sell it as dear as possible to others. He looks upon every man, distinguished by any title, not only as his friend, but his companion, and he treats him accordingly; but he disposes of his favours and regards, as methodically as Nash takes out the ladies to dance, and therefore speaks not to a marquess whilst a duke is in the room. As yet he is ignorant that my earldom lies in Ireland, and to keep him so, I have borrowed the only book of heraldry he has in his shop: by this method I shall be served many degrees above my place, and may have a squeeze of his hand in presence of an earl of Great Britain.

'His shop is a spatious room, filled from the cornice to the skirting. But I could not help observing to him that, the binding of his books did not make so glittering a figure as might be expected from the library of a person as illustrious as himself. He owned my observation was right, and added that, "Some fellows whose ancestors, he believed, were snails, had been daily expected from London, to illuminate and glorify his museum". I rejoiced at the good news, and told him, "I doubted not but he would shew the elasticity of his genius, and the nicknackatory of his understanding by binding Lord Bacon in hog's skin, Bishop Sprat in fish skin and Cardinal du Bois in wood". He seemed highly delighted with my proposal, and was going to enter it in his pocket book, when the Duchess of Norfolk, snatching him from my arms, allowed me an opportunity to assure you that I am, etc. Orrery.'

Leake had moved to Bath in 1722, when he married Hannah Hammond, daughter of a bookseller there. His better-known relative by marriage was Samuel Richardson, who married his sister, Elizabeth. Richardson would occasionally visit his brother-in-law and at least once asked him to comment on his work before it was published. In Leake's shop in 1752 Richardson was heard to say that he was going to dine that evening with Ralph Allen of Prior Court. 'Twenty years ago,' he added, 'I was the most obscure man in Great Britain; and now I am admitted to the company of the first characters of the kingdom.' Since it was almost exactly twenty years ago that he had married Leake's sister, Leake might have found a second meaning in this reflection, but there is no record that he did, and the two men seem always to have been friendly with each other.

Leake was also one of the 'best loved friends' of Ralph Allen, who would go daily to read the papers in Leake's 'cheerful, vaulted-roofed reading room'.[52]

In this same room Richard Brinsley Sheridan, during his time at Bath in 1771 and 1772, is traditionally said to have written *The Rivals*, though it was not staged until 1775 and then in London.

The obsequious Mr Leake, a friend of the admired and respectable Ralph Allen, and who, according to Dr Cheyne, ran 'one of the best bookshops in Europe', was not above dealing in pornography. In 1740 he printed (with a dedication to Cheyne) *A New Description of Merryland*, a 48-page pamphlet by one, Thomas Stretzer, writing under the pseudonym of Roger Phfuquewell. This fictitious gentleman was said, in the introduction, to be from an Irish family 'remarkable for their being red-headed, of great note and of long standing in that country'. Merryland was a woman's body, described topographically, as if a piece of landscape. Its latitude and longitude were not easy to define since they varied. 'This surprising increase . . . in Merryland seldom fails to happen after having a fruitful season in that country.' Fruitfulness was Merryland's chief drawback, and to guard against it the natives used a sponge which 'acted as an antidote to the juice above mentioned'. The book was a considerable success, selling ten editions, and next year Leake printed for Stretzer an illustrated version.

In 1741 he also printed an anonymous attack on Merryland, again by Stretzer, which was in fact a publicity device.

Booksellers, Stretzer wrote, were printing 'all the smutty stuff they could think of to humour the prevailing gout of the town, and scratch the callous appetites of their debauched readers'. He was sorry to say that 'some of the fair-sex as well as the men, have too freely testified their approbation' of Merryland, claiming that 'there is not a baudy word in it'. Ladies who thought so should consult Chaucer to see what meaning he gave to Phfuquewell, the supposed author's name.

William Warburton, Bishop of Gloucester, and Gertrude Tucker

The Rev. William Warburton (1698–1779), friend of Alexander Pope, a well-known controversial literary critic of his time, has been described as the eighteenth-century 'man who came to dinner'. In 1741 he arrived as a guest at Prior Park, Ralph Allen's country house, and there he stayed.

It was Pope and Allen, together, who invited Warburton. Pope had reasons for befriending Warburton, since Warburton had defended him against attacks on his *Essay on Man*. Pope was hoping that Warburton would write an introduction for a General Edition of his poetry; and he may also have wanted Allen to meet a clergyman who approved of his religious opinions. From Prior Park in 1741 Pope wrote to Warburton, 'If it were practicable for you to pass a month or six weeks from home, it is here I could wish to be with you . . . If the waters of Bath may be serviceable to your complaints (as I believe from what you have told me of them) no opportunity can ever be better . . . You'll want no servant here, your room will be next to mine, and one man will serve us. Here is a library, and a gallery ninety foot long to walk in and a coach whenever you would take the air with me . . .' Warburton came, and from the start Allen liked him.

Warburton was born at Newark, son of the town clerk; at school he was said by one of his teachers to have been 'the dullest of dull boys'. Another anecdote – not perhaps contradictory – tells how he was once so absorbed in his studies that he walked past a house without noticing that it was on fire.

After training as a lawyer he went into the church, and now held a living near Newark at Brant Broughton and another at

Frisby in Leicestershire, neither of which he often visited. He was, according to one acquaintance, a 'tall, robust, large-boned man',[53] and said by another to suffer from the 'natural conceit of his own superiority'.[54] Certainly his literary criticisms suggest that he was assertive, quarrelsome and commonly wrong. But he was good company, nevertheless. A young man who met him at Cambridge wrote, 'he strikes frequently into the province of paradox . . . spurns the dull earth, and soars above the skies',[55] though Bishop Thomas Newton admitted that he 'sometimes took the discourse too much to himself, if anything can be said to be too much of such an inexhaustible fund of wit and learning'. A sample suggests the style of his wit. 'Orthodoxy', he said, 'is my doxy and heterodoxy is another man's doxy.'

Bath water suited Warburton's complaints, which were described as 'bilious indigestion'.[56] Allen had it brought up the hill from Bath every morning and served to Warburton, still warm, in bed.

Five years after Warburton first came to Prior Park he made himself a more permanent connection with Allen by marrying his niece, Gertrude Tucker. Gertrude was eighteen – and Warburton forty-six. She had been living with Allen, who had no surviving children of his own, as an informally adopted daughter for eight years. She was a lively girl, and seems not to have objected to the marriage, or been intimidated by her formidable husband. Nor did Allen apparently object, though he mentioned it somewhat casually when writing to his sister (not Gertrude's mother, who had died): 'Gatty was married last ffryday.' Perhaps he was relieved to have found his lively niece a husband. According to his builder, Richard Jones, he had had to sack his chaplain, Mr Chapman, 'for being a little free with his niece, Mrs Tucker'. In Jones's opinion Chapman was not to blame. 'In short what I have seen myself Mr Chapman could not help being great with her, for she would play with him in an indecent manner.'

This story of teenage flirtatiousness seems more probable than the rumour spread (by Charles Churchill in his poem *Ghosts*) when Gertrude eventually had a child, that one Thomas Potter, not Warburton, was the father – though her failure for nine years to conceive gives circumstantial support to Churchill's scandalous assertions about Warburton's virility.

Continually Allen and other friends tried to get church promotion for Warburton. About the time of his marriage they obtained for him the preachership at Lincoln's Inn. When Warburton, somewhat reluctantly, accepted this position, Allen suggested that he should get a house in London, perhaps looking forward to an occasional respite from his company. But on the whole Warburton's sponging seems to have been resented more by Allen's friends than by Allen himself. 'Poor Mr A——n,' Samuel Richardson wrote, during his own quarrel with Warburton. The actor, James Quin, according to a well-known anecdote, was more direct. When visiting Prior Park one evening and asked to recite, 'Quin said that plays were then quite out of his head; however, he believed he remembered a few lines of *Pierre*; on which he got up, and looking directly at Allen, repeated . . .

> 'Honest Men
> Are the soft easy cushions on which knaves
> Repose and fatten.'

'Warburton gave him [Quin] no further trouble for the rest of the evening.'

Warburton dedicated several of his books to the Allens, of which the most notorious was his *Shakespeare*. When this, with its many idiosyncratic changes to the text, was criticised by a rival, Thomas Edwards, Dr Johnson said it was like a fly stinging a stately horse. But Edwards' criticisms were all too apt. He put them in the form of Canons, embodying the principles on which Warburton seemed to have worked. Canon II read, 'He had a right to alter any passage he does not understand.' Canon XII read, 'He may find out a bawdy, or immoral meaning in his author, where there does not appear to be any hint that way.'

Four years later Warburton published his nine-volume edition of Pope's works, in which he again improved the text with suggestions of his own, and in extensive footnotes continued various of his literary controversies. Typically, he took an introduction he had written to Richardson's *Clarissa*, which to his annoyance Richardson had omitted from a later edition, and transformed half of it into praise for the work of Richardson's great rival, Fielding.

At last Allen and William Pitt between them secured church

promotion for Warburton. In 1757 he was made Dean of Bristol. He rewarded Pitt with copies of his books, saying that he would be honoured to have them in Pitt's library. Two years later the *Bath Advertiser* announced the appointment of 'that masterly writer, uncommon genius, and prodigy of learning, the judicious Dr Warburton, to the See of Gloucester', adding that it 'filled the hearts of the studious and learned clergy with joy and gladness'.

In 1764 Ralph Allen in his will left Prior Park to his niece and the Bishop, and they kept it for five years before moving to Gloucester. When Warburton died ten years later, Gertrude married another clergyman.

Henry Fielding and his sister Sarah

When Sir Arthur Conan Doyle came to Bath on 5 June 1905 to unveil a tablet at Widcombe Lodge to celebrate the fact that Henry Fielding (1707–1754) and his sister Sarah had lived there, he explained, 'I do not propose to speak of her [Sarah] today . . . until I got this invitation I had never heard of the lady.' Sarah remains a more obscure figure than her brother, but she was a well-known writer in her time, author of one of the earliest children's books, *The Governess*. As a resident of Bath she helps to explain her brother's somewhat mysterious connections with the city. Neither Conan Doyle nor the organisers of the plaque seem to have realised that Widcombe Lodge (which was originally called Yew Cottage) was *her* house, not her brother's. Though he visited her there, the house in which he wrote some, perhaps much, of *Tom Jones* was at the other side of the city in the village of Twerton.

Sarah's residence at Bath does not solve the first mystery. She came here only in about 1739, but in November 1734 her brother was married at Charlcombe, a mile to the north of the city on the Lansdown Hills, where the register records that he and the girl he married, Charlotte Cradock, were residents of the parish of St James's, Bath. All other evidence suggests that at this time Henry and Charlotte were each living thirty miles away, near Salisbury. The most likely explanation is that they had eloped, because her mother opposed the marriage, and were in temporary lodgings at Bath. No doubt they chose

Charlcombe because they liked the place, as Sarah clearly did because she was eventually buried there.

When Sarah arrived in Bath she soon became the friend of Ralph Allen. The hill on which he was building his house, Prior Park, rises steeply behind Sarah's cottage at Widcombe. Richard Graves, rector of nearby Claverton, several times met Sarah dining at Prior Park, and she probably introduced her brother to Allen – his most important friend at Bath.

Allen first entertained Henry Fielding at Prior Park in November 1741. As always Fielding was in financial trouble. He had borrowed £200 which he could not repay and according to one story Allen settled the debt. Fielding's most memorable thanks to Allen was his kindly picture of him as Squire Allworthy in *Tom Jones*; but he also dedicated his last novel *Amelia* to him.

Charlotte, his well-loved first wife, had died at Bath in the autumn of 1744, though her body was carried back to London for burial. According to those who knew her, Fielding gave an accurate picture of her character as Sophia Western in *Tom Jones*, and of her looks as Amelia, 'even to her noselessness'. She had lost this in a 'frightful overturn of her carriage'[57] which destroyed its gristle, an accident which is also made to occur in the novel.

Whether or not she died at Twerton is uncertain, but it was to his house there, later called Fielding Lodge, that Fielding now began to come for summer periods of rest between his exhausting travels as a magistrate, and it was in the summers of 1746, 1747 and 1748 that he was writing *Tom Jones* there. The book was published in 1749. Meanwhile, in November 1747, he had married again, this time a girl named Mary Daniel. According to Horace Walpole, Fielding's comment on his second marriage was, 'if you talk of virtue, here's virtue! I married my whore yesterday.' Smollett described her as his 'cook-wench', and Fielding's second cousin, Lady Mary Wortley Montagu, confirmed this. 'His natural spirits gave him rapture with his cookmaid and cheerfulness when he was fluxing [purging] in a garret.' Mary was already six months pregnant, and their son was born in February 1748.

Bath again became important to Fielding when he began to suffer severely from gout. He was there, dining with Ralph Allen at Prior Park, in April 1751 when the Rev. Richard Hurd called him 'a poor, emaciated worn-out rake', and another guest wrote that he had to be wheeled from room to room. Nevertheless, this was the year in which he finished *Amelia*, which was published in 1752.

He might have come to Bath again in 1753, but was prevented by the Duke of Newcastle, who required him to stay in London and devise a plan for suppressing London's unusually active murder gangs. The following year he sailed to Lisbon for his health and died there.

Sarah survived him by fourteen years. She continued to live at Bath, and to publish novels, though she eventually moved from Widcombe to Bathwick Street. She was probably helped financially by Ralph Allen throughout her time at Bath. Allen also helped to educate Fielding's children after Fielding's death, and in his will left £100 legacies to the three of them who survived and to his widow.

James Quin, *actor*

'I am in Bath,' wrote the actor, James Quin (1693–1766), to the theatre manager, John Rich, in a gesture of reconciliation after quarrelling with him in London, hoping perhaps to be recalled. 'Stay there and be damned,' Rich replied. Quin stayed, and though for a few years he made occasional visits to London to play particular parts, his acting career was in effect finished.

For the thirty previous years he had been celebrated as the last great actor of the declamatory school. He excelled as Falstaff, had swollen to fit the part and was now enormous. The stories about Quin which must have been told and retold in the Pump Room for the next eighteen years were collected in an anonymous biography which was published in 1766, the year he died.

The first of these, though unsubstantiated, seems probable, judging by the others. During his early days in London he was conducting what he believed to be 'a very snug intrigue' with a married lady, Mrs L——. One day he met Mrs L—— when she had just failed to get into the theatre, and 'the opportunity was so favourable' that he invited her back to his chambers, forgetting that he had lent the key to a friend. Realising that 'such an excuse would look like coolness on his part . . . he prevailed on her, with much intreaty, to go to a bagnio, which was, perhaps, the first time in her life she had been in such a place. Her terrors were extravagantly great, till she thought there was no further danger to be apprehended, and gave a full loose to the indulgence of her passion. The hour of retreat now approached, when suddenly an ignorant waiter opened the door to introduce another company, not knowing the room was already occupied. But consternation – shame – horror – anguish – fury – rage – madness – all assist to delineate the scene! Who should appear but her husband! Quin was still in the room, and, perceiving Mr L—— ready to wreak all his vengeance upon his wife, he flew to his sword and drew it in her defence. In the conflict Mr L—— was wounded in the thigh; and this affair terminated for the present with a couple of prosecutions against Quin; the first for Crim. Con., and the next for an assault and battery.' Quin, his biographer concludes, escaped to Dublin and did not return till he learned that Mr L—— had died, though whether naturally or of his wound is not clear.

Soon afterwards Quin quarrelled with a fellow actor named Williams, a Welshman. When Williams, playing the part of Caesar's messenger and bringing a message from him, pronounced the name Cato as 'Keeto', Quin, in an aside to the audience, said, 'Would he had sent a better messenger.' Williams followed Quin to the Green Room and challenged him to a duel, then ambushed him in the street. In the sword fight which followed he was killed by Quin. Quin was found guilty of manslaughter but, because of the circumstances, only lightly punished.

The nineteenth-century edition of Quin's biography adds an even more circumstantial account of the trial of Quin for a third killing, including the evidence of seventeen witnesses. On this occasion the victim was another actor, William Bowen, and Quin was brought to court on 17 April 1718, accused of giving Bowen a 'mortal wound with a sword on the right side of the belly, of the breadth of one inch and the depth of four inches, of which wound he languished till the 20th, and then died'.

Quin produced evidence to establish that Bowen was quarrelsome by nature and had already made an unprovoked attack on someone else. But Quin had apparently made a habit for the previous two years of baiting Bowen. On one occasion 'when sitting by the fire behind the scenes he had been heard to say, "here comes that rascally, Whiggish, Tory fellow, Bowen, who deserves to be struck"'.

On the evening of 17 April, when Quin was drinking at the Fleece Tavern, he called Bowen to take a glass of wine with him, and 'as they drank *Mr Bowen* and *Mr Quinn* put pretty smartly upon one another with cutting jests'. They disparaged each other's acting, and Quin accused Bowen of dishonesty, and of drinking disloyal toasts to the Jacobite Duke of Ormonde. Although 'this discourse was all the while carry'd on with a jocular air', the last insult provoked Bowen into flinging down money for the bill and saying 'he could not bear it, but must be gone'.

Quarter of an hour later a messenger from Bowen called Quin outside where Bowen was waiting for him, and took him to the Swan Tavern. Here Bowen rejected one room because it smelled of paint and another because there were people in it, so they went to the Pope's Head. They sat down with wine, but Quin soon 'perceived a disturbance in Mr Bowen's countenance', saw him barricade the door with two chairs and was told by him that he had injured him 'past verbal reparation, and nothing but fighting' would make amends. A sword fight followed in which Bowen received the wound described in the accusation.

At first Bowen did not realise it was fatal, but when, by the following Sunday, his family saw his nails turning black, his son told him 'he would have to think of another world'. The surgeon who subsequently opened the body 'found the wound had gone several inches into the centre of his belly, slanting a little towards the left, and had touched a gut'. Quin was found guilty of manslaughter, but again not severely punished and soon afterwards returned to his employment on the stage.

That Quin could be provocative is confirmed by an incident which Philip Thicknesse watched in 1749, the year after Quin came to live at Bath:

It was after dinner. Quin was what he would call in another man, *sack-mellow*. At the time I was in conversation with a Wiltshire Esquire . . . to whom Quin walked as steadily up as he could, when putting his heels upon the Esquire's toes, made them *crash again*! and then, without saying another word, walked off. Whether pain, surprise or timidity overcame the Esquire's *upper-works* I cannot say, but as soon as he could speak he asked me whether I had observed Quin's conduct, and whether I thought it was an *accident*, or done with design to affront him? I replied that Quin had been drinking and probably did not know what he was about. But the next morning, meeting him on the parade, I asked him why he so treated a good-natured man with the whole weight of his *body corporate*? D——n him, replied the comedian putting on one of his most *contunding* looks, the fellow invited me to his house in Wiltshire, laid me in damp sheets; and seduced my servant; fed me too with red veal and white bacon; ram mutton and bull beef, adding, and as to his liquor, by my soul it was every drop sour except his vinegar, and yet the scrub had the impertinence to serve it upon dirty plate.

During his time at Bath Quin is said to have plotted to replace Beau Nash as Master of Ceremonies. By this time Nash was old and poor. In his life of Nash, Oliver Goldsmith printed a letter found among Nash's papers, which had been sent to a Lord in London, accusing Nash of losing his temper with a young lady who would not dance a minuet, and telling her 'G—dam yo madam what business have you here if yo do not dance.' Nash believed that Quin, who was known to dislike him, had written the letter, but Goldsmith doubted whether Quin – 'a gentleman who had mended Shakespear's plays so often' – would have written a letter full of so many 'faults, both of style and spelling'.

Quin did, however, quarrel with Samuel Derrick, the diminutive Irish-born poet, who was Bath's Master of Ceremonies after Nash's death. When there was general discontent with Derrick, Quin was reported to have said, 'If you have a mind to put him out, do it at once, and clap an extinguisher on him.'

Derrick, believing that Quin had been responsible for his suspension, wrote a twenty-line offensive verse about him, starting,

> When Quin of all grace and all dignity void,
> Murdered Cato the Censor, and Brutus destroyed,
> He strutted, he mouth'd; you no passion could trace
> In his action delivery or plum-pudding face . . .

Hearing how angry this had made Quin, Derrick wrote to a sea-captain friend at Plymouth to ask him to 'bring up as many John Dories as he could possibly cram into his post chaise'. Quin, 'upon receiving the present, was perfectly reconciled' to Derrick and helped to have him reinstated.

Quin's love of John Dories, a sea-water fish, was only the best known of his epicurean tastes. He had a reputation as a connoisseur of 'high-flavoured wines', and of 'choice dishes for dinner'.[58] He invented what he called a 'Siamese soup', claiming it was chiefly made from eastern ingredients. 'The peculiarity of its flavour became the topic of the day. The *rage* at Bath was Mr Quin's soup.' But he refused to reveal the recipe. 'A conspiracy was accordingly projected by a dozen *bons vivants* of Bath' to flood him with anonymous requests for it. Detecting this, Quin invited those he suspected to taste the soup and hear its secret. When they came he served them an old pair of boots, minced and stewed with sage, onions, spice, ham, wine and water. 'The company were in transports at its flavour',[59] but less amused when he told them its ingredients.

In Smollett's *Humphrey Clinker*, where Quin appears under his own name, he dines at his own table at the Three Tuns, Stall Street, then, with 'six good bottles of Claret under his belt', is carried home by servants whom he tells not to disturb him till midday the following Sunday.

Quin's wit was much admired, and a series of exchanges with Beau Nash was considered the height of sharp repartee. When Quin complained that a Bath shop had overcharged him, Nash said to him, 'Then they have acted towards you on truly Christian principles.'

Quin: 'How so?'
Nash: 'Why, you were a stranger and they took you in.'
Quin: 'But they fleeced me instead of clothing me.'

In spite of his passion for John Dories, Quin affected to consider angling a 'barbarous diversion', and once explained, 'Suppose now any being that was as much my superior as I am to the poor fish, were to say, "This is a fine evening, I'll go a *Quinning.*" If he were to bait with a haunch of venison, I should gorge; and how should I like to be dragged from Richmond to Kingston, floundering and flouncing with a hook in my gullet?'

When Quin died, a monument was erected to him in Bath

Abbey, with a ten-line epitaph by David Garrick. Another one, less respectful, ran,

> Alas, poor Quin, thy jests and stories
> Are quite extinguished, and what more is
> There's no *John Falstaff*, no *John Dories*.

Anstey's 'The New Bath Guide'

In 1766 Christopher Anstey (1724–1805), a country gentleman from Cambridgeshire and Member of Parliament for Trumpington, published a satirical collection of poems about Bath entitled *The New Bath Guide* which even Horace Walpole admired. 'What pleasure you have to come,' he wrote to George Montagu. 'It stole into the world, and for a fortnight no soul looked into it, concluding its name was its true name. No such thing. It is a set of letters in verse . . . describing life at Bath, and, incidentally, everything else; but so much wit, so much humour, fun, and poetry, so much originality, never met together before . . . the man has a better ear than Dryden or Handel.'

And Thomas Gray (prejudiced in Anstey's favour perhaps, because Anstey had previously translated Gray's *Elegy written in a Country Churchyard* into Latin) described the guide as 'the only thing in fashion . . . [a] new and original kind of humour'.

Anstey's guide was subtitled 'Memoirs of the B——r——d [Blunderhead] Family, in a series of Poetical Epistles'. Various members of the family write these epistles, in various verse forms, describing their experiences during a visit to Bath.

Typically, Simkin Blunderhead describes to his mother, Lady Blunderhead, how the family servant, Tabitha, is taken to the baths.

> This morning, dear Mother, as soon as 'twas light,
> I was wak'd by a Noise that astonished me quite,
> For in TABITHA's Chamber I heard such a Clatter,
> I could not conceive what the Deuce was the Matter:
> And, would you believe it? I went up and found her
> In a Blanket, with two lusty fellows around her,
> Who both seem'd a going to carry her off in
> A little black Box just the Size of a Coffin:

Pray tell me, says I, what you're doing of there?
Why, Master, 'tis hard to be bilk'd of our Fare,
And so we were thrusting her into a Chair:
We don't see no Reason for using us so,
For she bad us come hither, and now she won't go;
We've earn'd all the Fare, for we both came & knock'd her
Up, as soon as 'twas light, by advice of the Doctor;
And this is a Job that we often go a'ter
For Ladies that choose to go into the Water.

Simkin follows Tabitha to the baths where he hides himself under a table in the ladies' dressing-room.

'Twas a glorious Sight to behold the Fair Sex
All wading with Gentlemen up to their Necks,
And view them so prettily tumble and sprawl
In a great smoking Kettle as big as our Hall:
And to-Day many persons of Rank & Condition
We're boil'd by Command of an able Physician . . .

The doctors themselves, Simkin notes, were never seen bathing.

But, what is surprising, no Mortal e'er view'd
Any one of the Physical Gentlemen stew'd;
Since the Day that King BLADUD first found out the Bogs,
And thought them so good for himself & his Hogs,
Not one of the Faculty ever has try'd
These excellent Waters to cure his own Hide . . .

The visit is not a success. Simkin's sister, Jenny, discovers that Captain Cormorant, the man she had hoped would 'change her condition', has been cashiered and lives by gaming. And Tabitha, the servant, is seduced by a Methodist preacher.

But the *Man without Sin* that *Moravian* Rabbi,
Has perfectly cur'd the *Chlorosis* of TABBY;
And, if right I can judge, from her Shape & her Face,
She soon may produce him an Infant of Grace.

The Guide was so successful that after ten years the printer, Dodsley, gave the copyright back to Anstey. Though Anstey had written it at Trumpington, he moved permanently to Bath four years later and was one of the first to live in the newly completed Royal Crescent. Here he was a celebrity, and he continued to write occasional poems, for dropping into Lady Miller's urn (see page 157). Another, entitled *The Patriot*, was addressed to a well-known prize fighter named Buckhorse. But none had the success of *The New Bath Guide*.

Fanny Burney, the diarist and novelist and friend of Dr Johnson, met Anstey several times during her visit to Bath in the summer of 1780. On the first occasion she admitted that he had no opportunity of shining and it was unfair to expect wonders 'all at once; yet it was impossible to help being disappointed, because his air, look and manner are mighty heavy and unfavourable to him'.

Next time she reported, 'Mr Anstey opens rather more, and approaches to being rather agreeable. If he could but forget he had written the *Bath Guide*, with how much more pleasure would everybody else remember it.'

She could not doubt, she wrote the third time, that Anstey 'must sometimes be very agreeable; he could not else have written so excellent, so diverting, so original a satire. But he chooses to keep his talents to himself,' and once again was 'shyly important, and silently proud!'

Rector of Claverton

In the little church of Claverton, which lies over the downs from Bath and remains a charming hamlet today despite a nearby orbital road, a marble tablet records that Richard Graves (1715–1804) held the living for the last fifty-five years of his life without once being absent for more than a month. He also ran a school there for forty children, though where they can all have come from it is hard to imagine. Prince Hoare, the Bath artist (son of William Hoare), was one of his pupils. Another was Thomas Malthus, whose political and economic theories added a word to the language.

By the time Graves came to Claverton he had abandoned a career in medicine, and also been a fellow of All Souls College, Oxford. He lost his fellowship when he married Lucy, a beautiful but uneducated sixteen-year-old, whom he presently sent to London to acquire 'good manners and needful knowledge'.[60]

Though Graves was undoubtedly a responsible rector of Claverton, Bath became the centre of his life. To Bath he would walk every weekday till he was nearly ninety years old, occasionally varying his stride with a curious skip or hop. His essays, published in collections like *Senilities* (1801), and *The Triflers* (1805), tell us much of what we know about Bath, its residents and visitors during the second half of the eighteenth century. *The Triflers* was Graves's last book, and he never saw it published because of a printers' strike – described as a 'combination of the journeymen'.[61]

On a slight rise close outside the door of Claverton church stands evidence of Graves's special connection with the city: the Allen family mausoleum. The tomb at the centre of this small stone structure carries the names of many members of the family, including Ralph Allen himself, 'Man of Bath', his niece and adopted daughter, Gertrude Tucker Warburton, and her only son, Ralph Allen Warburton, who died at the age of nineteen. It was Allen who helped Graves to secure the living at Claverton and built for him the rectory which still stands opposite the church. Later he arranged to have him appointed chaplain to Lady Chatham, and obtained for him two more livings, the second of which, Croscombe, Somerset, Graves rarely if ever visited, referring to it as his 'warming pan'. Allen's niece, Gertrude, rented him her house at Claverton (now gone except for the terraced garden and elegant stone balustrade) in which he first lived and held his school, and her son Ralph was a pupil there.

Unlike many of his eighteenth-century contemporaries, Graves was a modest eater and drinker, claiming that this explained his good health and long life. In his mid-eighties he wrote,

> You're crippled with gout, at forty-eight,
> Yet wish for health – and ask for my receipt;
> My hale old age to temperance is due,
> *Which* rule for *Health* I'd recommend to you . . .

But he was an immodest collector, describing this as a 'propensity to purchase every thing we see . . . especially if it strikes our fancy, under the idea of being cheap or a great bargain', and had filled his house with 'such a multitude of pictures, that these have spread from the parlour into the passages; and from thence to the smoky walls of the kitchen'.

In his time his novel *The Spiritual Quixote* (1772) was much admired. It tells how a Quixote-like young man named Geoffrey Wildgoose sets out with the village cobbler as his Sancho Panza to convert the country to Methodism. Even Philip Thicknesse considered that it had 'some good strokes in it', and noted that although 'Mr G. by his address and manner seems a clown' he was clever.

If Graves satirised the excesses of Methodism, and enjoyed Bath, he was well aware of the essential triviality of social life there. 'Nothing can be more trifling,' he wrote, 'than the life of a lady, nor more insipid than that of a gentleman at Bath; the one is a constant series of flirting and gadding about, the other of sauntering from place to place, without any scheme or pursuit. Scandal or fashion engross the conversation of the former; the news of the day, the price of fish, the history of the preceding night at the tavern, or savoury anticipations of their next debauch, furnish out the morning entertainment of the latter.'

Graves survived his wife by twenty-eight years, and remained active and cheerful till he died. In his last illness he was attended by his old pupil, Thomas Malthus, now also a clergyman.

Beau Nash's successors – Collette and Derrick

When Beau Nash died in 1761 he was briefly succeeded as Bath's King and Master of Ceremonies by M. Collette, a French resident of the city. Collette, according to F. Fleming, the Bath musician who was his contemporary, 'glided smoothly through [rather] than cut any great figure in his sovereignty. – He was possessed of much agility, and very fond of exercising it in dancing with children publicly in the rooms. Among other antics which he shewed, he would in dancing with them spring from the ground several feet, and at falling, by a very sudden transition, contract his height in such a manner as to appear a little boy, leading one of the children to the bottom couple, rising to his usual stature gradually till he elevated the child in his arms extended . . .'

He was a great walker, would often walk the 106 miles to and from London, and was also fond of shuttlecock. He resigned as Master of Ceremonies because he considered his earnings inadequate.

He was succeeded by the Irish-born writer and poet, Samuel Derrick (1724–1769). Dr Johnson, when asked whether Derrick or Christopher Smart was the better poet, answered, 'Sir, there is no settling the point of precedency between a louse and a flea.' Had Derrick not been a writer, Johnson told Boswell, 'he must have been sweeping the crossings in the streets, and asking halfpence from everybody that passed'. More kindly he said that if Derrick's letters had been written by someone with a more established name they would have been considered 'very pretty'.

Women were Derrick's other interest. These were more indulgent to him than the muses, according to his obituary in the *Gentleman's Magazine*. 'From this universal partiality of the ladies to him,' it continued, one might suppose 'that the person was so *comely* and elegant as to be irresistible. This was far from the case. He was of diminutive size, with reddish hair and a vacant countenance; and he required no small quantity of perfume to predominate over some odours that were not of the most fragrant kind.'

At the Bedford Coffee House a fellow dramatic critic asked for snuff before he would talk to Derrick, because 'some people have such potent smells, they are insupportable'. When Derrick rose and challenged him the critic replied that he would 'fight him when he had washed his feet and got clean stockings on'. Derrick drew his ceremonial sword, but the critic grabbed and broke it, and there the matter ended.

Despite, or because of, his size and smell, Derrick wore fine clothes, but they were often dirty. 'He was a very imprudent fellow to have five embroidered coats, but only *one* shirt.' Until he came to Bath he needed to be well dressed to support his usual occupation: subscription-hunting. This consisted, the *Gentleman's Magazine* explained, of 'waiting upon the nobility and gentry with proposals for printing a book by subscription, and soliciting the honour of their names to the work, which is never intended to appear; and by perseverance and frequent teazing, many gentlemen will give a guinea to get rid of an impertinent fellow'.

When Dr Johnson heard that Derrick had been appointed Bath's Master of Ceremonies, he said, 'Derrick may do very well, as long as he can outrun his character; but the moment his character gets up with him, it is all over.' Derrick's appointment was an accident. He had happened to be at Bath when M. Collette resigned. As a joke a visiting lord suggested that Derrick should succeed him, and a visiting lady with influence, who had just been flattered by a poem Derrick had addressed to her, took the suggestion seriously and campaigned successfully for him.

In his new position he wore a white hat in imitation of Beau Nash, and affected an even greater elegance of dress and manner. Lydia, in Smollett's *Humphrey Clinker*, described him as 'a pretty little gentleman, so sweet, so fine, so civil and polite', who talked 'so charmingly, both in verse and prose', and was 'a great writer' who had 'got five tragedies ready for the stage'. Derrick did not have Nash's authority, and when two ladies quarrelled during his time in office, 'caps, lapets, curls, cushions, diamond pins and pearls strewed the floor of those rooms wherein during Nash's time order was supreme'.[62] But on the whole he carried out his duties adequately and he did at least one sensible thing when he gave William Herschel, later to become the country's most distinguished astronomer, a place in the Pump Room band.

Derrick's death after six years in office was said by gossip to have been caused by the quantity of cantharides (Spanish fly, an aphrodisiac) which he took. In his will he left 'My essence of cantharides, which has hitherto proved so effectual to me, but now my destruction, to Lord V——e.' He also left 'My last new set of teeth to Mrs Jullion, widow of the late Mr Paul Jullion, operator and dentist, they being not yet paid for.'

Soon afterwards, a violent disturbance occurred when the patrons of the two lower Assembly Rooms (the upper ones were still to be completed) supported rival candidates as Derrick's successor. On 28 March 'the *ladies* – who, by the bye, are said to have *begun* the affray – engaged in real combats: nor was it till the deputy town-clerk had read the *riot act three times* . . . that the hostile movements of the waring assembly could be reduced to decent decorum'.[63] The playwright Sheridan (who came to Bath with his family the following year) must have heard tales of the affair, and described it in his poem, *The Ridotto*:

Fair Nymphs achieve illustrious feats;
Off fly their tuckers, caps and *têtes*;
Pins and pomatums strew the room,
Emitting many a strange perfume:
Each tender form is strangely batter'd,
And odd things here and there are scatter'd.
In heaps confus'd the Heroines lie;
With horrid schrieks they pierce the sky . . .

The winning candidate was Captain Wade, nephew of General Wade, who held the position for eight years, before it was split: one Master of Ceremonies for the new upper Assembly Rooms, and one for the lower rooms.

Philip Thicknesse, his brother Ralph, and his three wives

Philip Thicknesse (1719–92) and his elder brother Ralph were two of seven sons of a Northamptonshire parson. Philip's connection with Bath is better known than Ralph's, but Ralph's was earlier. He had been a master at Eton College but became a soldier – because, according to his tomb in Bath Abbey, he thought arms more becoming the manly age, and therefore joined the laurels to the ivy.' He was also a composer, and it was while performing one of his own works at Bath on 11 October 1742 that he suddenly collapsed and died. He had just drunk a large draught of Bath water, followed by a breakfast of spongy Bath rolls, and these were generally thought to have killed him. Dr William Oliver (the inventor of the biscuit), who was standing next to him, considered that he died of a stroke brought on by over-excitement.

While Ralph was teaching at Eton, Philip Thicknesse had first been an apprentice apothecary in London to one Marmaduke Tisdale. Next he went with James Oglethorpe to help found the new colony of Georgia; and he was an army captain in Jamaica where he campaigned against the gangs of runaway slaves known as Maroons.

In these three early occupations he showed many of the interests which preoccupied him throughout his life and made him one of Bath's most notable eccentrics. As an apprentice apothecary he first took an interest in medicine. As a colonist in

Georgia he spread gossip about the relationships of the brothers Wesley with their young female converts, built himself a wilderness cottage, and sympathised with the misused native Indians, even considering marrying one. In Jamaica he quarrelled with a Scotsman, Makittrick, whose brother, Dr James Makittrick Adair, became the bitterest of his many enemies. Medicine, gossip, cottage building, taking the part of oppressed peoples and quarrelling, together with marrying for money and a little blackmailing, were Philip Thicknesse's obsessions for the next fifty years.

Between his times in Georgia and Jamaica Thicknesse showed early signs of the tactlessness which later caused some of his difficulties. When the board of trustees, which was considering his application to return to Georgia as a soldier, produced Oglethorpe's map of the colony he pointed out that it showed 'forts raised, where no ground had been broken, and flags flying, where no staff had been erected'. Thicknesse's application was rejected.

Soon after his return from Jamaica he heard, at Southampton, that a certain Lieutenant Briggs, who had been spreading malicious accounts of his conduct in Jamaica, was now about to escape by returning there. Deciding that such cowardly behaviour entitled him to cane Briggs rather than challenge him to a duel, he travelled to Portsmouth where, as he recounts in his memoirs, he found Briggs standing at a tavern door,

> very elegantly dressed for the ball, and to do his person justice, he was a very elegant man, he had a sword on, and a cane in his hand, and as I had only a sword, and a small riding stick, I drew a more substantial one out of a bundle which stood to be sold at the next door, and without staying to pay the owner for it, I determined to pay Mr Briggs with it. I believe he saw me draw it out, for before I got over to him, he was as white as the paper I am now writing upon. My word and my blow went in unison at his head and brought forth blood enough to spoil half a dozen brocade waistcoats. He did not draw his sword but struck at me with his cane. I then followed my blows till I had shivered my stick to pieces over him and then I took him, stick and all, and laid him at full length in the gutter of the High Street before the King's Arms door, gave him a blow or two with

his own cane, and told him he would find me at his service at Southampton . . .

When he returned to Southampton Thicknesse heard that Briggs was dying, and prepared to escape abroad to avoid a charge of murder, but fortunately Briggs recovered and they both survived a subsequent duel.

In Southampton Thicknesse fell in love with Maria Lanove, only daughter of French Huguenot parents. Though he claimed genuinely to love her, he noted in his journal, 'I believe it is no great matter of difficulty to make a woman who loves a man believe anything he says.' He had heard that she was due to inherit £40,000 and, to confirm this, he went to London to see her grandfather's will. Reassured, he courted her, but her parents objected, telling the girl that he was only interested in her money, and letting her out of the house only if heavily escorted. So Thicknesse waited for her in the street, then announced to her escort (one major and seven or eight French ladies) that he and Maria were already married. The shock this caused allowed him to escape with her down a long dark passage, where a 'little bakeress', who was in the plot, obstructed the pursuit by crying, 'Take care of the well.'

Thicknesse now had himself married to Maria by a fellow officer dressed in borrowed clerical clothes, and wrote to her parents saying that they were welcome to try to persuade their daughter to come home, but that whenever he and Maria were to be found, they would certainly 'be in bed together'. As a result the parents agreed to a proper marriage, and the father forgave Thicknesse, though not the mother who was, in Thicknesse's opinion, 'a gloomy, religiously disposed woman, who thought herself good, and perhaps meant to be . . . but . . . was of an unforgiving morose temper'.

Thicknesse now served in the Mediterranean as a captain of Marines with Admiral Medley, one of the few close acquaintances with whom he did not quarrel. He did, however, feel ill-used when he came home after a year ('being wife-sick') and so gave offence to the admiral with the result that he never received the 'large share of his fortune'[64] which he had expected. Back at Southampton, Thicknesse was put on half-pay, and lived in poverty with Maria's parents. It was they who forced him to move to Bath by withdrawing the £50 a year they were allowing him.

Here he arrived, accompanied by 'my *forty thousand pounder*', in April 1747, and soon began to support himself by gaming. But two years later, when a type of diphtheria – known as Pelham's fever because two sons of Henry Pelham, leader with his brother Thomas, Duke of Newcastle, of the 'broad-bottom' administration of 1743–54, had died of it – came to Bath, Thicknesse, his wife and their three daughters all caught the disease. Needing help, he wrote to his mother-in-law, Mrs Lanove, but instead of coming to Bath she told him to hire three nurses and sent no money. By this time it was anyway too late, and Thicknesse wrote again to her, 'Madam, your daughter is dead, your grandchildren are dead and I apprehend I am dying: but if I recover, the greatest consolation I can have, is, that *now*, I have no more to do with you . . .'

Thicknesse and his third daughter survived, but soon afterwards his father-in-law died in his sleep, first destroying his will, and his mother-in-law threw herself out of the window and was impaled on the spikes of her railings. Thicknesse inherited £5,000, not £40,000.

He was soon looking for a new wife, and considering a rich planter's widow, recommended by an old friend, Lord Chief Justice Willes, who suggested that Thicknesse compromise her by making his way into her bedroom and appearing at her window in a nightcap 'when the walks are full of company'. Instead Thicknesse married Elizabeth Touchet, daughter of the sixth Earl of Castlehaven, who brought him a further £5,000. Four years later, in 1753, he used £1,200 of this to buy himself the position of Governor of Landguard Fort, a coastal defence position at Felixstowe on the north side of the Orwell estuary.

For the next thirteen years Landguard was his home, although he kept his Bath house and returned there for visits. At Landguard he engaged in his most memorable quarrel – with a local landowner, Colonel Francis Vernon, son of Admiral Vernon. After his death Thicknesse's third wife admitted that he was a man 'susceptible in the extreme of every thing that bordered on insult and rudeness'. Both were likely when four of the companies he commanded at Landguard were also under the command of Vernon as Colonel of the Suffolk Militia.

A complicated succession of slights and counter-slights grew into a full-scale row, which culminated in Thicknesse buying himself a printing press to print attacks on Vernon, and publicly displaying in the streets of Ipswich a 'wooden gun', labelled as if sent to Vernon by one of his own officers as a symbol of his cowardice.

It was in fact a piece of driftwood in the shape of a gun which Thicknesse happened to find on the beach, and he made no effort to hide the fact that he had displayed it and written the label. He was taken to court by Vernon and found guilty of libel. Next morning he took breakfast with the jurors, and presently was sentenced to three months in the King's Bench prison and a fine of £100. Throughout his time there he remained Governor of Landguard, but, typically, neither his position nor his class prevented him from fraternising with the poorer prisoners. This 'rendered me rather obnoxious to the laced court gentry', he later wrote.

With him in prison was his third wife, Ann. During his quarrel with Vernon, one of his grievances was that Vernon's four companies had drilled under the window of Elizabeth, his second wife, while she was ill, and that this had caused her death. Ann Ford, the third Mrs Thicknesse, had been a friend of Elizabeth's.

Ann was a talented singer and player of the viol de gamba, who wished to perform not merely in friends' drawing-rooms but on the public stage. She had therefore arranged a concert at a theatre in the Haymarket, but her father objected and locked her in her room. It was then that she escaped to stay with the Thicknesses, where she continued to plan her concert. On the day of the performance her father had the streets around the theatre blocked by Bow Street Runners, and it was only after they were withdrawn under threat of being cleared away by a detachment of Guards that Ann was able to sing. She had also written a text book entitled 'Instructions for playing on the MUSICAL GLASSES etc.', and had had a well-publicised affair with the ancient Earl of Jersey. Thicknesse's marriage to Ann was happy, like his earlier marriages, and in contrast to his relationships with most of his male friends. It survived a two-year period during which Thicknesse tried to be a farmer in Wales but failed, before in 1768 they settled in the Royal Crescent at Bath.

While Thicknesse was at Landguard, he met the painter,

Gainsborough, and persuaded him to move to Bath. Ultimately he quarrelled with Gainsborough (see page 142), but his most prolonged feud at Bath was with Dr James Makittrick Adair. He and Adair wrote so many insulting things about each other that it is difficult to discover the underlying cause of their quarrel; but Thicknesse certainly believed that Adair had spread the story, first started by his brother in Jamaica, that Thicknesse had run away from the enemy there, and Adair believed that Thicknesse was a medical quack. They conducted their quarrel in long ironic dedications of their books to each other. Adair's eleven-page dedication of his *Medical Essays* called Thicknesse 'this celebrated gout doctor, rape and murder monger' among uncountable other insults. Thicknesse's dedication to Adair of the first volume of his memoirs called him a 'base defamer, vindictive libeller, a scurrilous indecent and vulgar scribbler', and continued in this vein for fourteen pages.

Thicknesse exposed himself to medical attacks by publishing *Man Midwifery Analysed* (1764), and *The Valetudinarian's Bath Guide*, or *The means of obtaining Long-life and Health* (1780). Some of his recommendations seem surprisingly modern. He considered that over-eating was more dangerous than wine drinking. 'After 40 years experience I know 20 intemperate eaters die early in life to one intemperate drinker – provided they were *boon* companions and wine not dram drinkers.' And he recommended the 'wonderful influence of music upon the frame of a man who has an ear'. Other suggestions are more curious. For long life he advised 'partaking of the breath of young virgins'. This was no euphemism, since he used as supporting evidence the longevity of schoolmasters. He himself had always 'partaken of the breath of young women whenever they lay in my way'.

He also wrote about gall stones, his own particular complaint, and one for which he had his own cure: opium. He had first suffered during his earlier period at Bath when his wife and two daughters were dying of diphtheria and he was ill with it. Then a stone had 'found its way into the gall-duct', causing 'the most acute pain the human frame is capable of feeling'. He and his family had taken refuge while ill with a certain Captain Rigg. Thicknesse in his memoirs continued,

> Captain Rigg knowing me to be an old offender even then in
> taking laudanum, had cautiously locked his bottle up, lest I

should be tempted to deal more freely with it than I ought. But being unable to prevail on my timid nurses to get me forty or fifty drops from the apothecaries, I crawled down on all four, broke open his closet, and took all he had at once; the consequence was, a great drought, a profuse sweat, passing the gallstone, and, I believe the preservation of my life.

Twenty-five years later Thicknesse advised Lord Chancellor Thurlow: the first thing to be done was to render the externals of the gall stones perfectly smooth, and that could only be effected by a hard trotting horse. Thurlow should then take up to twenty, thirty or forty drops of laudanum an hour, followed by a tepid bath. The Lord Chancellor took Thicknesse's advice and left Bath cured. Using such treatments, Thicknesse himself claimed to have 'passed seven and twenty gall stones in one day', one of them so large that his doctor had accepted it instead of payment. This was perhaps the huge stone which he illustrated in *The Valetudinarian's Bath Guide*.

Thicknesse recommended opium not only for gallstones but as a general prescription for health. It should be taken daily in doses of up to twenty drops – considerably more than doctors advised – by anyone over fifty for the rest of their lives. The Countess of Desmond had lived to be a hundred and forty with the help of regular opium. He himself had taken it for fifty years. He had, however, finally broken the habit, and adds in his memoirs:

> Since the above was written, I determined to conquer, what all the medical world say, no man could conquer, i.e. to leave off taking opium, after having been so long in the habit of taking it: and I must confess it an arduous task, and often thought, death was preferable to such a languid and miserable existence: but I have persevered long enough to be convinced I can do without it, as I find my usual strength encreases, and I can eat, drink, and sleep very well without it.

During his second period at Bath, Thicknesse made his living by writing. He published *New Prose Bath Guide for the year 1778*, hoping it would have the sort of success which Christopher Anstey's *The New Bath Guide* in verse had had twelve years before. It did not. He had also published *Sketches and Characters*

of the most Eminent and most Singular Persons now living (1770).
Some of the persons – Mr Nash, Admiral Byng, the late Rev.
Mr Laurence Sterne – were fully named; others were easily
identified, for example, 'L——d Sp——n——er', who had
'settled an annuity of two hundred pounds a year on F——y
M——rr——y, because it was supposed his f——r was her
seducer'.

More profitably, he wrote gossip which he was paid not to
publish. Lord Bute, George III's Prime Minister, bought from
him the complete edition of 1000 copies of some of Lady Mary
Wortley Montagu's letters which Thicknesse had printed, in
order to suppress them. In his memoirs Thicknesse is frank
about such extortions. 'I know not what I should have done to
make both ends meet, in my old age, if it had not been for the
repeated kindnesses of my enemies . . . I can at any time muster
ten or a dozen knaves and fools, who will put an hundred
pounds or two into my pocket, merely by holding them up to
public scorn . . . I got three hundred pounds for driving an
ignorant physic-monger out of Bath . . . The old bill sticker of
Pimlico still lives – for I would not shoot the poor devil for the
world, as he is about procuring me a hundred or two more –
but then he is a very old friend.'

This old bill sticker was Captain Crookshanks, who had
indeed been a friend for forty-five years before he became an
enemy. Thicknesse's thirteen-page dedication to Crookshanks
of the third volume of his memoirs contained so much malicious gossip that Crookshanks challenged Thicknesse to a duel.
If this had taken place Thicknesse would have been aged 72,
and Crookshanks 81.

It was another friend turned enemy, the actor and playwright
Samuel Foote, who named Thicknesse Dr Viper, after a quarrel
about one of Foote's typically libellous plays. When Thicknesse
helped the Duchess of Kingston to protest at the first version
of this play, Foote rewrote it and included Thicknesse as a
character of this name. Foote wrote elsewhere about Thicknesse
that he had 'the stupidity of an owl, the vulgarity of a
blackguard, the obdurate heart of an assassin and the cowardice
of a dung-hill cock'.

In 1774 Thicknesse let his house in the Royal Crescent and
moved to the village of Bathampton, a mile and a half to the
north. Here he bought and improved a cottage, naming it St

Catherine's Hermitage. It had fine views over the city and the
River Avon, and was sheltered from the north and east winds
by the Lansdown Hills.

One of his improvements was to erect a monument to
Thomas Chatterton, the dead poet, with the inscription:

> Unfortunate Boy!
> Short & Evil were thy Days,
> But the vigor of thy genius shall immortalize thee
> Unfortunate Boy!
> Poorly wast thou accommodated
> During thy short sojourning among us.
> Thou livedst unnoticed
> But thy Fame shall never die.

Monument erecting was one more of Thicknesse's enthusiasms,
and he had previously planned a Stonehenge, inscribed to
Liberty, on his Welsh farm.

Another series of improvements at St Catherine's Hermitage
was suggested to him by his discovery that its garden had been
an ancient cemetery. Here he displayed three stone coffins
which he had found. He claimed that one, because of its 'length
and narrowness', had contained 'a beautiful Saxon virgin'. In
another he found the body of a 'Roman knight', 'covered with
pickle' which had even preserved some of the flesh. This one he
was keeping to be his own coffin.

Thicknesse's improvements brought him the opposite of the
retired seclusion he claimed to want. So many visitors made the
'quarter of an hour's steep walk from the west end of the Royal
Crescent' that his gardener sometimes got no more than three
hours' work done in a day, and Thicknesse had to restrict access
to those who bought a copy of his prospectus, *A Sketch of St
Catherine's Hermitage'*.

Ever since his first wife and her parents had died twenty-five
years earlier, Thicknesse had been trying to obtain another
£12,000 from her family, but soon after he moved to the
Hermitage the House of Lords finally rejected his claim. Thicknesse left Bath in disgust, planning to settle in Spain; but he
was back at the Hermitage the following year.

The Hermitage was at the centre of his final quarrel, this with
Philip, his second son by his second wife. Philip, the son, and
his elder brother, George, had both taken their mother's name,

Touchet, and had both inherited money from their grandfather, Lord Castlehaven, who had excluded Thicknesse from his will.

Thicknesse sold the Hermitage to Philip when he went abroad, then bought it back from him. In these two deals he claimed that Philip had cheated him of £500. He had a further grievance which he described in his prospectus:

> The insolence of a fellow who possessed more land than manners or honesty, once drove me out of this sequestered shade, and I sold it to my youngest son. The house I then left (if a house it could be called) he was pleased to *improve*, and now its front resembles Alderman Pudding's house, over-against the Pack-Horse on Turnham-Green.

George Touchet, Thicknesse's elder son, had not only inherited money, but a title: Baron Audley. He (as well as Philip) was violently attacked by Thicknesse in Volume II of his memoirs, accused first of neglecting his father, then, when he became a peer, of being 'so addled with his own uncommon elevation that he chose to triumph it over his father'. When Thicknesse published his third volume of memoirs the title page described its author as Philip Thicknesse, late Lieutenant-Governor of Landguard Fort, and unfortunate father of George Touchet, Baron Audley. George and Philip destroyed all the copies of this volume which they could buy.

Meanwhile Thicknesse had finally left Bath to buy and convert a barn at Sandgate, near Hythe, Kent, from which he could sometimes see the coast of France, a country he liked better than England. He was travelling in France three years later when he died suddenly in his coach on the way to Paris. He was buried in the Protestant cemetery at Boulogne. In his will he left 'my right hand, to be cut off after death, to my son, Lord Audley, and I desire it may be sent him in hopes that such a sight may remind him of his duty to God, after having so long abandoned the duty he owed his father who once affection-ately loved him'.

Gainsborough at Bath

One day when Philip Thicknesse was in Ipswich, walking in the garden of the editor of the town's local paper, he inquired who was the 'melancholy faced countryman . . . leaning over the garden wall'. The editor 'said the man had been there all day and he pitied him, believing he was either mad, or miserable. I then stepped forward with an intention to speak to the *mad man*, and did not perceive, till I was close up, that it was *a wooden man* painted upon a shaped board'. It had been painted by Thomas Gainsborough (1727–89), then aged 27.

As a boy Gainsborough, the youngest of nine children of a wool manufacturer of Sudbury, Suffolk, had shown skill with his pen. To get a day off school he had forged a note from his father reading 'Give Tom a holiday'. When told, his father had said, 'Tom will one day be hanged.' When told also that the boy had spent his free day rambling and sketching in the woods, he said, 'Tom will be a genius.'

At fifteen the young Gainsborough had been sent to London where he trained for four years; but he showed no special talent and, by the time Thicknesse heard of him, he had returned to Sudbury, married Margaret Burr (a girl with an annuity of £200, rumoured to have been the bastard daughter of the Duke of Bedford, but more probably of a commercial traveller employed by Gainsborough's father) and set up as a painter in Ipswich. The painting which deceived Thicknesse had been made from a sketch which Gainsborough had drawn when a boy. Its subject had been a man Gainsborough had seen peering over an orchard fence, preparing to raid it. The sketch had been such a good likeness that although the man escaped he was identified.

Thicknesse visited Gainsborough the same day, arranged for one of his landscapes to be engraved, and when, a few years later, he persuaded him to move to Bath, found him lodgings there.

These were at 14 Abbey Churchyard, but Gainsborough later moved to 8 Ainslie's Belvedere, then to 24 The Circus, where the rent of £50 a year dismayed his cautious wife. During the fourteen years he spent at Bath Gainsborough's reputation rapidly increased. At first he charged 5 guineas a head, but eventually 40 guineas for a half-length portrait and 100 guineas for a full-length one. At Bath he painted many well-known citizens and visitors, including the novelists Sterne and Richardson; the actors Henderson and Garrick; Captain Wade, Master of Ceremonies; and Richard Graves, recorder of Bath gossip and Rector of Claverton.

His particular friend in the city was its carrier, Walter Wiltshire, 'who loved Gainsborough and admired his works'.[65] For taking Gainsborough's paintings to London, Wiltshire would accept no payment, so Gainsborough gave him a number of portraits, including those of James Quin and Samuel Foote, rewards which turned out to be a lot more valuable than any money payments would have been, when they were sold after the death of Wiltshire's grandson.

At Bath, Gainsborough pursued his other great interest: music. 'There were times,' the composer, William Jackson, wrote, 'when music seemed to be Gainsborough's employment and painting his diversion.' According to Jackson he 'never had application enough to learn his notes', but hoped to become proficient by using the instruments of the famous. In turn he bought 'Giardini's violin, Abel's viol-di-gamba, Fischer's haut-boy, the harp of a harper and the theorbo of a German professor'.[66]

His instrument-collecting contributed to his quarrel with Thicknesse. When Gainsborough offered to paint a portrait of Thicknesse to make a pair with one he had done of Ann Thicknesse before they were married he agreed to take for payment a viol belonging to Ann which he admired. But he wisely told her, 'Keep me hungry! – Keep me hungry!' until he had finished the portrait. She foolishly sent the viol to him next morning. As a result Gainsborough ceased to work on the painting, and gave further offence to Thicknesse by completing others he had begun later. Eventually he promised to return the viol, and sent Thicknesse the unfinished portrait, but Thicknesse was not satisfied. 'Every time I went into the room where that scare-crow hung, it gave me so painful a sensation, that I protest it often turned me sick, and in one of those sick fits, I desired Mrs Thicknesse would return the picture to Mr Gainsborough.' This Ann did, but enclosed with it a card asking Gainsborough to 'rub out the countenance of the truest and warmest friend he ever had, and so done, to blot him for ever from his memory.'

According to Thicknesse, Gainsborough at once left Bath, never to return, and set up in London. The move was as great a success as his move to Bath had been and, inevitably, Thicknesse in due course took credit for both.

Mrs Macaulay, James Graham, and the electric bath

Catherine Macaulay (1731–91), a well-known historian in her day, was no relation to the better-known Lord Macaulay, but took her surname from a Scottish doctor she had married. She was fifteen years younger than her husband and, when he died in 1766, had already published the first volume of her *History of England from the Accession of James I to that of the Brunswick Line* (1763).

As a child she had read much Roman history and become an egalitarian. This was the aspect of her character which critics ridiculed, including Dr Johnson, who told Boswell, 'Sir, there is one Mrs Macaulay . . . a great republican. One day when I was at her house, I put on a very grave countenance, and said to her, "Madam, I am now become a convert to your way of thinking. I am convinced that all mankind are upon an equal footing; and to give you an unquestionable proof, Madam, that I am in earnest, here is a very sensible, civil, well-behaved fellow-citizen, your footman; I desire that he may be allowed to sit down and dine with us." I thus, Sir, shewed her the stupidity of the levelling doctrine. She has never liked me since.'

Nonetheless, further volumes of her history appeared, and in 1774 (between the fifth and sixth volume) she moved to Bath, where she became a bigger fish in a smaller pond. Here she began to dress splendidly (Johnson said she was better employed reddening her cheeks than blacking other people's characters). The citizens of Bath were kinder and on her birthday, 2 April 1777, presented her with six odes. Mrs Macaulay sat on a throne and was crowned, honours for a republican which amused the critic of the *Monthly Review*.

At Bath she met two people who were to alter her life. The first was the Rev. Thomas Wilson, an absentee rector of the London parish of Walbrook. At her birthday celebration he presented her with a large and curious gold medal. Infatuated with her, he had invited her to live at his Bath house, No. 2 Albert Street, and, five months after the celebrations, erected in his Walbrook church a white marble statue to her. It represented Mrs Macaulay as the Goddess of Liberty, pen in one hand, the other laid on some volumes of her history. Also at Walbrook he built a vault for her body when she died.

The second person to affect her life importantly was a

Scottish quack, James Graham. His remedies at this time included placing his patients on a magnetic throne or in an electric bath. When he left Bath for London he developed a 'celestial bed' guaranteed to cure sterility. It was surrounded by magnets, he wrote, which were 'continually pouring forth in an ever flowing circle, inconceivable and irresistibly powerful tides of magnetic effluvium'. They gave 'that charming spring-yness – that sweet undulating, tittulating, vibratory, soul dis-solving, marrow-melting motion; which on certain critical and important occasions, is at once so necessary and so pleasing'.

Still later he advocated earth-bathing, a treatment which became a personal obsession. During one session he had himself buried naked, except for his head, for six hours each day for eight days, then for twelve hours on the ninth day. And at Newcastle he and a young lady patient 'stripped unto their first suits', were buried side by side up to their chins, 'their heads beautifully dressed and powdered, appearing not unlike two fine full-grown cauliflowers'.[66]

Back temporarily at Bath, he announced that he regretted his ill-spent younger days, which had not been curbed by Christi-anity. Presently he settled in Edinburgh, where he was for a time confined to his house for lunacy. He became an even more enthusiastic Christian, and dated his publications of 1787 'In the first year of the New Jerusalem Church'. For a fortnight during the year before he died he ate nothing, but kept alive by massaging himself with his own 'nervous aethereal balsalm' and dressing in cut turfs.

James Graham claimed later that having Mrs Macaulay as his patient first made his reputation. At her birthday celebra-tion he 'with GREAT MODESTY AND DIFFIDENCE presented her with a copy of his works, containing his surprising discoveries and cures',[67] and when the six odes were published he wrote an introduction for them. Precisely which of his remedies he prescribed for her we do not know, but she was well satisfied, writing to him that 'a great part of my disease immediately gave way to your aerial, aetherial, magnetic and electric appliances and influences'. But it was his younger brother, William Graham, whom she married.

She was forty-seven, William twenty-one. He was also a medical man of a sort, described as a surgeon's mate. Little more is known of him at this time except that he had 'such a fondness for money, as to oblige her to live without a servant, and to officiate himself in the character of cook and chamber-maid'.[68]

The friends of Mrs Macaulay Graham, as she now called herself, were dismayed, especially the Rev. Thomas Wilson. Though he realised that he could not turn her out of his house at Bath, he had her statue removed from his Walbrook church. He may have been glad to have an excuse for doing this because his parish 'was determined to carry the matter into the Ecclesiastical Court, if the Doctor had not thought proper to have it taken down almost as suddenly as it was put up'.[69] The vault he sold to a wealthy family of the parish.

Some years after her death the *Gentleman's Magazine* published a fierce correspondence between Isaac Disraeli (father of the Prime Minister) and William Graham, her second husband, now in Holy Orders and holding a living in Leicestershire, in which Graham defended his wife against Disraeli's accusation that she had destroyed inconvenient historical evidence. Disraeli had written,

> Mrs Macaulay, when she consulted MSS at the British Museum, was accustomed in her historical researches, when she came to any passage unfavourable to the Stuarts *to destroy the page*. These delapidations were at length perceived and she was watched. The Harleian MS No. 7379 will go down to posterity as an eternal testimony to her historical impartiality. It is a collection of state-letters. The MS has three pages entirely torn out; and it has a note, signed by the Principal Librarian, that on such a day the MS was delivered to her; and the same day the pages were found to be destroyed.

Graham suggested that the final pages had either been missing before or never existed, and was able to prove that his wife had never been banned from using the museum. But Disraeli was unconvinced, writing in his final letter, 'I never understood, or suspected that Mrs Macaulay had been *officially* refused access to that learned respository . . . I heard, *as many others have*, that the lady had been watched, and, when accused, looked fiercely and replied insolently.'

Sarah Siddons, rage of the town

It was her success at Bath that made Sarah Siddons (1755–1831) a celebrity and forced London theatre managers to call her back to the capital.

She was a West Country girl, the daughter of strolling players, born in a private room at a Brecon pub, the Shoulder of Mutton. Soon she showed promise and began to perform with her family. When she was only eleven they staged an entertainment in which she took part at the King's Head, High Street, Worcester, to which the audience was admitted only if they each bought a packet of tooth powder. But she fell in love with a fellow actor, William Siddons, of whom her parents disapproved. He was dismissed from the company, his ears boxed by Sarah's mother, and Sarah went to work as a lady's maid in Warwickshire, where she would entertain fellow domestics in the servants' hall by reciting Milton and Shakespeare.

But she was faithful to William. They married, and then went to Bath where they worked for Chamberlain and Crump's Company and lived in poverty. Here, and at other country towns, she was enough admired to persuade Garrick to give her her first London parts at Drury Lane. She was not a success and in May 1776 returned to the provinces. She blamed her failure on Garrick's jealousy: 'In short, I found I must not shade the tip of his nose.'

Two years later, on 24 October 1778, she was back at Bath, recommended by the actor John Henderson to John Palmer (famous for his mail coaches – see page 159), and here she quickly made her reputation. By 5 November the *Bath Chronicle* was reporting that her playing of Elvira in the tragedy *Percy* had 'established her, in the judgment of the town, as the most capital actress that has performed here these many years'. During the next four seasons she played over one hundred different parts, either at Bath or at Bristol where Palmer was also her manager. Eventually the theatres would fill only on nights when she was to perform.

She even played Hamlet, in a version of the play written by Garrick and Lee. But her Lady Macbeth was most admired. On one occasion the audience refused to hear any more of the play after her final exit and insisted on the curtain coming down.

Fellow actors were sometimes so moved by her speeches that they were unable to reply. She believed that she was now successful, whereas before she had failed, because tragedy was once again fashionable. 'This was more favourable to my cast of powers,' she wrote. But her professionalism was as important. She 'excels all persons in paying attention to the business of the scene', 'Dramatic Miscellanies' reported. 'Her modulation of grief, in the pronunciation of the interjection "Oh!" is sweetly moving and reaches the heart.' She was equally successful as the mad character, Belvidera, in Otway's *Venice Preserv'd*. 'The many accidents of spectators falling into fainting fits in the time of her acting bear testimony to the effects of her exertions.'

At first at Bath she complained that she had to play subordinate roles because the leading parts were 'by contract, in the possession of another lady'. And her life there was hard: 'after the rehearsal at Bath, on a Monday morning, I had to go to act at Bristol on the evening of the same day, and reaching Bath again, after a drive of twelve miles, I was obliged to represent some fatiguing part there on the Tuesday evening . . . When I recollect all this labour of mind and body, I wonder that I had strength and courage to support it, interrupted as I was by the cares of a mother, and by the childish sports of my little ones, who were often most unwillingly hushed to silence, from interrupting their mother's studies.'

On the night when Thomas Sheridan (father of the playwright) saw her at Bath her costume had failed to arrive from Bristol, and she appeared in her ordinary dress, but he was so impressed that he went to her dressing-room and told her she was wasting her talents in Bath. She replied that she had tried London and failed. Just the same, he spoke to the management of Drury Lane about her and, in 1782, when his son had become the manager there, she was called back and given a new contract. At her final appearance at Bath she produced her three children on stage and explained that they were the reason she was leaving the city.

Soon she became London's most celebrated actress, converting even Horace Walpole, who had not at first been enthusiastic. ('Her hair is either red or she has no objection to its being thought so, and [she] had used red powder.') She impressed Dr Johnson, when she went to visit him, with her modesty. ('Neither praise nor money, the two powerful corrupters of

mankind, seem to have depraved her.') Almost the only criti-
cism acquaintances had of her was that she behaved off stage as
if on stage. Sir Walter Scott would parody her blank verse style
at the dinner table:

> 'You've brought me water, boy; I asked for beer.'

When she was young she was slim, but later she grew so fat
that on stage she had to be helped to rise. To prevent this being
noticeable, actresses appearing with her were also helped to rise.
Though London became her principal scene, she made four
return visits to Bath, the last in 1808 when she was fifty-three.
Her husband died there the same year. By then they were
informally separated, and for some years he had lived at Bath
for his health.

Richard Sheridan and Eliza Linley

When *The Rivals*, Richard Brinsley Sheridan's first play, was
performed at Bath, his sister-in-law wrote to his wife, 'In my
life I never saw anything go off with such uncommon applause
. . . I suppose the poor creatures never acted with such shouts
of applause in their lives . . . They lost many of Malaprop's
good sayings by the applause; in short I never saw or heard
anything like it; – before the actors spoke they began clapping.'

This was hardly surprising. To the people of Bath the play
must have seemed like a great private joke. It was set in Bath,
and in all they heard and saw they heard and saw themselves.
As a young man Sheridan, born in 1751, had lived among
them, and he knew intimately what he was writing about. The
first sketch for his later play, *The School for Scandal*, for example,
he subtitled 'The Slanderers, a Pump-Room Scene'.

He had not merely lived at Bath but played the central part
in the most celebrated of its many scandals. This began when
he, his elder brother Charles, and his writing collaborator,
Nathaniel Halhed (as well as a great many other gentlemen of
Bath of all ages) all fell in love with the same girl.

She was Eliza Linley, eldest daughter of Thomas Linley,
the director of Bath Concerts. Several of Linley's twelve
children were musically talented and Eliza was a fine singer.

She was also sensationally beautiful. The Bishop of Meath said that she 'formed the connecting link between angel and woman', and Huge Walpole wrote, 'Miss Linley's beauty is in the superlative degree. The king [George III] admires her and ogles her as much as he dares to do in so holy a place as an oratorio.'

Richard Sheridan kept his love for Eliza secret, even when his brother Charles had left Bath (rejected by Eliza) and Halhed had been forced to go to India. Her father, anyway, had other plans for Eliza, and when she was still sixteen set about marrying her to a wealthy sixty-year-old Wiltshire landowner named Long. This plan and Eliza's reluctant agreement to it became so well known at Bath that the playwright Samuel Foote took it for the plot of a play which was staged at the Haymarket, London, in June 1771. Foote made no attempt to hide his play's inspiration; it was called *The Maid of Bath*, the first act took place in Bath's well-known Bear Inn, and Eliza Linley became Miss Linett. As for Mr Long, he was Solomon Flint, described by another character as 'an old fusty, shabby, shuffling, money-loving, water-drinking, milk-marring, amorous old hunks'.

In Foote's play Miss Linett's mother argues her into agreeing to the marriage by telling her to consider Flint as a kind of mortgage or encumbrance, well worth accepting when it was attached to such a valuable property, and anyway soon likely to be removed because of Flint's age. But another character, Major Rackett, persuades Flint that marrying such a young girl will be bad for his pocket, not to mention his health, so instead Flint makes an improper proposal to the girl. While he is doing this, Major Rackett and others interrupt him, threaten to blackmail him and force him to abandon the seduction as well as the marriage. In real life Long behaved more honourably, withdrawing his offer when Eliza told him she was in love with someone else and voluntarily giving her £3,000 and the wedding jewels when her father threatened to sue him for breach of promise.

At this point the real-life original of Major Rackett, a married man named Major Mathews, began to pursue Eliza and to threaten suicide for love of her. Richard Sheridan now re-entered the story. When Eliza told his sisters about Mathews, Sheridan, who was a friend of Mathews, persuaded him to stop harassing her.

Sheridan may not have believed Mathews, and nor perhaps did Eliza. She was anyway tired of singing for her father. Whatever the explanation, she soon afterwards decided to leave Bath for a convent in France, and Sheridan agreed to help her. She chose an evening when her father was giving a concert, told him she was too ill to take part, then went by sedan chair to a pre-arranged place where she joined a waiting post-chaise which drove her to London. Here she and Sheridan boarded a boat for Dunkirk.

It was only now that Sheridan told Eliza that he loved her, and persuaded her to undergo a marriage ceremony at a village near Calais, where the priest was 'well-known for his services on such occasions',[70] on the grounds that this would make their elopement seem less improper. But they agreed to keep their marriage secret, presumably treating it as something of an insurance policy to be used only if they were too severely blamed for what they had done. They then went on to Lille where Eliza entered her convent. But not for long. Her father soon arrived, forgave his daughter and persuaded her to return to England.

Meanwhile at Bath, Major Mathews had been thrown into wild anger by Eliza's escape. A friend wrote to Sheridan and described his state of mind: 'The morning after you left Bath, Mathews came to me, and has repeated his visit several times. It is impossible to give an account of his conversation. It consisted of dreadful oaths and curses upon himself and his past life.' But what particularly infuriated Mathews was his conviction that Sheridan had persuaded him to cease pursuing Eliza to make it easy for him to escape with her. He did not stop at oaths and curses but wrote threatening letters to Sheridan and, when he got no answer, published a notice in the *Bath Chronicle* which began,

Mr Richard S******* having attempted, in a letter left behind him for that purpose, to account for his scandalous method of running away from this place, by insinuations derogating *my* character, and that of a young lady, innocent as far as relates to *me*, or *my* knowledge; since which he has neither taken any notice of letters, or even informed his own family of the place where he has hid himself; I can no longer think he deserves the treatment of a gentleman, and therefore shall trouble myself no further about him than, in this public method, to post him a L★★★, and a treacherous S★★★★★★★★.

The notice threatened anyone who continued to spread 'this infamous lie' that they might 'depend on receiving the proper reward of their villainy, in the most public manner'.

Sheridan now received Mathews's delayed letters and also heard of the published notice. At once he set off for London, where Mathews had gone, swearing that from the moment he reached England he would not sleep till he had found Mathews and 'thanked him as he deserved'.[71] At Canterbury on the first night he kept his promise then travelled on to London.

Here he discovered Mathews's lodgings and determined to call on him the same evening. He arrived there at half past midnight, equipped with two pistols, but it was two in the morning before he persuaded Mathews to let him in. Mathews then received him in alarm – not surprising, since 'one of the pistols peeped out of his pocket'[72] – called him his 'dear friend'[73] and claimed that he never meant to quarrel with him. He kept him talking till seven in the morning, by which time he had persuaded him that his brother Charles had been to blame for the notice.

As soon as Sheridan reached Bath he obtained a denial from Charles. The same night the two brothers set out for London, now determined on a duel. This they arranged with Mathews and that evening the two men and their seconds spent some time searching Hyde Park for a convenient place, Mathews continually refusing to fight, either because the ground was uneven or they were being watched. Eventually they went to the Castle Tavern, Henrietta Street. Describing this first duel Sheridan later wrote, 'almost immediately on our entering the room we engaged, I struck Mr Mathews's point so much out of the line, that I stepped up and caught hold of his wrist, or the hilt of his sword, while the point of mine was at his breast. You [Mr Knight, Mathews's second] ran in and caught hold of my arm, exclaiming, "*Don't kill him*". I struggled to disengage my arm, and said his sword was in my power. Mr Mathews called out twice or thrice, "*I beg my life*". – We were parted. You immediately said, "*There, he has begged his life*, and now there is an end of it".'

When Mathews did not agree, claiming that it was Knight's

intervention which had caused his defeat, Sheridan made Mathews give him his sword and broke it in half. Much furious argument followed, Sheridan suggesting that they should fight again, but Mathews refusing to fight with someone who claimed to have spared his life. Pistols were also suggested, but eventually Sheridan forced Mathews to give him a written apology in return for a promise that Sheridan and his second would not mention the breaking of the sword.

Mathews's apology read, 'Being convinced that the expressions I made use of to Mr Sheridan's disadvantage were the effects of passion and misrepresentation, I retract what I have said to that gentleman's disadvantage, and particularly beg his pardon for my advertisement in the Bath Chronicle.'

Sheridan now returned to Bath, where Eliza had also returned, but they were not reunited because, as far as anyone knew, they were not married. Nor did they feel any need to reveal their marriage because, far from being blamed for escaping together, they were considered to have reacted properly to Mathews's persecution. There was general sympathy for Eliza, and Sheridan was admired for his gallant rescue.

When Mathews returned from Wales, where he had temporarily retired, his own unpopularity and Sheridan's popularity were more than he could bear and he soon began to spread his own version of the duel at the Castle Tavern. Hearing of this, Sheridan felt free to do the same. As a result Mathews now challenged Sheridan to a duel. By this time it was midsummer, 1772, and they agreed to meet outside Bath, on Kingsdown.

Here Sheridan again tried to disarm Mathews by rushing at him and grabbing his sword, but failed and was wounded in the chest by Mathews. A confused brawl followed in which both swords were finally broken and Mathews, the heavier man, ended sitting on top of Sheridan on the ground. First he jabbed him in the neck with the broken hilt of his sword, then recovering its point he wounded him in the belly. Eventually their seconds separated them and Sheridan was taken to the White Hart, where his wounds were dressed by Ditcher and Sharpe, Bath's two 'most eminent surgeons'.[74]

Meanwhile Eliza was at Oxford, due to sing for her father at one of his concerts. But, knowing the effect that hearing of Sheridan's serious wounds might have on his daughter, he kept the newspapers from her. The result was an astonishing occasion at which the audience knew what had happened but Eliza did not. It was described to Sheridan by his friend, Thomas Grenville:

'Miss Linley's appearance on that day inspired the greatest interest in the company present. As her ignorance of the duel and its consequences was known to every person, and her beauty joined to the effect of her truly enchanting powers could not fail of exciting a degree of sympathy in young and susceptible minds when they thought of the heavy calamity that hung over her.'

Eliza had almost reached Bath on her way home before a clergyman met her carriage and told her. In her shock she described Sheridan as her husband and demanded to be allowed to nurse him. Sheridan's father did not allow this, and during the following days the young couple both denied that they were married, but he and Eliza's father began to suspect that they might indeed be, and to try to make them admit it, so that they could separate them. And though Sheridan's father got no admission, he did persuade Sheridan to agree not to see Eliza. When he discovered that he was meeting her in secret he sent him to stay at Waltham Abbey, while Eliza's father took her to Wells.

Throughout the winter of 1772/3 they were separated, and though Sheridan received loving letters from Eliza, he kept a further promise not to write to her. But he was still hopelessly in love with her, and with so little interest in anything else that he wrote to a friend, '*Amo, ergo sum.*'

Meanwhile Mathews had returned to Bath where, finding himself even more unpopular because of his behaviour during the second duel, he wrote his own account of it and even persuaded Sheridan's second to sign this. Among other things, Mathews claimed that Sheridan had been drunk and that he would have had no difficulty in killing him if he had wished. Once more Sheridan was furious, and would have challenged Mathews to a third duel if his friends had not dissuaded him.

He did, however, want to answer in a London paper a particularly offensive description of the two duels which was published about now in a Bath paper, and went for help to 'Memory' Woodfall (a journalist who had earned his name from his phenomenal memory of what was said in parliament at a time when reporters were forbidden to take notes). The result was curious. Woodfall agreed to help Sheridan and, at Sheridan's suggestion, to republish the offensive article first, so that Sheridan's answer would be understandable. But 'day after day . . . elapsed and, notwithstanding frequent applications on the one side, and promises on the other, not a line of the answer was ever sent by Sheridan'.[75]

Separation from Eliza was hardest for Sheridan to bear when she came to London to sing at Covent Garden. In order to meet her he is said – not too reliably – to have several times disguised himself as a cabman so that he could drive her home from the theatre. The separation also distressed Eliza, and led to a violent quarrel during which she wrote that she would never willingly marry Sheridan. Rumours had reached Bath that he had been unfaithful to her with a certain Miss C——y. But when spring came a friend reconciled them without much difficulty, and they were married in London on 13 April 1773.

From this time onwards Sheridan was chiefly known at Bath through his plays. The plot of *The Rivals*, which was first performed at Covent Garden in 1775, included exactly the sort of duels, plans for elopements and romantic rivalries in which Sheridan himself had been involved, and though it is clearly not autobiographical, many of his contemporaries thought that it might be.

William and Caroline Herschel

A regular visitor to the Pump Room, who heard in 1816 that the country's most distinguished astronomer, William Herschel (1738–1822), had been knighted by George III, might have remembered a young Hanoverian of that name who used to play in the Pump Room's band fifty years before. This was the same man. Herschel had been given a place in the band by Samuel Derrick, when he was Bath's Master of Ceremonies, after he heard him play in the Assembly Rooms at the New Year's benefit concert of 1767. Herschel had been the soloist, playing the violin, the hautboys and the harpsichord. His official position at Bath was organist to the Octagon Chapel.

He was one of ten children of a Hanoverian regimental bandsman, and at the age of fourteen he joined the same band himself as an oboist. But five years later, when he became unwell, his parents sent him to England where he landed at Dover in 1757, his only money a French crown. Twenty-five years later he was officially pardoned by George III for deserting his regiment. For the next nine years he worked in the north of England, at one time as trainer of the band of the Durham militia, before getting his 'agreeable and lucrative'[76] position as organist at Bath.

Presently William brought his brother Alexander to Bath, and his sister Caroline to keep house for him. Caroline, who also became a distinguished astronomer, had been refused education by her mother, and taught only to knit, though occasionally she was given surreptitious lessons on the violin by her father. When he died she taught herself to sing 'by imitating the violin parts of concertos with a gag between her teeth'.[77] In Bath William continued to train her, and after a few years she began to give concerts at Bath and Bristol. Sometimes she gave as many as five a week, always with her brother as conductor, and her earnings helped to support their musical household. 'By way of relaxation,' she wrote, 'we talked of astronomy.'

The relaxation became an obsession, and the two brothers set about building large, then larger, telescopes. Soon 'his lodgings resembled an astronomer's much more than a musician's, being heaped up with globes, maps, telescopes, reflectors etc., under which his piano was hid, and the violoncello like a discarded favourite, skulked away in a corner'.[78] During concert intervals the people of Bath would see Herschel 'running still in lace ruffles and powder, from the theatre to the workshop'.[79] He once polished one of his mirrors for sixteen hours continually, and Caroline would place food in his mouth to keep him alive.

Mirrors were essential at a time when it was not possible to make lenses of the size that Herschel wanted. But mirrors had to be viewed from a seat on a scaffold or a suspended cradle, the viewer's back to the sky, with the result that the complete apparatus was large. The Herschels moved house several times to find the garden space they needed, eventually to 19 New King Street, where he set up a seven-foot telescope. With this, on 13 March 1781, he made his greatest discovery: the planet Uranus. 'It was that night,' he wrote, '*its turn* to be discovered. I had gradually perused the great volume of the Author of Nature and was now come to the page which contained the seventh planet.' Herschel called it Georgium Sidus, in honour of George III, but the name did not survive.

The discovery brought to an end his time at Bath. Next year he was invited to take his seven-foot telescope to London, where it was compared to those at Greenwich and shown to be superior. In July he demonstrated it to the king at Windsor. 'Last night,' he wrote to Caroline, 'the king, Queen, the Prince of Wales, the Princess Royal, Princess Augusta, etc., saw my telescope and it was a very fine evening. The instrument gave a general satisfaction; the King has very fine eyes and enjoys observations with telescopes exceedingly.' Soon afterwards George III appointed him his court astronomer at £200 a year.

Herschel and Caroline now moved to Datchet, then to Windsor, and finally to Slough. Here he bought a house close behind the Crown Inn, where, with contributions totalling £4000 from the king, he completed the largest of all his instruments, a forty-foot telescope. It stood close enough to the Bath Road to become a sight which visitors would look for from their carriage windows. 'On the left of the road to Eton and Windsor,' Archibald Robertson wrote in 1792, 'stands the house of the celebrated Dr Herschel; by whose extraordinary improvements in the construction of telescopes many discoveries have been lately made in the noble and useful science of astronomy. The apparatus, which gives motion to his telescope, is seen from the high road.'

It was already an object of interest while it was being built, and many visitors had come to walk through the tube, including George III and the Archbishop of Canterbury. 'Come, my Lord Bishop,' the king said, 'I will show you the way to heaven.' When erected, fifty-foot ladders were needed to reach the viewing platform. As soon as it was first turned on Saturn, it showed a sixth moon and, the next month, a seventh.

Meanwhile Caroline had continued to work for Herschel, even when, in 1788, he married, though she then went to live on her own. She made her own discoveries, including eight new comets. But she always gave her brother William the entire credit for their work together. 'I did nothing for him but what a well-trained puppy-dog would have done,' she wrote. She was certainly no mathematician, and admitted that she could never remember the multiplication tables.

Eventually Herschel's forty-foot telescope was found less

successful than his smaller ones. Seventeen years after he died, his son, Sir John, and his family sang a requiem (composed by Sir John) inside its tube before sealing it and laying it horizontally on three supports in the garden.

Lady Miller and the Batheaston vase

In 1765 Anna Riggs (1741–81), a girl with a fortune, married a relatively poor Irish soldier, John Miller, who had fought in the Seven Years War (1755–62) but was now retired. Miller was sufficiently pleased with his good luck to add his wife's name to his own, making himself John Riggs Miller. He soon set about spending her money on a fine villa at Batheaston, close to Bath. By the time it was built they were so poor they needed temporarily to go abroad where they lived in France and travelled in Italy.

On their return, Mrs Miller's light-hearted letters from Italy were anonymously published (1776). 'The poor Arcadian Patroness', wrote Horace Walpole, who knew who the author was, 'does not spell one word of French or Italian right through her three volumes of travel.'

By this time the Millers (now Sir John and Lady, since he had been made an Irish baronet) had begun the entertainment which made them locally famous. From Italy they had brought an Etruscan vase, found by a workman at Frascati in 1769. They set this on an altar in a bow window, surrounded by laurel leaves, and each Thursday transformed their villa into a temple of Apollo, Lady Miller playing the part of high priestess. Here they invited '"the mob of gentlemen who wrote with ease" and the still more numerous mob who thought they could write',[80] and asked them each to drop an anonymous verse into the vase.

At first these were merely what were called in France *bouts rimés*, or rhyming terminations, but presently they became original verses on a subject announced the week before. Then, according to Richard Graves, Rector of Claverton, who was occasionally a guest, 'some young nymph put in her delicate arm, and took out a single poem which . . . someone who either had, or fancied he had an agreeable elocution, read to the assembly. When in this manner, the whole collection was gone through, the gentlemen retired into a contiguous apartment; where amidst a profusion of jellies, sweetmeats, ice-creams and the like, they decided on the merits of the several performances; from which they selected three, which were deemed the best; and of course entitled to prizes; which her ladyship distributed to the respective authors; a pompous bouquet of flowers to the first, a myrtle wreath to the second, and a sprig of myrtle to the third. These were then usually presented, by the successful candidate, to some lady who wore them in her hair or her bosom, the next evening, to the publick rooms.'

The Millers and their Thursday salons became fashionable. 'Nothing is more tonish than to visit Lady Miller,' Fanny Burney wrote in 1780. Graves once counted fifty carriages outside and on another occasion four duchesses inside. Horace Walpole also went, and described the occasion mockingly, perhaps because his own verse was not chosen. About Lady Miller herself, Fanny wrote that she was 'a round, plump, coarse looking dame of about 40, and while her aim is to appear an elegant woman of fashion, all her success is to seem an ordinary woman in very common life, with fine clothes on. Her manners are bustling, her air is mock important, and her manner very inelegant.'

According to the *Dictionary of National Biography* the entertainments ceased when Lady Miller died in 1781 (still only forty). Pierce Egan, writing in 1819, gives a different explanation: 'After several years the wicked wit of an unknown wag having contaminated the purity of the urn by some licentious and satyrical composition, to the extreme horror of the ladies assembled to hear the productions recited, and the equal chagrin of the host and hostess, who expected the usual weekly tribute of adulatory compliment, the sacred vessel was thenceforth closed and the meetings discontinued for ever.' He adds that Wilkes was in town at the time and suspected, but another account accuses a young naval officer, Malcolm Graeme.

Four volumes of the verses were published under the title of *Poetical Amusements at a Villa near Bath*. In 1865 the supposed vase itself was rediscovered in a builder's yard at the village of Box and placed in Bath's Victoria Park. Here it was vandalised in 1895, when the Bath historian, R. E. M. Peach, wrote to the *Bath Herald* suggesting that 'the wretch or wretches' who had done such a thing should be punished by being made to read

Above: Prior Park, Bath.

Below: The Upper Rooms (the Grand Ball Room) referred to in
Jane Austen's novel *Persuasion*.

Right: Hester Lynch Piozzi, formerly Mrs Thrale, friend of Dr Johnson, by George Dance, 1793.

Below: Louisa, Countess Craven.

Opposite above: "A Peep at the Fancy". Theatre Royal, 23rd April 1824.

Opposite below: A View of King's Bath *c.* 1800.

Portrait of the actress Mrs Siddons by Gainsborough.

aloud to their fellow prisoners a poem addressed to Lady Miller on 'Envy'. Peach, however, had apparently failed to compare the vandalised vase with the vase shown in the frontispiece of the first volume of *Poetical Amusements* . . . which clearly shows that it was not the original one.

John Palmer and the mail coach

John Palmer, born at Bath in 1742, son of a brewer and tallow-chandler, inherited from his father the management of Bath's Orange Street Theatre, and acquired the Theatre Royal, Bristol. At these he would put on performances on alternate days, and use as his performers such celebrities of the time as John Henderson and Sarah Siddons.

At this time, in spite of Ralph Allen's improvements to postal services, letters were still carried by post-boys on horseback, who had become so unreliable that the post office advised those sending bank notes to cut them in half and send the halves separately; and so slow that, in spite of the extra cost, people would wrap letters as parcels (which were carried by faster stage-coaches). Even these in the 1770s were still taking thirty-eight hours to make the journey from London to Bath.

Palmer proposed and eventually had accepted a scheme by which all mail would be carried by special mail coaches. To save time (and money) they would pay no tolls. As they approached the toll gates they would sound their horns, and toll-gate keepers who delayed them would be fined. Palmer believed that such coaches could make the journey between Bath and London in sixteen hours, and the first two runs did better. One left Bristol at 4pm on 2 August 1784 (Palmer was there to see it go), and arrived, via Bath, in London at 8am the next morning. The first return coach reached Bristol in only fourteen hours.

Within one month, mail coach services were suggested between London and four more towns, and within fifteen months they were actually running to these and another twelve towns. Palmer was made Surveyor and Comptroller-General of the Post Office.

He held this position for only six years, before he quarrelled with the Postmaster-General, Lord Walsingham, and with his own assistant, Charles Bonner. Palmer had rescued Bonner financially – he had previously been a coach builder's apprentice, then an actor – but in the process had written him compromising letters which Bonner now published. As a result Palmer was sacked.

At Bath, however, he remained a respected figure. He became mayor of the city and was four times elected its Member of Parliament. The country in general also rewarded him. Eighteen cities gave him their freedom, and soon after he had been dismissed he was given an annual pension of £3000. He considered this grossly inadequate, and campaigned for more. Eventually, some twenty years later, Parliament at a fourth attempt voted him an extra £50,000. His attempts to get it had cost him, he calculated, £13,000.

Palmer died at Brighton, five years after this, in 1818, but his body was brought home to be buried at Bath Abbey.

7

VISITORS

Stephen Duck's tour

Stephen Duck (1705–56), known as the Thresher Poet because he grew up a poor agricultural labourer, included Bath in a tour of the West Country. While others went to explore the Italian coast, he wrote, he could only holiday at home, being 'more bounded in my Fancy and my Purse'.

He crossed Hounslow Heath, famous for its robbers, but unafraid because 'A *Poet's* Purse, like *Virtue,* dares a thief', stayed the night with a one-time fellow worker where he was tempted to show his old skill at mowing, then came on the second day to the village of Charlton where he had once been a thresher. Here it was the village feast-day, funded by his patron, Lord Palmerston, at which

> All eat enough, and many drink too much:
> Full twenty *Threshers* quaff around the Board;
> All name their Toast, and ev'ry one my Lord.
> No Cares, no Toils, no Troubles now appear;
> For Troubles, Toils and Cares are drown'd in Beer.

Presently he reached Bath, where an unnamed 'son of Aesculapius' (perhaps Dr William Oliver) charmed him ('Polite his Manners and his Temper sweet'), and he noticed Ralph Allen's landscaping of Prior Park, thus dating his visit in the 1740s at the earliest. He also met the wife of the Rev. Stanley, Rector of Pewsey, who had been the first to encourage his writing. Duck approved of the disapproving attitude which Mrs Stanley took to Bath's frivolities.

> Various Diversions here employ the *Fair*;
> To Dancing some, and some to Play repair;
> Not MUSIDORA [Mrs Stanley] so consumes her Days,
> The Dame who bad me sing JEHOVAH's Praise:

> Uncharm'd with all the flutt'ring Pomp of Pride,
> Heav'n, and domestic Care her Time divide:
> In her own Breast she seeks a calm Repose,
> And shuns the crouded Rooms of *Belles* and *Beaux*:

On his way home he met the Rev. Stanley himself,

> . . . the Friend, who first my Lays approv'd
> Who loves the Muse, and by her is belov'd;
> Who taught her tender Pinions how to fly,
> Told when she crept too low, or soar'd too high.

Duck had other patrons, one of whom had introduced him to George II's Queen Caroline. The queen had in turn sent his poems to Pope and, more usefully, given him a pension and made him keeper of Merlin's Cave, the curious folly she was having built in the grounds of Richmond Palace. In 1735 the *Gentleman's Magazine* reported that 'Her Majesty has order'd also a choice collection of English books to be placed therein; and appointed Mr Stephen Duck to be cave and library keeper, and his wife to be necessary woman there.'

The queen died two years later, but Duck remained in royal favour, and, when he had been ordained a priest, became preacher at Kew Chapel. A year later he was appointed Rector of Byfleet, Surrey. But his private life was not happy. His first wife, by whom he had three children, had died many years earlier, and in 1733 he had married Sarah Big, housekeeper to the queen at Kew. It was his failure to satisfy this lady that caused the trouble since he was 'not able to give his yoke-mate that satisfaction and content which a weak mind with a vigorous constitution is generally apt to do'.[81] As a result he drowned himself in a trout stream behind the Black Lion Inn at Reading.

Alexander Pope and Miss Blount

> Let low-born Allen, with an awkward Shame,
> Do good by stealth, and blush to find it Fame.
> Virtue may chuse the high or low Degree,
> 'Tis just alike to Virtue, and to me.

So Alexander Pope (1688–1744) wrote about Ralph Allen, Bath's philanthropic postmaster, in his satirical dialogue *One*

Thousand Seven Hundred and Thirty Eight. Pope had been coming to Bath for twenty-four years and by this time he and Allen were good friends. He had been helped by Allen, who had offered to pay for the publication of a full and correct edition of Pope's letters – after an unauthorised edition had been published in 1735. In the end Allen was one of the subscribers to the new edition, taking fifty copies. On the other hand, Allen was receiving advice from Pope about the pictures he should commission for Prior Park. And he was undoubtedly looking forward to Pope's advice about laying out its grounds, since Pope, with his own celebrated garden at Twickenham, was one of the foremost gardeners of the time.

Even before the publication of his poetic tribute, Pope had been including fulsome compliments to Allen in letters to him. 'I really esteem you as a friend to all virtue and an impartial Christian', he had written in 1736. And seven months after the poem appeared he wrote to Allen to tell him that he had revised it. Humility was the new virtue he had discovered in Allen, and he 'must therefore in justice to my conscience of it, bear testimony to it, and change the epithet I first gave you, of *Low-Born* to *Humble*'. He would tell everybody, Pope continued, that he had made the change because Allen deserved it, not because Allen or anyone else had asked for it.

By now Allen was sending regular gifts of Bath Water to Twickenham for Pope and his guests. He also sent guinea-hens, oil and wine. In return Pope sent Allen a Great Dane puppy and a Bible.

Next autumn Pope stayed with Allen and his second wife (he had remarried in 1737) for three months. Prior Park was still not finished but the Allens had left Bath to live in the village of Widcombe near the new house. Here Pope was given a special little green chair to sit in and copiously provided with medicinal waters. At this time he visited Allen's quarries, and became inspired by their coloured stones to make dramatic improvements to his famous fifty-foot grotto at Twickenham, which he thought he had finished fifteen years earlier. Soon after Pope left, Allen was sending him stone, and Pope was inviting Allen to come and see the effect.

In 1739 Pope introduced the literary divine, William Warburton, to Allen; and in 1741, when the Allens moved to Prior Park, Pope and Warburton both became regular visitors. The first apparently harmless hint of what was to follow occurred two years later when Pope wrote to tell them that he was accepting their invitation to bring Martha Blount with him.

Pope had known Martha ('Patty') Blount (1690–1762) for almost forty years. Her parents, Catholic gentry living near Reading, had been close friends of his own. In 1714, during Pope's earliest visit to Bath, he had written to Martha to tell her that she would be the finest mermaid in Christendom if she would come there. Later he addressed his *Epistle to a Lady* to her. At first he had been equally fond of her sister, Teresa, but he quarrelled with Teresa and when, about 1723, rumours began to spread that he was Martha's lover, he claimed that Teresa had started them. Meanwhile Martha had made a number of visits to Bath, some with her friend, Lady Suffolk (George II's nearly deaf one-time mistress, Mrs Howard). She was now fifty-three years old.

The house-party of the autumn of 1743 was a disaster. The underlying cause was that Mrs Allen and Martha Blount took a strong dislike to each other – described by the tolerant Allen as a 'mutual dissatisfaction'. The one person in the household whom Martha Blount did not dislike was Allen's sixteen-year-old niece, Gertrude Tucker. Ironically, Gertrude Tucker could have been the cause of the disaster. She later (after, at the age of eighteen, marrying Warburton) revealed that she had heard from her bedroom, next to Pope's, the regular visits which 'Mrs Blount' would pay him between 6am and 7am when they would 'talk earnestly together for a long time', adding that when they met at breakfast Martha Blount would always 'ask him how he had rested that night'. Gertrude may well have gossiped to Warburton or to her aunt, Mrs Allen.

Allen's sister, Mrs Elliott, on the other hand, believed the explanation lay in Miss Blount's defiant Roman Catholicism; and this was supported by the Bishop of Bristol's story, told him by Allen, so he claimed, that while at Prior Park Miss Blount had wished to go to Mass in Bath, and that although Allen had offered her his carriage he had refused to accompany her. Pope, who described Mrs Allen as 'a minx and an impertinent one', offered yet another explanation: on an earlier visit he had passed Mrs Allen's family home at Bathampton, now usually empty, and suggested that he and a friend should set up house there. It would ultimately make a good permanent home for Martha Blount, he told Allen. Though Allen had agreed to neither of these suggestions, Mrs Allen could well have been annoyed that someone she already disapproved of for her Catholicism, and for carrying on a clandestine affair under her roof, was trying to take possession of a house to which she was sentimentally attached.

Whatever the explanation, Mrs Allen was first rude to Pope, then Pope was blunt with Allen before departing for Cirencester. Miss Blount described her embarrassing final days at Prior Park in a letter to Pope:

> I hope you are well. I am not. My spirits are quite down, though they should not. for these people deserve so much to be dispised, one should do nothing but laugh. I packed up all my things yesterday, the servants knew it, Mr and Mrs Allen never said a word, nor so much as asked me how I went or where, or when. In short from every one of them much greater inhumanity than I could conceive any body could shew. Mr Warburton takes no notice of me. tis most wonderfull. they have not one of them named your name, or drank your health since you went. they talk to one another without putting me at all in the conversation. Lord Archibald is come to Lincombe, I was to have gone this morning, in his coach, but unluckily he keeps it here. I shall go and contrive something with them to day. for I do really think, these people would shove me out, if I did not go, soon.

Presently Pope began to write again to Allen. In a gesture of reconciliation, Allen sent Pope four hampers of Bristol water. And they were on good enough terms by the following March for Allen to take his wife to stay the night at Twickenham.

Next day, however, he and Pope had a fresh discussion of their autumn quarrel. And when Pope died two months later, he made his final contribution to the matter in his will. To Warburton and Allen jointly he left his library but in addition he left to Allen the sum of £150 which was 'to the best of my calculations, the account of what I have received from him; partly for my own, and partly for charitable uses'. According to one report Allen smiled when he read the amount and said that Pope was always a bad accountant. According to another, he was 'extremely enraged'.[82]

To Martha Blount Pope left £1000, sixty of his books, his

household goods and plate, the furniture of his grotto, the urns in his garden, and the residue of his estate after legacies had been paid.

Samuel Richardson and his doctor

Samuel Richardson (1689–1761), novelist and printer, had two reasons for visiting Bath: his brother-in-law and his doctor. His brother-in-law was the Bath bookseller, James Leake (see page 112). Richardson had known Leake in London where he had worked for Leake's father. When James, the son, moved to Bath in 1722, Richardson began to rent James's London house at the entrance to Salisbury Square. By this time Richardson was married to his first wife, Martha Wilde, the daughter of another ex-employer. He and Martha had six children, but they all died young; and in 1733, soon after she also had died, he again married an employer's daughter, this time James Leake's sister, Elizabeth.

Richardson's doctor was the Bath physician, George Cheyne, famous as the exponent of his milk and vegetable diet. Richardson had business, as well as medical, dealings with Cheyne. In 1733 he printed his *The English Malady*, and from then onwards printed all Cheyne's works till Cheyne died in 1743.

Throughout this time Cheyne gave Richardson stern if eccentric medical advice. He deplored Richardson's tendency towards rotundity. 'Fatness is but another word for dropsy of the flesh,' he wrote. A proper diet was the first cure. Richardson should abandon meat eating and abstain from fermented liquor, except 'on occasions of gallantry, gaiety or lowness'.

He recommended vomiting. 'Your short neck is rather an argument for a vomit now and then than against it for no long necked animal can vomit, and vomits are the best preservative from apoplexies.' Although he was against the drugs used by his fellow physicians, he prescribed a few medicines, for example, 'a tea spoonful or two of tincture of soot and Assa Foetida made on penny water in a cold infusion' to be drunk in peppermint water. This would help Richardson to 'break wind plentifully'.

Cold baths were useful. So was exercise, something which Richardson disliked. To convert him to it, Cheyne recommended a device he called a chamber-horse, a complicated machine which consisted of a chair set on a board with hoops for arms and a rest for the feet, which Richardson should ride when reading or dictating. Cheyne told Richardson that the machine 'rides double better than single'. It is pleasant to imagine Richardson, his recent biographers write, 'dropping Pamela's advice to her little family from this gently bouncing perch, perhaps balanced by Mrs Richardson'.[83]

Later, Cheyne suggested that Richardson should take up the 'charming manly diversion' of billiards. Best of all, he should 'give up business intirely to live in the country and follow a post-boy's life a horse-back with a good deal of evacuation and apothecary's poison'. Then 'perhaps you might be enabled to live on dog's meat some years longer'. Although for seven years Richardson took Cheyne's advice and gave up meat he found this did him no good, and remained, in Cheyne's words, 'full puffed short neck't and head and face bursting with blood'.

Cheyne also gave Richardson advice about his writing, on the whole preferring his dull, moralising novels to Fielding's bawdier ones. About Fielding's *Tom Jones* he said, 'it will entertain none but porters or watermen'. On the other hand he suggested that the later volumes of *Pamela* should have a little more action. 'An excellent physician', Richardson wrote to another friend, 'was so good as to give me a plan to break legs and arms and to fire mansion houses to create distress.' He rejected Cheyne's suggestions.

From early in their acquaintance Richardson kept Cheyne's letters, unlike those of other friends, although Cheyne told him to burn them. When he died he left a note with them reading, 'This book, and the lettters in it, on no terms, or consideration what so ever, to be put (or lent) into such hands, as that it may be printed or published.' In an obituary for Cheyne, Richardson wrote, 'Those who best knew him most loved him.'

In spite of these agreeable connections with Bath, Richardson did not like the city, considering it 'a gay, sauntering good-for-nothing place for a young woman to live in . . . the town's people, though ever so genteel . . . despised by the guests of the place'. He wrote this in 1757 when he heard that his daughter Mary (Polly) might marry a Bath surgeon, Mr Ditcher. Richardson disapproved of Ditcher, and of the proposed marriage settlement. Polly, he believed, was marrying him on the rebound, and wrote that 'Mr Ditcher's task was as easy as he could wish; too easy I think, between you and me, considering another affair was so recently gone off . . .' The night of the signing of the marriage treaty was a dramatic one in the Richardson household. 'The dear girl, I am sure, meant not either disregard or slight: but was hurried only by her timidity. But what a wasp's nest did I disturb, by mentioning what I had expected and desired, when we were returning among ourselves, that night of signing! – from hysterical girls, Polly, Miss Lintot etc. the paroxysm catching one from the other . . .'

Long before this, Richardson had become a close enough friend of Ralph Allen to be asked to dine at Prior Park during his visits to the city. He was also on friendly terms with Allen's permanent house-guest William Warburton, until they quarrelled about the preface which Warburton provided for the later volumes of *Clarissa*. Richardson claimed that he had always planned to drop Warburton's preface when the novel was published as a whole, but when he did so Warburton not only took offence but became a supporter of Fielding in the literary squabble between the two novelists. Richardson printed the fifth edition of Thomas Edwards's devastating attack on Warburton's Shakespearean scholarship.

Richardson's relationships with the Fielding family were complicated. 'I love four worthy sisters of his [Fielding's] with whom I am well acquainted,' Richardson wrote. He was particularly friendly with Sarah Fielding and he printed her books, including *The Governess*. He and her brother, Henry, both had an exaggerated opinion of this now forgotten lady's work; others were more guarded, and one critic wrote to Richardson, 'I have read Miss Fielding with great pleasure. Your *Clarissa*, is, I find, the Virgin-mother of several pieces; which, like beautiful suckers, rise from her immortal root.'[84] But Richardson never forgave Fielding for parodying him, first in the anonymously published *An Apology for the Life of Mrs Shamela Andrews*, and then in *Joseph Andrews*.

The Duke of Kingston and his bigamous duchess

In the second half of the eighteenth century, when the King's and Queen's Baths became so crowded and insanitary that the better class of visitor would not use them, the Duke of Kingston (1712–73) built private baths nearby. Though they were not so large – Smollett's Lydia Melford wrote, 'I was almost suffocated for want of air; the place was so small, and the steam so stifling' – they became smart. 'They are now the only place where persons of condition or delicacy can bathe decently,' Philip Thicknesse wrote in his *New Prose Bath Guide*. Kingston owned other property in Bath and, at about the time of his marriage to Miss Elizabeth Chudleigh, he built a house there which was later called Kingston House.

Earlier in his life Kingston's aunt, Lady Mary Wortley Montagu, had written 'he has hitherto had so ill an education, 'tis hard to make any judgment of him; he has spirit, but I fear will never have his father's sense but, as young gentlemen go, 'tis possible he may make a good figure amongst them.' Handsome he certainly was, said by Horace Walpole to be 'possessed of the greatest beauty and the finest person in England'; but despite his fine figure and his building at Bath, it is because of his marriage to Elizabeth Chudleigh that he is remembered.

He brought his duchess to Bath twice, on the first occasion for a nine-day stay soon after their wedding in 1769, when they used his house there; on the second occasion, four years later when they first stayed in Mrs Hodgkinson's fashionable lodgings, then moved to Kingston House, then to 5 South Parade. On both visits Elizabeth showed her talent for causing confusion by changing her mind. In 1769 she hired two chair-men for a fortnight, but because she had stayed only nine days she refused to pay them the agreed amount till they appealed to the mayor. In 1773 she refused to pay Mrs Hodgkinson, then 'gave her a piece of plate worth ten times the amount'.[85] The second visit ended with the death of the duke.

It was in the following years that the Duchess of Kingston's problems reached a climax, but they had begun in the years before she married him. Early in life she had had a connection with another Bath property-owner, William Pulteney, who commissioned the bridge. Pulteney had met Elizabeth during a shooting party, and been charmed by this beautiful, fatherless girl. He had tried to educate her, without much success, then sent her to London where he arranged for her to become a maid of honour to Augusta, Princess of Wales.

Here she was courted by the Duke of Hamilton (who later married one of the beautiful Gunning sisters one midnight, in such a hurry that they had to use a bed-curtain ring). But Hamilton went on the Grand Tour, and his love letters were kept from Elizabeth, who, assuming that he was ignoring her, secretly married a young naval officer, John Hervey, second son of Lord Hervey, author of the memoirs.

They spent a single night together, but it was such a failure that Hervey rejoined his ship to sail for the West Indies, and Elizabeth returned to court, determined never to see her husband again. When she became pregnant next year she pretended to be ill. The truth was suspected. 'The world says I have had twins,' she told Lord Chesterfield. 'I make a point of believing half what it says,' Chesterfield replied. The child conveniently died soon after it was born.

Back at court, she attracted the Duke of Kingston's attention, as she did that of many others; George II, now in his seventies, 'had a mind to believe himself in love' with her, Horace Walpole wrote, and gave her a watch worth thirty-five guineas. She held the most elaborate firework entertainments, the duke in attendance and no doubt paying the bill. When taking part in a masque at one of these she appeared as Iphigenia dressed for sacrifice, wearing such a skin-tight costume that Princess Augusta threw a veil over her.

Eventually the Duke of Kingston offered to marry her, so Elizabeth, to free herself for this (and because Hervey, back in England and jealous of her court success, was threatening to disclose their marriage), went to the parish church at Lainston, Hampshire, where the wedding had taken place and, while a friend distracted the clerk, tore the page which recorded it out of the parish register.

Now, however, Hervey's elder brother became seriously ill, making it likely that Hervey would succeed him as Earl of Bristol, and Elizabeth, perhaps thinking that an earl in the hand was better than a duke in the bush, went back to Lainston and persuaded the rector to re-enter her marriage in the register. And when Hervey now asked for a divorce she at first refused, remarking, 'I can either be Countess of Bristol or Duchess of Kingston.'

Eventually, however, she and Hervey colluded to have their marriage declared null and void on the grounds of non-consummation, and in February 1769 she married the Duke of Kingston.

For four years all seemed well, and might have remained so after the duke had died, leaving her a life interest in his real estate and the rest of his huge fortune outright. She went to Italy to start spending it, delighting the Romans by having her yacht sailed up the Tiber. But while in Rome she heard that Evelyn Meadows, the late duke's nephew, who had by accident been left out of the future inheritance of the duke's estate, had brought a charge of bigamy against her. In a hurry to return to England, she found that her Roman bank manager, for some unexplained reason, would not advance her money for the journey, and had to threaten him with a pistol before he would agree.

Hannah More, the lady of letters from Bristol, who may perhaps have met the duchess at Bath during her two brief visits, and certainly knew her reputation, vividly described the first day of her trial:

[It was] a sight of which, for beauty and magnificence, exceeded anything which those who were never present at a coronation, or a trial by peers, can have the least notion. Mrs Garrick and I were in full dress by seven. You will imagine the bustle of five thousand people getting into one hall! yet, in all this hurry, we walked in tranquilly. When they were all seated, and the king-at-arms had commanded silence on pain of imprisonment (which, however, was very ill observed), the gentleman of the black rod was commanded to bring in his prisoner. Elizabeth, calling herself Dowager-Duchess of Kingston, walked in, led by Black Rod and Mr La Roche, curtseying profoundly to her judges. The peers made her a slight bow. The prisoner was dressed in deep mourning; a black hood on her head; her hair modestly dressed and powdered; a black silk sacque, with crape trimmings; black gauze, deep ruffles, and black gloves. The counsel spoke about an hour and a quarter each. Dunning's manner is insufferably bad, coughing and spitting at every three words, but his sense and his expression pointed to the last degree: he made her Grace shed bitter tears. The fair victim had four virgins, in white, behind the bar. She imitated her great predecessor, Mrs Rudd, and affected to write very often, though I plainly perceived she only wrote, as they do their love-epistles on the stage, without forming a letter. The Duchess has but small remains of that beauty of which kings and princes were once so enamoured . . . She is large and ill-shaped; there is nothing white but her face, and, had it not been for that, she would have looked like a bail of bombazeen.

After five days, on the evidence of a servant, of the sergeant surgeon who had delivered her child and of the widow of the rector of Lainston, the duchess was found guilty. The penalty should have been burning on the hand, and Hannah More was told by Lord Camden, the attorney-general, that he was angry that she had escaped this, but (as he was once a professed lover of hers) 'he thought it would have looked ill-natured and ungallant for him to propose it' and the peers accepted that her title (now presumably Countess of Bristol) exempted her from corporal punishment. When, however, she heard that Mr Meadows planned a further action against her she fled to Dover where she persuaded the captain of her yacht to take her to Calais in an open boat, just in time to avoid an order forbidding her to leave the country.

Mr Meadows's subsequent attempts to claim back his rights from the countess failed, and meanwhile she continued to live abroad, buying various large estates including one near St Petersburg where she established a brandy manufactory. She named it Chudleigh. Another was at Montmartre. Realising that she had been cheated by the vendor of this, she brought an action against him. When told at dinner one evening that it had failed, she suffered a stroke. A day or two later she ordered two glasses of mid-morning madeira, rose from her bed to drink them, lay down again and was soon afterwards found to have died.

The 'Great Commoner'

Of all Bath's Members of Parliament, William Pitt (1708–78), known as Pitt the Elder, later Earl of Chatham, was the most famous. Since, politics apart, the best-known fact about Pitt is his chronic gout, it is ironic that Bath with its healing waters should have been his constituency.

As a young cornet in the army Pitt had been picked out by his commanding officer, Lord Cobham, for patronage. He later married one of Cobham's nieces. Pitt and Cobham were prominent members of the Whig splinter-group known as the Boy Patriots, which opposed the official Whigs under Walpole, and as a result it was many years before Pitt held office. In 1756, however, he at last became Secretary of State and Leader of the House of Commons. The following year he became Member of Parliament for Bath.

It was Thomas Potter, rumoured seducer of Ralph Allen's niece, Gertrude Warburton, who made the arrangement. Potter himself replaced Pitt at Okehampton so that Pitt could move to Bath where the sitting member, Robert Henley, had vacated his seat to become Lord Keeper. The next few years were those of Pitt's most memorable successes when, as the king's chief minister during the Seven Years War, he organised the defeat of the French in India and Canada. Bath celebrated appropriately when General Wolfe captured Quebec, and Prior Park 'in splendour out-shone any thing in imagination, being one great appearance of light, and gave a very fine idea of the Chinese Feast of Lanthorns, which with a large bonfire a little on its right, made the most sparkling and lively appearance ever yet seen'.[86]

When peace was made in 1763, however, Pitt for the first time quarrelled with the mayor and corporation. He was violently opposed to the peace, believing that the war should have been continued until France was more thoroughly beaten, and he objected strongly to the congratulatory address which they wished him to deliver to King George III. Ralph Allen claimed to have had the word 'adequate' inserted in the address to qualify the word 'peace' and so make it acceptable to Pitt, but it was precisely to this word that Pitt objected. To Allen he wrote, 'The epithet of *adequate* given to the peace contains a description of it, so repugnant to my unalterable opinion . . .

that it was impossible for me to obey the Corporation's commands in presenting their address.'

In further letters Pitt pressed Allen to pass on his 'sentiments' to the corporation, and Allen eventually replied, 'With the greatest anxiety and concern, I have in obedience to your positive and repeated commands executed the most painful commission that I ever received', adding obsequiously, 'it is impossible for any person to retain higher sentiments of your late glorious administration than I do'.

When, the following year, Allen died, he left Pitt £1000 in his will. Meanwhile, at the end of 1763 Pitt had sold No. 7, The Circus, the house he had used on visits to Bath since 1755 when he bought it. In due course he was painted by the Bath artist, William Hoare, and came again to the city for his health in 1766, but the same year his official connection with it ended when he became the Earl of Chatham.

Selina, Countess of Huntingdon, and her chapel

Selina, Countess of Huntingdon (1707–91), founded her chapel at Bath as part of her plan to bring her Christian message to the upper classes. She founded others at Tunbridge, Brighton and London. About the Bath chapel John Wesley wrote in 1767, two years after it opened, 'I know not when I have seen a more serious, a more deeply attentive audience. Is it possible? Can the gospel have a place where Satan's throne is?'

Selina's commitment to low-church Christianity was the indirect result of a mass conversion of her husband's family. When the four sisters of the ninth Earl of Huntingdon, to whom she was married, were taken to hear the Yorkshire Methodist, Benjamin Ingham, all four were converted, and one of them, Lady Margaret, married Ingham. It was Lady Margaret who told her sister-in-law, Selina, that 'since she had known and believed in the Lord Jesus Christ . . . she had been as happy as an angel', so persuading Selina to 'turn Methodist' – to the distress of other friends and relations.

When two of her sons, George and Ferdinando, died of small-pox in 1743 she became more fervently religious, and her husband's death three years later freed her to devote her life to spreading her message. 'There was a publicity in her religion', her biographer wrote, 'which no other, dissenter, puritan, churchman, or reformer, had ever displayed, at least since the Reformation. Wherever she was, in whatever company, her conversation was on religion.'[87]

She began to come to Bath in the early 1740s, when Beau Nash was its dominant figure, and did not spare 'this man of pleasure . . . a monument of irreligion, folly and vice'. Her acquaintance with him allowed humorists of the city to spread the rumour that Nash had been converted. 'Verses were written on her Ladyship and Mr Nash, which were fastened to the walls of the Pump-room and Assembly-room', and a story was started that the countess was to preach one morning at the Pump Room, and that Nash, 'to be known as the Rev. Richard Nash',[88] would preach in the evening at the Assembly Rooms. Nash was not amused and would never afterwards visit the countess.

Some twenty years later, on 24 October 1765, when her Bath chapel was opened, she invited many of her aristocratic friends to the ceremony. Her special disciple, George Whitefield, preached the sermon.

She befriended most of the well-known Methodists of the time, from the Wesley brothers to Augustus Toplady, author of *Rock of Ages*, to William Grimshaw, the so-called 'mad parson' of Haworth. A number of them, including Whitefield, she made her chaplains to protect them from persecution, taking advantage of her right, as a peeress, to appoint as many as she liked. Romaine, the London preacher, and Fletcher, the Swiss parson of the mining village of Madeley, both spent periods as resident ministers at Bath.

'It was truly delightful', her biographer wrote about the Bath chapel, 'to behold the powerful, the resistless effects of the gospel-words amongst those, who, before that time, had seldom or never heard it proclaimed in its purity. Many despisers were overawed and confounded . . . and many careless lovers of pleasure were impressed with a solemn sense of eternal things.'

In 1981 the chapel was finally made redundant. Three years later it was acquired by the Bath Preservation Trust, which launched an appeal for its restoration to celebrate its own fiftieth anniversary. The Trust has now moved its offices into the group of buildings attached to the chapel, which include the manse the countess had built for her personal use when she visited Bath.

Dr Johnson visits Bath

On 26 April 1776 James Boswell followed Samuel Johnson to Bath, and at the Pelican Inn found a note from Johnson, who was with the Thrales. 'I went to him directly,' Boswell wrote, 'and before Mr and Mrs Thrale returned, we had by ourselves some hours of tea-drinking and talk.' Boswell collected together Johnson's sayings during their time at Bath. Among them was one about the father of his friend, Bennet Langton, who 'never clarified his notions, by filtering them through other minds. He had a canal upon his estate, where at one place the bank was too low. "I dug the canal deeper," said he.'

Boswell records no comment by Johnson on Bath or his accommodation, but it presumably contrasted well with their inn when they made an excursion to Bristol, which did not please them. '"Let us see now," said I, "how we should describe it." Johnson was ready with his railery. "Describe it, Sir? – why it was so bad that Boswell wished to be in Scotland".'

Fanny Burney, the young celebrity

When Fanny Burney visited Bath in 1780, at the age of twenty-seven, she was already a widely admired novelist. Her first novel, *Evelina* or *A Young Lady's Entrance into the World*, had been published two years earlier. Various celebrities of the day told stories of its effect on them. Sir Joshua Reynolds had sat up all night reading it, then brought it to table where it so absorbed him that he had to be fed. Dr Johnson had learned much of it by heart and would imitate its characters with roars of laughter. It was in part her connection with Johnson that had made her famous, and this she owed to her father, Dr Charles Burney, a music teacher and writer on the history of music, who had been giving Mrs Thrale's daughter piano lessons. He had told Mrs Thrale about his daughter's book and she had told Johnson. Fanny became something of an adopted daughter of the Thrales, and stayed with them at Streatham for months at a time.

Today her novels are forgotten, but her diary and letters are read for the vivid account they give of eighteenth-century life, not least of society at Bath. It was with the Thrales that she planned to travel there. Johnson came to see them off.

The next morning we rose at four o'clock, and when we came downstairs, to our great surprise, found Dr Johnson waiting to receive and breakfast with us; though the night before he had taken leave of us, and given me, the most cordial and warm assurances of the love he has for me . . . and I failed not to tell him the affectionate respect with which I return it; though, as well as I remember, we never came to this open declaration before.

On their way Mrs Thrale was in very good spirits, Fanny reported, and Mr Thrale could not help being charming, whether he was ill or well. They made stops at Maidenhead, Speen Hill and Devizes. It was here, at the Bear Inn, that they met the innkeeper, Mr Lawrence, his charming daughters, and 'the wonder of the family', his son Thomas, who was already showing precocious skill at drawing (see page 59).

At Bath the Thrales hired a house in the South Parade, where Fanny's room had a view of 'meadows, hills, Prior Park [and] "the soft flowing Avon"'. They were soon involved in Bath's busy social round of calls and counter-calls, early visits to the Pump Room, public breakfasts, afternoon card-playing and evening balls. Fanny reported sharply on many of her new acquaintances. A certain Mr L—— was 'a sensible man of eighty-two, strong, healthy and conversable as he could have been at thirty-two', but had a wife who was 'a dull, muzzy old creature; his sister ditto'. A second Mrs L—— was 'a fat, round, panting, short-breathed old widow, and her daughter a fubsy, good-humoured, laughing, silly, merry old maid'.

Some occasions were dull. About an evening party at Dean Ossory's she wrote, 'our party tonight . . . by no means proved entertaining'. Others were amusing, as when 'Mrs Montagu and Mrs Thrale both flashed away admirably'. Mrs Montagu, whose house, Sandleford Priory, lay close to the Bath Road at Newbury, became one of Fanny's particular friends, and inevitably Fanny compared her to Mrs Thrale: 'allowing a little for parade and ostentation, which her power in wealth, and rank in literature, offer some excuse for, her conversation is very agreeable; she is always reasonable and sensible, and sometimes instructive and entertaining; and I think of our Mrs Thrale, we may say the very reverse, for she is always entertaining and instructive, and sometimes reasonable and sensible'.

'Us Bluestockings,' Fanny wrote at one point, about herself and Mrs Montagu; and she clearly enjoyed her reputation at Bath as a successful young writer, regularly reporting the flattering comments of admirers of *Evelina*. 'So my fame is now made,' she wrote when, during a visit to the Millers at their Batheaston villa with its celebrated vase, a certain Mrs G—— at first 'cut' her, then 'suddenly came up, and with a look of equal surprise and pleasure at sight of me, most graciously and smilingly addressed me. My coldness in return to all these sickening, heartless, *ton*-led people, I try not to repress . . .'

Her visit ended in panic, when the Bath newspapers reported the Lord George Gordon anti-popery riots in London. Soon Bath had a riot of its own and the mob surrounded 'a new Roman Catholic chapel. At first we disbelieved it, but presently one of the servants came and told us they were knocking it to pieces; and in half an hour, looking out of our windows, we saw it in flames! and listening, we heard loud and violent shouting.'

Fanny's account of the riot was an abbreviated one and what she probably saw burning was not the chapel itself but either its contents which the mob was burning in St James's Parade, or the next-door house rented by the priest, Father Brewer. Brewer tried to take refuge at two inns which both turned him away, then at the Guildhall where he was driven off by the beadle. Finally he slipped unnoticed into the White Lion and from there escaped by a back door and across the river.

Meawhile the riot continued, the mob 'only pausing to consume all the wines and other liquors' in the burning house's cellar. Soon the magistrates of the city 'bestirred themselves'[89] to read the Riot Act, and when this had no effect, one Captain Molesworth and some volunteers forced their way into the chapel, but could do no more than prevent it being set alight.

Around midnight a new body of twenty volunteers arrived with fixed bayonets but were met by 'a shower of brickbats, logs of wood and fire-brands'.[90] In the confusion a shot was fired, probably by a rioter, and one of them was killed. Infuriated, they drove the volunteers from the chapel.

The magistrates now sent for reinforcements which arrived in the early hours of the morning: forty dragoons from Devizes at 5am, then sixty more at 7am. By this time, besides the priest's house, the chapel and four neighbouring tenements were alight, casting 'a lurid light over the whole city'[91]. By 9am, however, when 240 men of the Hereford Militia arrived from Wells, the mob had dispersed, so the corporation entertained the officers to an elegant breakfast.

It is not surprising that Fanny Burney and the Thrales, when they read in a Bristol newspaper the same morning that Mr Thrale was a Papist, were alarmed. 'This villainous falsehood terrified us even for his personal safety, and Mrs Thrale and I agreed it was best to leave Bath directly.' Subsequently the supposed leader of the riot, John Butler, footman to the architect, Thomas Baldwin, was hanged in St James's Place in front of a large crowd, and in due course Father Brewer was awarded damages against the Hundred of Bath of some £3,750.

Fanny did not return to Bath for eleven years. Five of these (1786–91) she spent as Second Keeper of the Robes to George III's queen, Charlotte, a position for which she was quite unsuited since it reduced her to no more than a lady's-maid and put her at the mercy of her superior, the gross, frog-keeping, bullying Mrs Schwellenberg. It was only when she grew ill that her family and friends at last with difficulty persuaded Queen Charlotte to release her. At once she celebrated with a tour of the West Country, which brought her, after a month, to Bath. She found many of her earlier friends gone or dead and the city dramatically changed:

> Bath is extremely altered since I last visited it. Its circumference is perhaps trebled; but its buildings are so unfinished, so spread, so everywhere beginning and nowhere ending, that it looks rather like a space of ground lately fixed upon for erecting a town, than a town itself, of so many years' duration.
>
> It is beautiful and wonderful throughout. The hills are built up and down, and the vales so stocked with streets and houses, that, in some places, from the ground-floor on one side of a street, you cross over to the attic of your opposite neighbour. The white stone, where clean, has a beautiful effect, and, even where worn, a grand one.

Fanny soon settled again into the old routine of card-leaving and calling. It was less her career as a writer that now made her interesting (this had anyway been in abeyance during her time at court) than the inside information she might have about the great story of the time: George III's first madness. One political party wished to minimise this, the other to exaggerate it so that the Prince of Wales could become Regent, and Fanny was quizzed by a leading member of the latter, the Duchess of Devonshire. This 'was a tender subject,' Fanny wrote, 'considering her heading the Regency squadron; however, I have only one line to pursue, and from this I can never vary. I spoke of my own deep distress from his sufferings without reserve, and of the distress of the Queen with the most avowed compassion and respect . . . I fancy no one has just in the same way treated it with Her Grace before; however, she took all in good part, though to have found me retired in discontent had perhaps been more congenial to her.'

By the time Fanny came to Bath again, twenty-five years later in 1816, there had been even greater changes in her life. She was now Madame d'Arblay, wife of a French general, whom she had married when he was in England as a refugee. After he had made his peace with the French revolutionary government, they had gone to live in France for ten years, before escaping back to England so that their only son, Alexander, would not be conscripted into the French army. During the Waterloo campaign she had been in Brussels, where she wrote vivid descriptions of the city as it waited for news of the battle. The general, meanwhile, was kicked by a horse, and as a result he had to retire. After spending the summer visiting Bath, Fanny decided that this would make a better home for them than either London or the country. It was 'the only place for us, since here, all the year round, there is always town at command, and always the country for prospect, exercise, and delight'. But they were forced to live with 'the greatest economy' in order to pay for their son to be educated at Cambridge. And a friend who visited them reported that the general was 'now a miserable object with the jaundice'.[92]

His jaundice did not improve, though he went to France and tried various cures. He returned to Bath in 1817, at about the time of a royal visit by Fanny's old employer, Queen Charlotte. Almost as soon as the Queen arrived she received the appalling news that her granddaughter, Princess Charlotte, had died in childbirth.

But the queen's own health was so bad that, after the funeral, she returned to Bath, and here 'deigned to say "she should be very glad to see the General." Ill he was!' Fanny continued, 'suffering, emaciated, enfeebled! But he had always spirit awake to every call; and just before Christmas 1817, we went together between seven and eight in the morning, in chairs to the pump-room.

'I thought I had never seen him look to such advantage. His fine brow so open, his noble countenance so expressive, his features so formed for a painter's pencil. This, too, was the last time he ever wore his military honours . . . decorations which singularly became him, from his striking martial port and character.'

When the queen eventually turned to the general, 'highly sensible to the honour of her distinction, he forgot his pains in his desire to manifest his gratitude; – and his own smiles – how winning they became . . . Alas! the Queen no sooner ceased to address him than the pains he had suppressed became intoler-able, and he retreated from the circle and sunk upon a bench near the wall; he could stand no longer, and we returned home to spend the rest of the day in bodily misery.'

The general died the following May. Though Fanny was deeply affected, and four months later had left Bath for ever, she presently transferred her father worship back to her genuine father, Dr Burney, and spent many years writing his memoirs, a book 'disfigured by an elaborate affectation of style', and 'singularly vague in dates'.[93] She died at the age of eighty-seven and was buried with her husband at Walcot, near Bath, where there is a tablet in the church to their memory.

Mrs Thrale – Mrs Piozzi

Hester Lynch Piozzi, the lively and intelligent Welsh-born lady who was Dr Johnson's close friend, paid an increasing number of visits to Bath during her long life (1741–1821), and eventually when both her husbands had died she came to live there.

She was at Bath in 1775 soon after her only son by her first husband, the brewer, Henry Thrale, had died, for the health of her eldest daughter, Queenie. During her visit she had a violent quarrel with Queenie's tutor, Joseph Baretti, about the treatment she was giving Queenie for worms. In 1776 she and Thrale came with Dr Johnson and in 1780 they came again, with Fanny Burney.

By the time Mrs Thrale came once more, in 1783, Thrale had died and she was trying to escape from London where her intimacy with the Italian singer, Gabriel Piozzi, had become a scandal, and where her children were ill with whooping cough (a disease which frightened her). She had been at Bath only a few days when she received news that her daughter, Hester, had died. 'I have taken a vomit, and just received your letter,' she wrote to Dr Johnson; 'I will set out the first moment I am able.' But after burying her child she came back to Bath and awaited Piozzi with an impatience which was considered highly improper. Eventually he came, and in July they went to London for a Catholic marriage, then two days later back to Bath for an Anglican one. On 10 August 1783 the *Morning Herald* published these lines:

> Most writers agree, and I know it a truth,
> We all love a frolic in the days of our youth,
> But what shall one say, when such grave ones engage
> And frolic in love, in the days of old age.

The new Mrs Piozzi was forty-three. She and Piozzi now travelled abroad for the best part of three years. Back in England they began to remake lost friends and to visit Bath again. Their homes were at Streatham and in Wales, where she built a villa known as Brynbella on her family estate. Here she was described by a neighbour as 'skipping about like a kid, quite a figure of fun, in a tiger skin shawl, lined with scarlet, and . . . a white beaver hat and plume of black feathers – as gay as a lark'.

Piozzi, on the other hand, began to suffer increasingly from gout. When he and she arrived to winter in Bath in 1805 she wrote to Queenie, 'Mr Piozzi has *walked upstairs* today – *with help*, but in short not carried in arms. . .' When a girl of five asked Piozzi why his distorted fingers were bandaged in black silk he told her, 'They are mourning for my voice.' At Bath Fanny's father, Dr Burney, who was also there for his health, reported that Mrs Piozzi nursed Piozzi 'with great affection and tenderness'. But he was so ill there in 1807 that he was given the last sacraments (by an Anglican). In March 1809 he died in Wales.

For a time Mrs Piozzi returned to Streatham but when, in 1814, she gave her Welsh properties to Piozzi's nephew and her adopted son, John Salusbury, her income was so reduced that she was forced to move to Bath. Though now seventy-four, she had not lost her ability to fall in love. In succession she became obsessed by a retired naval surgeon, Sir James Fellowes, and an indifferent actor, William Augustus Conway. For both she wrote accounts of her life on which much of what is known about her early years has since been based. For Conway she involved herself in a gossipy intrigue to further his own love affair with a young Bath girl who did not fancy him. John Salusbury, afraid that she would give Conway the £6000 capital which Piozzi had left her and on which she lived, persuaded her to give this to him so that he could buy a baronetcy. 'My poor 6000 £. gone – Addio! I trust they will leave me the dividend', she wrote, after she had had 'a long business talk – unpleasant of course' with Salusbury. Salusbury did not get the baronetcy but kept the £6000.

Earlier that year she had staged the most spectacular event of her final period at Bath: the great party to celebrate her seventy-ninth birthday. This was held at the Assembly Rooms on 27 January 1820, and consisted of a concert, ball and supper. Between six and seven hundred guests attended, and she took the floor first, to dance with Salusbury 'with astonishing elasticity'.[94] She stayed late at the ball, but was eating breakfast by ten the next morning, when she reported that a caller had been surprised to see her up.

The birthday party reduced her to poverty, and although Salusbury did presumably allow her the dividends on her lost £6000 – since she was never destitute – she was forced to let her Bath home; but she visited the city once more a year later – in March 1821 – to dine with Fellowes and to see Conway act. Five weeks after this she died at Clifton.

Rowlandson's 'Comforts of Bath'

The twelve caricatures of Bath life drawn by Thomas Rowland-son (1756–1827), and entitled *Comforts of Bath*, give a vivid picture of Bath towards the end of its great period. They were not published as a series till 1798, but some if not all were clearly drawn well before then. Rowlandson's Pump Room, for example, is the old one, opened in 1706 and enlarged in 1751, not the one which replaced it in the early 1790s. And an earlier caricature, *Comfort in the Gout*, was dated 1785. There is no evidence, however, that he drew them as illustrations either for Anstey's *The New Bath Guide* (1766) or for Smollett's *Humphrey Clinker* (1771).

The twelve *Comforts of Bath* illustrate in grotesque detail all the well-known events of a Bath day: water-drinking at the Pump Room, bathing in the King's Bath, dancing at an Assembly Rooms ball, breakfasting in public; as well as less well-known scenes and events: the fish market, a doctor's surgery, the Bath races, a portrait artist at work in his studio.

Rowlandson had shown his drawing skill from childhood (when he could draw before he could write), and revealed his special talent at his school in Soho Square where he filled his exercise books with mischievous sketches of his teachers and fellow pupils. At the Royal Academy School, according to the Librarian, Richard Wilson, he 'once gave great offence by carrying a pea-shooter into life-class, and, whilst old Moser [the Academy's Keeper] was adjusting the female model, and had just directed her contour, Rowlandson let fly a pea, which making her start, she threw herself entirely out of position and interrupted the gravity of the study for the whole evening. For this offence Master Rowlandson went near to getting himself expelled.'

By the age of twenty-one Rowlandson had set up in London as a portrait painter and between 1777 and 1781 he regularly sent portraits and landscapes to the Royal Academy. But he had already studied in Paris where he had an aunt, and now the sketches he made on a continental tour of Flanders, Holland and Germany persuaded him that his real talent was for humorous drawings. From then onwards he made huge num-bers of these. Many, during the years of the Napoleonic wars, ridiculed Bonaparte. Among the rest, some of the best known illustrated the tour of a schoolmaster and were published as *The Tour of Dr Syntax in Search of the Picturesque* (1812), with verses by the poet, William Combe.

Rowlandson probably came to Bath less in search of humorous subjects to draw – he was able to find these wherever he went – than for the gambling, to which he was addicted. Oddly, No. 8 of *Comforts of Bath*, entitled 'Company at Play', which shows tables of card players, including two white-gowned ladies so alike they could be twins, is the least grotesque of the series.

Gambling had another effect on Rowlandson's work, compelling him to produce more to pay for his losses. His father, a tradesman living in Old Jewry, had gone bankrupt and Rowlandson was determined that this should not happen to him.

Comforts of Bath was a success in its time, several editions selling out, and shows that even if late-eighteenth-century Bath still took itself seriously, the country as a whole could and did laugh at it.

PART THREE

Tales of Later Times

BATH WATERS YESTERDAY AND TODAY

Though Bath gradually became less fashionable as a resort after about 1790, its baths continued to attract the sick. By the middle of the nineteenth century they had an enema or lavement apparatus, which Dr Randle Falconer described in his brief guide *The Baths and Mineral Waters of Bath* (1860).

> This apparatus is supplied from a cistern, at some height from the floor, which will hold fourteen gallons of water, exerting a pressure of two pounds three quarters to three pounds on the square inch, and discharges two quarts of water a minute. The temperature of the water may be estimated at 110°F.

Falconer listed lavement and douching as the third way in which the waters could be used, but concentrated on the traditional ways: drinking them and bathing in them. Drinking produced 'a glow of warmth in the stomach, an increased appetite, an improvement of the spirits, an augmented secretion of saliva and an excitement of the urinary discharge.' If it produced the opposite effects, including nausea and sickness, he recommended drinking less, at different times of the day. Bathing produced a higher pulse-rate and body temperature, a better appetite and a 'consciousness of elasticity and vigor of the frame'.

He divided patients discharged from the Bath General Hospital during the previous year by their complaints; while 345 out of 583 were rheumatic, others had had leprosy, palsy from lead, visceral obstruction and paralysis. And though his full list of complaints which the waters could cure or modify was not so all-embracing as the lists of seventeenth- and eighteenth-century doctors, it included gout, anaemia, and syphilis and gonorrhoea, particularly if previously treated with mercury. Twenty-eight years later Dr Freeman still listed syphilis and gonorrhoea, together with rheumatics, gout, Henerdens nodes, sciatica, digestive disorders, anaemia and chlorosis, diseases of women, palsy, and respiratory complaints.

Bath's twentieth-century doctors make more modest claims. Drinking mineral waters, they say, may help to prevent the formation of kidney and bladder stones, can help prevent certain sorts of dyspepsia, liver or gall bladder diseases and, if they contain magnesium sulphate (Epsom salts), can act as a laxative. Bath waters do not contain magnesium sulphate, but they do contain other magnesium compounds, and an adequate intake of magnesium may help to prevent heart attack.

About bathing, modern-day doctors are more positive, saying, with additional scientific explanation, much what doctors were saying a hundred years ago. 'The pool of warm water causes relaxation, pain relief, enhancement of circulation and is the ideal medium for exercise and rehabilitation as the water reduces the force of gravity, so that a twelve-stone man bears the weight of only twelve pounds when he moves. Recent research has also shown a long-lasting diuretic effect, reducing oedema and swelling of the rheumatoid joints.'[1]

Sceptics may wonder whether warm water of any sort would not be as effective, and suspect that faith, together with Bath's relaxing charm, may be the real explanation for its healing reputation.

2

NEW DISCOVERIES

Thomas Baldwin – Guildhall to bankruptcy

The architect Thomas Baldwin (1750–1820) made his contribution to Bath in the later years of its great period between 1776, when his design for the new Guildhall was accepted, and 1793 when he went bankrupt. But because his work formed the architectural background which residents and visitors of the following two centuries knew, he belongs in a sense to this later period. Apart from the two John Woods, father and son, he had more influence on Bath than any other architect.

As a young man he worked for Bath's city surveyor, Thomas Atwood, a councillor and member of the building committee who used his positions to such effect that, after over thirteen years of discussion, he managed to have his own design for a new Guildhall accepted. Work had started on Atwood's plan but it was still being challenged by supporters of another plan when Atwood was killed by falling through the floor of an old house in Market Street, which collapsed on top of him.

This allowed the corporation to commission Baldwin to produce yet another plan (the sixth), which it accepted. By general agreement its banqueting hall was its most impressive feature, described as 'beyond any question the finest interior in Bath, and a masterpiece of late eighteenth-century decoration'.[2]

To the casual visitor Baldwin's work across the river is more obviously impressive. Here, as a continuation of Pulteney Bridge, he built Great Pulteney Street, Bath's finest, 1000 feet long and 100 feet wide.

Meanwhile in 1785 Baldwin had produced plans for redeveloping the whole area around the baths, including the making of a proper connection (which would not pass through an inn yard) between the new upper town and the old lower town, and the complete rebuilding of the Pump Room. Though he had been dismissed by the corporation (because he would not show his accounts) before this was finished, his design was followed by his successor, John Palmer, and the Duchess of York opened the new Pump Room three days after Christmas 1795.

During his work on the Pump Room Baldwin had made his own contribution to the discovery of the Roman Temple of Minerva, which lay north and north-west of the Roman bathing complex, in an area below the Pump Room and Stall Street. At twelve feet below ground level, when digging foundations, his men had found a solid Roman pavement, which they used as a basis for their own new building. In the process they removed some seventy blocks of Roman sculptured stone. A study of these enabled the antiquarian, Samuel Lysons, to produce, twenty years later, his classic work, *Reliquiae Romano Britannicae* (1813) which so closely forecast what we know today about the shape and site of the temple.

Baldwin's discoveries and Lysons's descriptions of them confirmed what the Roman name for Bath – Aquae Sulis – had always suggested: that the Celtic god Sulis was as important at Bath as the Roman goddess Minerva. Though the temple, as Lysons drew it, was of classical design and would not have been out of place in Rome itself, it had features which were Celtic, in particular the magnificent male gorgon's head which formed the centrepiece of its pediment. Below and to the left of the shield on which the head was carved was a plumed Corinthian helmet, below and to the right was an owl perched on a helmet, typical symbols of Minerva. But the head itself is Celtic in style – Roman gorgons are always female – with wild hair, heavy brows and big moustaches. Furthermore, tombs and altars throughout Bath, some discovered by Baldwin, some later, are as often dedicated to Sul as to Minerva. Archaeologists have concluded that the god of Bath's Roman temple was half Roman, half Celtic, and generally name him/her Sulis Minerva.

James Thomas Irving's scrapbooks

James Thomas Irving came to Bath in 1864 as Clerk of Works to the architect, Sir Gilbert Scott, who had been commissioned to 'restore' Bath Abbey. Irving's private interest was Roman archaeology, and his job at Bath gave him a perfect opportunity to indulge it. He was the first person to record Bath's Roman remains, as they were discovered, with a modern archaeologist's precision. Every note he made he preserved and today, at Bath's Reference Library, his papers fill many boxes, and consist of everything from huge plans measuring some 7 feet by 5 feet, to newspaper cuttings and scraps of old envelopes covered with barely decipherable sketches and measurements.

By the time he arrived at Bath the White Hart Inn, which stood across Stall Street from the Pump Room and had in its time accommodated so many of Bath's distinguished visitors, had gone out of business. Irving's first move was to obtain permission from the city architect, Major Davis, to excavate in the derelict inn's cellars. Three years later, when the inn was pulled down so that the Grand Pump Room Hotel could be built, he made some more extensive excavations.

He discovered – as he had guessed he would by studying the descriptions of Baldwin's 1790 work on the new Pump Room's foundations – the base or podium on which the Roman temple itself had stood. In 1870 he was able to give a full description of his results in a lecture to Bath's Literary and Philosophical Association.

By this time he had also worked on the east and west ends of the Roman bathing complex, as well as on an entirely separate set of Roman baths around the old Hot Bath. When Francis Haverfield wrote his article for the *Victoria County History* on Bath's Roman remains he largely ignored Irving, but today Irving is considered the most important nineteenth-century archaeologist to have worked at Bath.

Major Davis and the Roman lead

It was Major Charles Edward Davis (1827–1902), Bath's city architect and surveyor for forty years at the end of the nine-teenth century, who made the most exciting of all the discov-eries of Roman remains at Bath, and who did most damage to them. Even at the time, when archaeology was still a treasure hunt as much as a science, antiquarians protested. Davis was short of money, and this partly explains what he did, but he also resented interference, and was often on bad terms with his builder, Richard Mann, who carried out the excavations for him. About one of Davis's rare visits to the site Mann wrote,

'This is the first time he [Davis] has been below since a cursory visit with his clerk just before we broke through the 3ft Roman wall . . . he caught cold then, he says, and has not been able to get rid of it since.'

Davis made the first of his major discoveries in 1871, when investigating a leak from the King's Bath. To cure this he excavated at a point between the King's Bath and the abbey. When he reached a depth of twenty feet he came to the north-west corner of the Great Roman Bath, and presently to the bath's large flight of steps. At its bottom he cut a foot-square hole in its lead lining to discover what lay below – the place can still be seen. But the powerful pumps he used to keep his excavation dry so depleted the water in the nearby Kingston Baths that he had to desist.

Some seven years later, again investigating a leak from the King's Bath, he undertook his most dramatic excavation. To understand this, it is best to know what Davis did not know, that today's King's Bath had been built in mediaeval times on top of, and thus entirely hiding, a Roman octagonal stone-walled reservoir, which itself stood directly above the spring. The Romans had led the water from here to the south and east, to the Great Bath, the Large Bath, and various subsidiary baths. Surplus water they had fed into a long drain which led away towards the abbey.

It was up this partly blocked drain that Davis now began to tunnel, from the abbey towards the King's Bath. Not only were his workmen working twenty feet below ground in a tunnel three feet wide, but they were constantly facing a flow of water coming in the other direction which became hotter as they advanced.

Davis was forced to raise his tunnel and turn north, but he eventually found the Roman reservoir, full of a mixture of rubbish and Roman votive offerings. These included curses scratched on pieces of lead, one of which (written backwards for the benefit of the gods) asked for punishment for the person, male or female, who had absconded with a lady by the name of Vilbia. 'May he who carried off Vilbia from me become as liquid as the water, may she who so obscenely devoured her become dumb, whether it be Velvinna, Exsupereus, Severinus, Augustalia, Comitianus, Catusminianus, Germanilla or Jovina.' As soon as he had cleared the reservoir Davis sold its lead lining to finance further excavation, then laid over it a concrete raft which hid it for a hundred years.

The money he raised, and the general excitement about his discoveries which brought new support from the city corporation, enabled Davis to continue his excavations for about twenty years. In the process he removed the mediaeval Queen's Bath, finding below it the Roman circular bath. And above the Roman Great Bath he bought and demolished properties till it was totally exposed. But he cleared it as carelessly as he had cleared the reservoir, carting off haphazardly the refuse which filled the bath without keeping a record of what had been found where. He thus destroyed all but the larger fragments of the roof which had once enclosed the Great Bath, and which made it a vastly more civilised bathing place than the city's mediaeval baths.

The most important discoveries of the present century were made between the wars, in 1923, and more recently in the twenty years between 1963 and 1983. After the Large Bath had been discovered in 1755 and described by Dr Lucas (it is sometimes called the Lucas Bath) it was covered by the private Kingston Baths. In 1923 the Kingston Baths were demolished and W. H. Knowles was able to re-expose the Large Bath and its surrounding rooms. Knowles's excavations were particularly interesting because they revealed that the destruction done to the Roman floors when the Kingston Baths were built had exposed earlier Roman levels of building. These demonstrated that the Romans had made major alterations to their baths during the three centuries in which they used them.

The 1963–83 excavations were more extensive and have made it possible to map in detail the Roman temple area as well as the bathing complex. In the process, the concrete raft which Major Davis had built above the reservoir to form a new floor for the King's Bath was removed and the reservoir re-excavated. More Roman offerings were found, including a total of 12,000 coins. In Roman times the reservoir, within its chamber, had been an open pool, and the people of Bath no doubt had wished or prayed as they threw in coins, just as tourists do today although, because this was a sacred pool, more hopefully.

3

VISITORS AND RESIDENTS

Strata Smith

> In this house
> William Smith
> The Father of English Geology
> dictated
> 'The Order of the Strata'
> December 11th 1799

reads a plaque on the elegant front of 29 Great Pulteney Street. These words, with their flavour of the first chapter of Genesis, or suggesting at least that Smith wrote a whole book in one day, record in fact the literal if more modest truth. Here William Smith (1769–1839), a man reluctant ever to put his original geological theories into print, dictated to his friend, the Rev. Benjamin Richardson, in the house of another friend, the Rev. Joseph Townsend, a list of the geological strata which lay below the English countryside, from chalk downland to coal measures. Richardson made a copy for each of them and, thirty-two years later, Smith presented his copy to the Royal Geological Society.

Smith had been born a poor boy, in the village of Churchill near the forest of Wychwood in Oxfordshire, and gone to the village school there. Afterwards he taught himself surveying, then spent much of his early life as a civil engineer, working on the building of canals. In 1794 he had so impressed his employers that they sent him on a journey to Newcastle and back by different routes, to make a general survey of canal construction. This journey helped to confirm his idea that geological strata occurred in the same order throughout the country.

By 1795, the year in which he moved to Bath, he was working on the Somerset Coal Canal. At Bath he first lived in the central house of Cottage Crescent, high up to the south of the city. Its position also helped to form his ideas. 'From this point', he later wrote, 'the eye roved anxiously over the interesting expanse which extended before me to the Sugar-Loaf mountain in Monmouthshire, and embraced all in the vicinities of Bath and Bristol; then did a thousand thoughts occur to me respecting the geology of that and adjacent districts continually under my eye . . .'

At Bath he met Benjamin Richardson, rector of the nearby parish of Farleigh, an amateur naturalist and collector of fossils. When Smith arranged Richardson's fossils in order, and told him that the same fossils were always found in the same geological stratum, and these occurred always in the same order, Richardson was 'both astonished and incredulous'.[3]

That year, 1799, the West Country weather gave Smith another useful experience. 'An exceptional degree of wetness in the year 1799 had produced, in the vicinity of Bath at Combegrove an extraordinary phenomenon. Vast mounds of earth displaced by the augmented force of the springs and the direction of water into new channels below the surface, were sliding down the sides of the hills, and bearing to new situations houses, trees, lawns and fields.'

After his second visit Smith reported that he was sorry to find the slip 'of much greater extent than upon my first survey I had reason to expect, for there is not a building of any sort that has not more or less felt the effect of its fatal consequences. Therefore I am of the opinion, that the whole of this beautiful place, in a few years, must inevitably fall a sacrifice to the irresistible pressure of the rocks moving down upon it, if some effectual means are not speedily taken to prevent their further progress.' Smith prevented further damage by tunnelling into the hills and draining the springs.

Up to this time he had been in regular employment, and he had bought himself a property near Bath which his nephew and biographer, John Phillips, describes but does not identify. It lay in a deep valley 'almost overgrown with wild wood, hiding in its bosom a sheet of water and a mill'. It was also in 1799, however, that his work on the Somerset Coal Canal ended, and in December that Richardson, together with Joseph Townsend, a traveller who had written *Travels in Spain*, persuaded Smith to dictate his list of twenty-two strata. From then onwards Richardson always referred to him as 'Strata Smith'.

Earlier that year the two clergymen had been trying to

persuade Smith to put his accumulated knowledge into a book, and they continued to do so, but Smith preferred to continue travelling the country in pursuit of his great aim: the drawing and printing of a complete geological map of England. To finance this he took casual work, first at a guinea a day, eventually at three guineas per day.

In 1810 another and potentially greater disaster struck Bath: the springs of the King's Bath began to fail. About this time a mining shaft was being sunk in the nearby village of Batheaston, and since warm water was flowing into this shaft, it was blamed. Smith was consulted and, against much opposition, 'was allowed to open the hot-bath spring to its bottom, and thus to detect the lateral escape for the water. The spring had in no sense failed, but its waters were flowing away in new channels. The men in the excavation thus opened, found the heat oppressive; wax candles were employed for illumination, and the gushing water raised the thermometer of Fahrenheit to 119° . . . The operation was perfectly successful, and the cure complete, the baths filling in less time than formerly.'[4]

Some five years later Smith at last published his geological map of England. Unfortunately it was in this year that he also tried to make his fortune from Bath stone. The result was disastrous. At his property near the city he opened new quarries, and built a railway to take the stone down to barges on the Avon, just as Ralph Allen had done successfully eighty years before. But the project 'failed utterly by the unexpected deficiency of the stone'.[5] After some four years Smith was forced to sell his Bath property as well as a house he had bought in London.

He was in the north of England when this happened, and he continued to live, homeless, in that part of the country for some seven years, taking work as it was offered and continually travelling in order to extend his geological knowledge. He would cover as much as 10,000 miles a year, often walking, but hurrying over uninteresting stretches by post-chaise.

Eventually he was given a position by Sir John Johnson, a north country baronet, as his land steward. Johnson encouraged Smith to 'publish more of his vast stores of geological information',[6] but Smith continued to fail to do so. One of his last commissions was to help select the stone to be used for Sir Charles Barry's new Houses of Parliament.

Jane Austen's Bath

'The sun was got behind everything and the appearance of the place from the top of Kingsdown hill was all vapour, smoke and confusion,' Jane Austen (1775–1817) wrote to her sister, Cassandra, immediately after arriving at Bath in May 1801. By this time she had often visited Bath and had written – though not published and perhaps not revised – her first novel, *Northanger Abbey*, which was largely set at Bath.

Her family had many connections with the city. Her grandmother, her mother's mother, had lived there as a widow. Her aunt, Mrs (Jane) Cooper, and her uncle, James Leigh Perrot, both had houses there. It was with the Leigh Perrots at No. 1, Paragon that Jane had often stayed, though she liked neither that part of the town nor Mrs Leigh Perrot (another Jane). About a letter from Aunt Jane Leigh Perrot to her own mother, Jane once wrote, 'The discontentedness of it shocked and surprised her – but *I* see nothing out of nature – though a sad nature.'

Jane had probably stayed with the Leigh Perrots during her first visit to Bath of which there is any record (1797), but when she came with her brother, Edward, and his family in 1799 they rented No. 13, Queen's Square. Jane soon noted with satisfaction that the newspapers reported a long list of visitors, and she began to attend Bath's well-established social occasions. She went, for example, to a concert in Sydney Gardens, looking forward to it 'with pleasure as the gardens are large enough for me to get pretty well beyond the reach of its sound'. And she went to the theatre. Though she does not name the play, the *Bath Herald and Register* records that on this night it would have been 'The pleasing spectacle of Bluebeard', together with the curtain raiser, *The Birthday Day*, by the German dramatist Kotzebue. Kotzebue had a reputation for 'the immorality of his products for the stage', but this particular piece was 'calculated to promote the best interests of virtue, and the purest principles of benevolence'. About her brother's medical programme Jane wrote that 'he drinks at the Hetling Pump, is to bathe tomorrow and try electricity on Tuesday'.

Before Jane came to Bath again there was a family scandal: Aunt Jane Leigh Perrot was accused of shoplifting. She had bought and paid for some black lace at a shop at the corner of

Bath Street kept by a Miss Gregory. Later that morning when she and her husband were passing the shop again, Miss Gregory emerged and accused her of stealing some white lace. Her parcel was opened and the white lace discovered.

Aunt Jane returned it, explaining that it must have been accidentally included in the parcel with the black, but shortly afterwards a male assistant from the shop stopped her and demanded her name. This man and Miss Gregory then went to the Guildhall and charged her with attempted larceny.

Ten days later Aunt Jane was arrested and sent to Ilchester gaol, where she had to remain for seven months since she could not be released on bail and the Taunton assizes were not due to take place till the following March. The punishment for such an offence was fourteen years deportation, but Mr Leigh Perrot not only went to live at Ilchester to be with his wife during her detention, but said that if she was found guilty he would sell all his English property and go with her to Botany Bay.

Though she was in fact allowed to live in the house of the gaoler, these seven months were distressing for Aunt Jane. Her sister, Mrs Austen, suggested sending her daughters, Jane and Cassandra, to keep their aunt company, but Aunt Jane refused the offer because she would not allow 'these elegant young women [to] be inmates of a prison'.

On 29 March 1800 the six-hour trial took place. A quarter of an hour later the jury found Aunt Jane innocent. The affair was a national as well as a family scandal and, within a month, a bookseller in London and another in Bath were offering a printed account entitled, *The Trial of Mrs Leigh Perrot*, priced at eighteen pence, with marginal notes.

Jane Austen, now twenty-five years old, had lived her whole life at Steventon, Hampshire, where her father was the rector. But the year of her aunt's trial her father decided to retire to Bath. Jane was not consulted, and was shocked when told. By the following January, however, she was able to write, 'I get more and more reconciled to the idea of removal . . . We plan having a steady cook, a young giddy housemaid with a sedate, middle-aged man, who is to undertake the double office of husband to the former and sweetheart to the latter.'

In May 1801 Jane and her mother went ahead to Bath and began to search for a house which would match their social position but which they could afford. During the search Jane again attended Bath's social functions, including card parties and a ball at the new Assembly Rooms. Since the season was ending, this was 'shockingly and inhumanly thin' for Bath, but full enough 'to have made five or six very pretty Basingstoke assemblies'.

Eventually they rented No. 4, Sydney Place, a four-storey terrace house across the river from the old city at the far end of Pulteney Street. It looked east over Sydney Gardens, the gardens which had been big enough two years earlier to enable Jane to avoid hearing the concert. They were more peaceful in Jane's time than they became in 1840 when Isambard Kingdom Brunel made a cutting through them for his Great Western Railway line.

Within a year of settling at Bath Jane had two romantic encounters, neither of them at Bath, and neither of them happy. When on holiday at Sidmouth she met and fell in love with a young man who died soon afterwards. Next year, when visiting Manydown Park she was unexpectedly proposed to by a young man, Harrison Bigg-Wither, with whom she was *not* in love. She accepted him, then next day refused him and returned quickly to Bath. These two incidents probably explain why no letters survive for the period. They would have contained intimacies which would have made her sister Cassandra destroy them.

Both Jane's parents were ill during the years she lived at Bath, and this could explain why she did not write much fiction. After three years at Sydney Place the family moved to No. 27, Green Park Buildings, lying a little west of the old city, and it was there, in January 1805, that her father died. By April, Jane and her mother had moved to Gay Street, the street which runs north from Queen's Square to the Circus, and they finally lodged for a short time in Trim Street before, in the summer of 1806, leaving Bath for Clifton. They were now poorer than they had been, though not desperately so. Jane's brothers made allowances which brought Mrs Austen's income to £450 a year, as against £600 when her father was alive. Jane's dislike of Bath was probably a more important reason for their leaving it. In *Northanger Abbey*, Isabella Thorpe says, 'I get so immoderately sick of Bath; your brother and I were agreeing this morning that though it is vastly well to be here for a few weeks, we could not *live* here for millions' – perhaps also Jane's feelings.

This novel was originally called 'Susan' but had been given its final title by the time it was published, the year after Jane's death. It describes the amorous adventures of Catherine Morland when she comes with the Allen family on a visit to Bath and how she eventually captures her young man, Henry Tilney. Here she first meets him:

> Every morning now brought its regular duties; – shops were to be visited; some new part of the town to be looked at; and the Pump-room to be attended, where they paraded up and down for an hour, looking at every body and speaking to no one. The wish of a numerous acquaintance in Bath was still uppermost with Mrs Allen, and she repeated it after every fresh proof, which every morning brought, of her knowing nobody at all.
>
> They made their appearance in the Lower Rooms; and here fortune was more favourable to our heroine. The master of the ceremonies introduced to her a very gentlemanlike young man as a partner; – his name was Tilney. He seemed to be about four or five and twenty, was rather tall, had a pleasing countenance, a very intelligent and lively eye, and, if not quite handsome, was very near it. His address was good, and Catherine felt herself in high luck. There was little leisure for speaking while they danced; but when they were seated for tea, she found him as agreeable as she had already given him credit for being . . . After chatting some time on such matters as naturally arose from the objects around them, he suddenly addressed her with . . . 'Have you been long in Bath, madam?'
>
> 'About a week, sir,' replied Catherine, trying not to laugh.
>
> 'Really!' with affected astonishment.
>
> 'Why should you be surprized, sir?'
>
> 'Why, indeed!' said he, in his natural tone – 'but some emotion must appear to be raised by your reply, and surprize is more easily assumed, and not less reasonable than any other . . .'

Persuasion, Jane's last completed novel, was the other which she set partly at Bath. To Bath Sir Walter Elliott, father of Anne, the heroine, moves when he has to retrench, because here 'He might be important at comparatively little expense'. He takes a house in Camden Place (now Crescent), a 'lofty and dignified situation such as becomes a man of consequence'. In the shops of Bath Sir Walter counts 'eighty-seven women go by, one after another, without there being a tolerable face among them'.

Anne is equally unenthusiastic, though for different reasons. 'She persisted in a very determined, though very silent, disinclination for Bath; caught the first dim view of the extensive buildings, smoking in rain, without any wish of seeing them better.' She by no means shared the enthusiasm of her friend, Lady Russell, for 'the dash of other carriages, the heavy rumble of carts and drays, the bawling of newsmen, muffin-men and milk-men, and the ceaseless clink of pattens'.

But at Bath Anne meets once more the naval officer, Captain Wentworth, whom she originally rejected seven years before, first in Molland's, the pastry cook's in Milsom Street, later and more encouragingly at the Octagon Room where his behaviour persuades Anne, as she sits to listen to the concert, that 'all, all declared that he had a heart returning to her at last'.

The affair reaches a happy climax when Captain Wentworth at last takes Anne's arm to escort her up Union Street to Camden Place, and 'as they slowly paced the gradual ascent, heedless of every group around them, seeing neither sauntering politicians, bustling housekeepers, flirting girls, nor nursery-maids and children, they could indulge in those retrospections and acknowledgements . . . which were so poignant and so ceaseless in interest'.

A Regency coach journey (1816)

I started at six on a winter's morning outside the Bath *Regulator*, which was due in London at eight o'clock at night. I was the only outside passenger. It came on to snow about an hour after we started – a snowstorm that never ceased for three days. The roads were a yard deep in snow before we reached Reading, which was exactly at the time we were due in London. Then with six horses we laboured on, and finally arrived at Fetter Lane at a quarter to three in the morning. Had it not been for the stiff doses of brandied coffee swallowed at every stage, this record would never have been written. As it was, I was so numbed, hands and feet, that I had to be lifted down, or rather, hauled out of an avalanche

or hummock of snow, like a bale of goods. The landlady of
the White Hart [demolished 1898] took me in hand, and I
was thawed gradually by the kitchen fire, placed between
warm pillows, and dosed with a posset of her own
compounding.

According to Charles Harper, who gives this account in *The
Bath Road* (1899) but does not name the traveller, such an
experience was not unique. On another occasion three outside
passengers were found at Chippenham to have frozen to death.
And after the great snowstorm of Boxing Day, 1836, when
there were fourteen- to sixteen-foot drifts on the Marlborough
Downs, the Duke of Wellington's carriage and four became
stuck in a wheatfield and had to be dug out by local labourers.

Queen Victoria fails to return

Queen Victoria made her only visit to Bath in 1830 when she
was a ten-year-old princess. She came accompanied by her
mother, the Duchess of Kent. It was already generally assumed
that she would one day be queen, and the corporation literally
laid down a crimson carpet for her visit to the Guildhall. She
was then taken by the mayor on a tour of the city – though this
was interrupted when it was her one o'clock lunch time and she
had to return to York House Hotel. Afterwards she saw Bath
Abbey, and next morning Beckford's tower, at Lansdown.
Before leaving she and her mother graciously agreed to the
park, which was being laid out south and west of the Royal
Crescent, being named Victoria Park.

Eight years later the city celebrated her coronation. 'Cannon
and fireworks awoke the citizens soon after dawn,' and the
church bells were rung at 6am. The day-long festivities included
a parade of 7,000 'clean, healthy and happy' children which
took forty minutes to pass the Guildhall. At night there were
elaborate illuminations and a party of gentlemen 'paraded the
streets singing the national anthem in parts, in very excellent
style'.

But when year after year passed and the queen failed to revisit
Bath, the people of the city began to wonder why, and to
remember (or invent) explanations. One was that the young

princess had overheard a comment on the fatness of her ankles when she appeared on the balcony of her hotel. Another was that the Prince Consort (who visited Bath in 1843 on his way to Bristol to launch the *Great Britain* and was given a reception at the railway station) had heard himself called a German and had told the queen. Neither story has been verified.

The only time the queen was ever again seen in the neighbourhood was in 1899 when she passed through the city by train, also on her way to Bristol. Her train slowed sufficiently as it approached the station for the crowds of watchers to see her stand up and look northwards over the city – but they were not able to see her expression.

Beckford and his tower

William Beckford (1760–1844) finally sold Fonthill Abbey, greatest of English follies with its 276-foot Gothic tower, and moved to Bath because there was no other way in which he could pay his debts. The following year he was already planning a new tower, this time a Saxon one on Lansdown Hill. From its 154-foot summit he would be able to see Fonthill's tower, twenty-six miles away to the south-east.

When Beckford was only ten he had inherited from his father, a City of London alderman and the owner of large Jamaican sugar plantations, a fortune which rumour said brought him an annual income of £100,000, as well as £1 million in cash. Though his true income only averaged between £27,000 and £29,000, this still made him comfortably rich. He also inherited Fonthill Splendens, the mansion which his father had built close to the River Nadder, considered the finest in the south-west of England.

But he took little interest in business or in politics, his two most obvious careers, and preferred to travel abroad, collect books and manuscripts and lead either in practice or imagination a life of oriental fantasy. Though he married and had children, he was undoubtedly homosexual, and his pursuit of a young man, William Courtenay, heir to Powderham Castle near Exeter, led to a great scandal which deprived him of a promised peerage and wrecked his life.

Beckford's most persistent enemy was the young man's uncle

by marriage, Lord Loughborough. Loughborough trapped Beckford into accepting an invitation to stay at Powderham Castle, then, when Beckford left, spread the rumour and promoted newspaper articles which claimed that Beckford and Courtenay had been discovered in a locked room making love. One version of the story was sent in a letter by Charles Greville to his uncle, Sir William Hamilton, at Naples. 'It seems,' Greville wrote, 'young C was put to a school with a clergyman near Fonthill; he [Beckford] went over very early one morning before they were up and into Courtenay's room. Mr Moore, the tutor's name, heard a creeking and bustle, which raised his curiosity, and through the key hole he saw the operation which it seems he did not interrupt, but informed Lord Courtenay [William Courtenay's father] and the whole was blown up.'

Though this was obviously inaccurate, since the supposed incident occurred at Powderham, not Fonthill, and the boy's tutor was not named Moore, similar stories, supported by indiscreet letters Beckford had written to Courtenay and a confession Loughborough had extracted from the boy, eventually forced Beckford to fly the country. He spent most of the next eleven years abroad and, even when he made brief visits to England, he found himself ostracised by respectable society.

Before he left the country he had completed (in French) his best-remembered book *Vathek*, an oriental fantasy, and left this with his old tutor, Samuel Henley, for translation into English. While he was abroad Henley published his translation, without Beckford's permission and anonymously. To establish his rights Beckford had it translated back into French (he had no copy and the translator had to work from Henley's English) and published it under his own name in Lausanne.

On his brief returns to Fonthill during these years Beckford commissioned one of his more remarkable (and symbolically significant) projects: a great wall, six miles long, twelve feet high, around his Fonthill estate. In theory it was meant to keep out the local fox hunt, but it was also a gesture of defiance. If polite society did not want him, he did not need it.

From his return in 1796 he began to build in earnest the hilltop tower and semi-ruined convent which were eventually combined to form the abbey. His architect was the dilatory and incompetent James Wyatt, who used wood and a material he had invented which he called compo-cement. Beckford had no objection to this since what he wanted was more in the nature of a stage set than a permanent building. But, as a result, in May 1800 a gale blew the tower down. To his friends Beckford said that his only regret was he had not been there to watch. Secretly he determined to build it again, in stone and taller.

The abbey was still unfinished that Christmas when it received its most celebrated visitors: Nelson, Emma Hamilton and her husband, Sir William Hamilton. The house party stayed at Fonthill Splendens, but were taken one evening at dusk, uphill through the torchlit woods, to a supper of monastic food in the abbey. Afterwards Emma Hamilton, dressed as Agrippina, entertained them with her well-known 'Attitudes'. All was magnificently staged, with scarlet, purple and crimson drapery, lit by candles in gold and silver sticks and wax torches held by hooded figures.

During the next few years the compo-cement of the rest of the abbey began to decay so that much of it needed rebuilding, and it was another six years before Beckford finally decided to move there. He then demolished Fonthill Splendens, using the stone for extensions to the abbey.

He lived there for only fifteen years. By 1821 he had debts of £150,000, partly the result of his chronic extravagance, partly because of the low price of sugar during the Napoleonic wars, and partly because of the thieving of his legal adviser, Thomas Wildman. By good luck he managed to sell the abbey for the £300,000 which he considered it worth. Its buyer was John Farquhar, an ancient merchant and speculator who had originally made his fortune by dealing in gunpowder in India, and was now said to be worth half a million. He lived in such squalor in his Baker Street rooms, however, that Beckford nicknamed him 'Old Filthyman'. The sale made Beckford comparatively rich again, and he used his money to buy in succession three houses at Bath.

He first considered Prior Park, but eventually chose the house now numbered 21 Lansdown Crescent. Soon he added its neighbour, No. 20, and, because a roadway divided it from No. 21, connected them with a bridge. A few years later he bought No. 19, to prevent himself being annoyed by 'the ticking of some cursed jack, the jingling of some beastly piano, horrid-toned bells tinkling, and so on'.[7] He then connected the three houses on the drawing-room level so that there was a continuous vista through No. 19 and No. 20, across the bridge and through No. 21. In 1832 he sold No. 21, but not the bridge, placing a mirror at its far end to maintain the illusion of a vista.

Meanwhile Beckford had bought land behind his houses, reaching uphill for a mile to the 800-foot summit of Lansdown. It was here that he began to build his new tower. It would, he said, have the finest prospect in Europe. Like the abbey, it was not intended to be his residence, but a retreat where he could read, contemplate and keep some of his furniture, books and manuscripts.

The tower was unfinished when Beckford received an alarming piece of news. He was called to the deathbed of the man who had been his clerk of works at Fonthill, who now told him that, when the tower of the abbey had been rebuilt of stone, the foundations had not been strengthened as they should have been to support the extra weight. Beckford at once told Farquhar, but Farquhar replied that it would last his time. He was wrong. On 21 December 1825, as the story went, before Beckford had received any news of disaster he discovered for himself, from the scaffolding of his new tower, that the tower of the abbey was missing from the south-eastern horizon.

Farquhar had been on the lawn at Fonthill when cracks were seen in the tower, and had been carried into a wing of the abbey, where he did not hear the tower fall. It collapsed on itself rather than toppled sideways. According to a witness,

> It first sank perpendicularly and slowly, and then burst and spread over the roofs of the adjoining wings on every side, but rather more on the south-west than on the others. The cloud of dust which arose was enormous, and such as completely to darken the air for a considerable distance around for several minutes. Such was the concussion in the interior of the building, that one man was forced along a passage, as if he had been in an air-gun, to the distance of 30 feet among dust so thick as to be felt. Another, on the outside, was in the like manner carried to some distance.[8]

Farquhar's comment was that the abbey had always been too big for him.

During the next nineteen years Beckford became well known at Bath, where he would be seen in its book shops or picture galleries, a small figure, dressed like a country squire in 'white neckcloth, green tail coat, buff-coloured waistcoat, knee-breeches and brown top boots'.[9] But he was never accepted by polite society. He had private revenge on the aristocracy by writing an account of its ancestry entitled *Liber Veritatis*, in which he particularly attacked the families of his one-time boy-friend, William Courtenay, his one-time legal adviser, Thomas Wildman, and his one-time guest, Emma Hamilton, 'the too seductive enchantress . . . who proved the bane of our most triumphant admiral and fixed a foul and sanguine spot upon his glorious memory'.

When Beckford died in 1844, aged eighty-three, he wanted to be buried with his dog near his tower, but was not because the ground was unconsecrated. He was therefore buried at Luncombe and his prepared sarcophagus moved there. He left the tower to his daughter, wife of the Duke of Hamilton, who allowed it to be sold, but when she heard that it had fetched only £1000 and the buyer planned to turn it into a beer garden, she bought it back and gave it to the parish of Walcot. Its grounds were then made into a cemetery and her father's body moved there (though his dog had first to be removed). The cemetery survives, somewhat unkempt, and his tomb can be seen there. The tower survives too. For many years it was used as the cemetery chapel but, in 1972, the Church Commissioners sold it to a private buyer for £5000. Today the lower parts are privately occupied, but the tower is open at certain times to visitors.

Walter Savage Landor

The phenomenally quarrelsome and extravagant, but generous writer, Walter Savage Landor (1775–1864), who was a name in his time but correctly wrote, 'I neither can nor ever shall be popular', set up house at Bath in 1805 when his father died. Already he had quarrelled with his father who had disapproved of his firing a gun at a fellow undergraduate's window at Oxford, and had been rescued financially by his father who had had to sell property to pay his debts.

Now that Landor had money of his own, and expected more when his mother died, he began to live in style. At Bath, according to his brother, he soon got 'a reputation for very great wealth', and confirmed it with 'a fine carriage, three horses, two men-servants, books, plate, china, pictures, in everything a profusion and wasteful outlay'. In winter he would live in the old city in South Parade. In summer he would cross the river to a house in Pulteney Street.

Early in the nine years of this first stay in Bath he went to Spain to fight for the rebels there and gave them a large sum of money. He also bought (with money advanced by his mother) the Welsh estate of Llanthony Abbey, which he subsequently managed so incompetently. And it was then (1811) that he met his wife at a Bath ball. 'That's the nicest girl in the room,' he said when he saw her, 'and I'll marry her.' To his mother he explained that 'she had no pretentions of any kind, and her want of a fortune was the very thing which determined me to marry her'.

When he was forced by quarrels, law suits and debts to sell his Welsh estate he left England and for some twenty-three years lived abroad, quarrelling as he moved from place to place, ending at Fiesole, outside Florence. Here he finally quarrelled with his wife and, as a result of settling on her most of his remaining income, was left with only £200 a year when, in 1838, he returned to Bath.

During the next twenty-one years, first in St James's Square, later in River Street, he and his dog Pomero became equally well-known Bath figures. Aged sixty-three, he was now, according to his friend Sidney Colvin, 'beautifully venerable': his forehead was 'bald and singularly imposing . . . beneath its thick white fringe of backward flowing hair'. But he was also notably clumsy and impractical:

> He would put his spectacles up over his forehead, and after oversetting everything in the wildest search for them, submit himself with desperate resignation to their loss. In travelling he would give himself worlds of trouble to remember the key of his portmanteau, but utterly forget the portmanteau itself; and when he discovered that he had lost it, he would launch out into an appalling picture of the treachery and depravity of the railway officials concerned, and of their fathers and grandfathers to the remotest generation. Next, after a moment's silence, the humorous view of the case would present itself to him, and he would begin to laugh,

quietly at first, and then in louder and ever louder volleys, until the room shook again, and the commotion seemed as if it would never stop. These tempests of hilarity seemed to some of Landor's friends almost as formidable as the tempests of anger to which he continued to be subject at the suspicion of a contradiction or a slight.

Landor was particularly fond of children. On the High Common he would make Pomero do tricks for them. And they were in sympathy with him. 'It was impossible for a child . . . to listen to his *crescendo* roars, mixed with those of . . . Pomero, without wanting to take part in the fray.'[10]

He was eventually forced to leave Bath by another quarrel. When he received a legacy of £100 he passed this on to a lady friend. She in turn gave half of it to another lady. The two ladies then quarrelled and the second accused the first of having received Landor's gift in return for improper services.

In fury Landor published a book entitled *Dry Sticks Fagoted*, which libelled the second lady. Friends who knew he would lose the action which she brought against him advised him to assign to his children and separated wife his remaining property and leave the country.

This did not protect him and the £1000 damages she was awarded was deducted by court order from the small sum he had set aside for his own support. As a result for the last six years of his life, which he spent at Fiesole, Florence and Siena, he depended on his family's generosity and on help from friends like the poet Robert Browning.

Dickens and Mr Pickwick

Charles Dickens (1812–1870) first visited Bath in 1835 as a journalist to report a speech by Lord John Russell. In the following years he would come with his friend and biographer, John Forster, on 30 January to visit Walter Savage Landor, who was another of Forster's subjects, and celebrate jointly Landor's birthday and the execution of Charles I. It was at one such celebration in 1840 that Dickens invented the character of Little Nell. At first she was to form part of a story, but the story expanded to a novel, and the title changed from 'The Old

Curiosity Dealer and the Child' to *The Old Curiosity Shop*.

Dickens was at Bath ten years later for the first provincial performance of the comedy, *Not So Bad As We Seem*, which Bulwer Lytton had written for his company. Dickens insisted on staging the play in the Large Room at the Assembly Rooms, in spite of warnings that its acoustics were deplorable. The result was disastrous. 'We well remember', wrote R. E. M. Peach, who was in the audience, 'the expressions of blank disappointment on the countenances of those present . . . not because they were listless or indifferent, nor because the actors failed, but simply that from within the *proscenium* set up by Dickens within the room, not one distinct syllable could be heard.' Dickens took the audience's disappointment as an insult and, according to Peach, this was why he was prejudiced against the city.

He was at Bath for the last time in 1869, the year before he died. It was mid-winter (27 January) and Bath, without its visitors, was empty and depressing. To Forster Dickens wrote, 'Landor's ghost goes along the silent streets here before me . . . The place looks to me like a cemetery which the dead have succeeded in rising and taking. Having built streets, of their old gravestones, they wander about scantly trying to "look alive". A dead failure.'

Dickens's early visits to Bath almost certainly gave him the name Pickwick. About nine miles down the road to London stands the village of Pickwick; and at Bath itself there was a coach owner named Moses Pickwick (great-grandson of a postboy at the Old Bear, who had later become landlord of the White Hart). When the fictional Pickwick sets off for Bath from the White Horse Cellar, London, his servant, Sam Weller, notices a coincidence: they are about to travel in a coach *labelled* Pickwick.

'I'm wery much afeerd, sir, that the proprietator o' this here coach is a playin' some imperence vith us,' he tells Pickwick, showing him the name in capitals on the coach door. '. . . that ain't all,' he adds, telling Pickwick to look again. '. . . they puts "Moses" afore it, vich I call addin' insult to injury . . .' When Pickwick won't allow him to fight the guard and coachman Weller becomes 'wery much afeerd that somethin' queer's come over the governor'.

At Bath Mr Pickwick is given tickets to an Assembly Rooms

ball by the Master of Ceremonies, Angelo Cyrus Bantam, Esquire, a man preposterously decorated with gold ornaments. There, in the tea room, he sees 'a vast number of queer old ladies and decrepid old gentlemen, discussing all the small talk and scandal of the day with [an evident] relish and gusto . . . three or four matchmaking mammas, appearing to be wholly absorbed in the conversation in which they were taking part, but failing not from time to time to cast an anxious sidelong glance upon their daughters . . .' and 'various knots of silly young men, displaying various varieties of puppyism and stupidity'. Presently he is persuaded to play whist with three ladies who 'were so desperately sharp, that they quite frightened him'. He plays so badly that his partner, Miss Bolo, 'rose from the table considerably agitated, and went straight home, in floods of tears, and a sedan chair'. (This is the phrase which Fowler's *Modern English Usage* quotes as its first example of syllepsis.)

Pickwick goes each morning to drink the waters at the Pump Room, where he finds 'a large bar with a marble vase, out of which the pumper gets the water; and . . . a number of yellow-looking tumblers, out of which the company get it'. '. . . after every fresh quarter of a pint, Mr Pickwick declared, in the most solemn and emphatic terms, that he felt a great deal better: whereat his friends were very much delighted, though they had not been previously aware that there was anything the matter with him'.

At a loss, perhaps, to find anything more intrinsically amusing about Bath, Dickens then involves Pickwick's friend, Winkle, in an adventure which begins at three o'clock in the morning when Winkle, in his dressing-gown, opens the door to let Mrs Dowler in, and instead gets himself locked outside. To avoid approaching ladies, Winkle flings himself into Mrs Dowler's sedan chair, but Dowler, now awake and believing that Winkle and his wife are eloping, chases Winkle twice round the Royal Crescent with a supper-knife, before Winkle is able to reach his bedroom and barricade himself inside.

Lord and Lady Lytton

The earliest visit that Lord Lytton is known for certain to have made to Bath was in 1833 when he was thirty. He was then plain Edward Bulwer, and came with his friend Benjamin Disraeli, at that time better known as a novelist than as a politician. 'We have lodging at £2 per week in an unfashionable part of town,' Disraeli wrote, 'with no servant and do everything but cook our own dinners to which Bulwer was very inclined – we have two sitting-rooms, and scribble in solitude in the mornings until two.'

Lytton was probably writing *The Last Days of Pompeii*, the best remembered of his many historical novels, which was published the following year. He was working hard to support himself since refusing an allowance of £1000 a year from his mother on the grounds that she was still refusing to meet his wife, a lady whom she disliked.

Lytton's own well-known quarrel with his wife reached a climax three years later in 1836 when they separated. It then became Lady Lytton's obsession that she had been badly treated by her husband and she did herself further damage by bringing expensive law suits against him. She also published a novel, *Cheveley, or the Man of Honour*, with a villain who was clearly identifiable as Lytton.

In 1840, soon after this had been published, she moved to Bath where she lived at 7 Johnstone Street. Her aim now was to become a lady of letters and write more novels, using them as evidence that her husband was a fake and all his better books had been written by herself. She spent more money on negotiations with a London publisher, but these ended in failure.

At an Easter Fancy Dress Ball at the Assembly Rooms she came dressed as Madame de Pompadour. 'She was in truth a magnificent woman,' an observer reported, though he thought it a mistake to have impersonated a king's mistress. R. E. M. Peach, who could have known her – or at least known many who did – was less generous. 'Beautiful once she might have been,' he wrote, 'but her beauty was no longer attractive. She had grown large, and her manner and carriage were of that defiant character that repelled, and excited curiosity and surprise rather than admiration. You looked at her and passed on with the happy reflection that your destiny was not cast with that of such a resolute-looking lady . . . Her career in Bath was in every way discreditable. She lived beyond her income; she showed a vulgar loquacity; she left her tradesmen in debt, and never made an effort afterwards to pay them.'

By 1858 her grievance had driven her mad. On election day at Hertford, where Lytton was standing as a candidate, she publicly abused him to the crowd. A fortnight later she was put in the charge of a doctor and certified insane. Later the same year her son wrote to *The Times* denying that she had ever been sent to a lunatic asylum and enclosing letters from two doctors who said she had now recovered.

Meanwhile Lytton, by 1844, had been reduced by overwork to a condition in which 'the least attempt at exercise exhausted me', and to restore his health had taken up water therapy. But he practised it at Malvern under Dr Wilson and at Petersham under Dr Weiss rather than at Bath where he might have met his wife. *Confessions of a Water Patient*, 1845, was an account of his experiences. (He wrote it as a letter to the *New Monthly Magazine*; the editor, his fellow historical novelist, Harrison Ainsworth, was so grateful that he gave him two suits of antique armour.) Nor did Lytton apparently come to Bath in 1850 when Dickens's troupe of actors staged, *Not So Bad As We Seem*, the play Lytton had written for them, at the Assembly Rooms.

Eventually, however, he began to visit Bath again, and in December 1863 he wrote from 15 Royal Crescent to Lady Combermere, 'Certainly Bath seems to be a place favourable to longevity; it reminds me of those tranquil ponds in which carps, forgotten by the angler, live to a fabulous age . . . Its mild and misty melancholy gains upon one and engenders a languid affection . . . If I come to Bristol I will certainly pay my respects to your ladyship, but at present I have fallen into the carp-like state of meditative laziness, and my excursions are limited to a slow swim up and down the pond.'

Three years later he took up residence at 9 Royal Crescent, and next year moved to 2 Great Pulteney Street, which was then Stead's Hotel. For the rest of his life he made visits to Stead's. By this time he was deaf and took little part in the life of the city. But its citizens observed him. 'One could never quite realise,' Peach wrote, 'that the dapper gentleman, with dyed hair and whiskers, and who certainly was not above

middle height, was the *puissant* Edward Bulwer Lytton . . .
with all his faults . . . he was a gentleman, kind to his inferiors,
scrupulously honourable in his dealings . . . the reverse of his
wife, who, thirty years before, had made Bath her home and
tradesmen her victims.'

Inventor of Pitman's shorthand

Isaac Pitman, inventor of the world's most successful short-
hand, first came to Bath in 1839 when he was twenty-six, and
the city remained his home till he died there fifty-eight years
later, in 1897. Before he arrived he had been a schoolmaster,
but he had been dismissed by his school managers at Wotton-
under-Edge, Gloucestershire, for joining the New Church of
Emmanuel Swedenborg. At Bath he also founded a school,
which he conducted at his house, 5 Nelson Place.

By this time he was already engaged in his life's principal
interest, phonetic writing. In 1837 he had published a 4d.
pamphlet, *Stenographic Sound-Hand*. Gradually this interest took
up more and more of his time and after four years he closed his
school in order to devote himself exclusively to it.

He now founded the Phonetic Institute, which he at first ran
from his home. Later it had four different headquarters: in
Upper Bath Street, in Parsonage Lane, in Kingston Buildings,
and finally in Lower Bristol Road. He himself eventually moved
to 12 Royal Crescent, then to No. 17. He loved Bath, considering that 'of the many beautiful cities in this fair country, Bath is
unquestionably the most beautiful'.

He had many other interests or obsessions. He tried without
much success to promote the reform of English spelling, also to
introduce a duodecimal system of mathematics. In 1875 he
helped to establish a free library and to maintain it for six years
by voluntary subscription. It collapsed when the city council
was offered a freehold in which to continue it, but refused
because it would add a halfpenny to the rates.

Throughout his life he was a teetotaller, vegetarian, non-
smoker, anti-vaccinationist and obsessive worker. At 6.30 every
morning he was at his desk. When a journalist asked to see his
study Pitman told him it was his office. 'I do not study, I
work,' he said.

The journalist reported that phonetic literature lay in piles on the tables and floor but there was no disorder.

The day before he died Pitman wrote to Gordon Drummond, the minister of the New Church, Bath, 'To those who ask how Isaac Pitman passed away, say, Peacefully, and with no more concern than in passing from one room to another to take up some further employment.'

A Bath waif

While Bath in the early twentieth century outwardly became a city of retired army officers and wintering invalids, many of its citizens remained as poor as the occupants of Avon Street had been in the eighteenth century. Few of these poor are remembered, but one, Louie Stride, has published an account of her childhood – which began in 1907 when she was born in the old Gaol, Grove Street.

She was the illegitimate daughter of a Welshman from Merthyr Tydfil, but she hated her father and saw him only at weekends. Her mother was a shop-cleaner, but badly paid and improvident. As a result many of Louie's earliest memories are of midnight escapes from lodgings where the rent could no longer be paid. This was a well-known Bath practice, usually carried out at about midnight, using a handcart which could be hired for 1s. 6d. deposit at the rate of 6d. an hour.

To supplement her earnings her mother would steal from her employers, in particular from Mr Potts, the chemist, coming home with his sheets and pillow cases wound round her waist, which she would then take one by one to the pawn shop in Upper Borough Walls. But she managed money so badly that Louie was always ill-dressed and dirty. Her hair was close cropped against lice, and when she started school she was known as 'Lulu no-drawers'. After she had been weaned – at three years old – she was invariably hungry, and would grab younger schoolchildren's pieces of bread and run to bolt herself in the lavatory to eat them.

She was seven when the First World War began and food became still scarcer. She would beg for bread at bakers' shops – sometimes one would give her a sack of stale pieces for 3d. – and take home any piece she saw in the gutter for a feast of toast. Now her mother 'went on the street', and at the same time began to take 'drugs' to prevent venereal disease. But she eventually found and married a Canadian soldier, one of those billeted at Prior Park. Louie's life seemed transformed now that she, like everyone else, had a father. She did not at once realise that he was a hopeless alcoholic.

Meanwhile Louie's schooling became more and more irregular, until she chose a new school for herself – Kingsmead Board School – and enrolled there, using her stepfather's name. She said she had come from Birmingham, where her stepfather had been born, and where she had memorised the address. At her new school she would regularly faint on Monday mornings from hunger, until the teachers realised what was wrong and fed her. At this school she was happy, until the school board man recognised her as a truant from schools in other parts of town and she was dismissed.

After the war poverty at Bath was even more acute. Some of its inhabitants would try to make a living as rag-and-bone men – known as 'totters'. Others would solicit charity by doing remarkable things. One, named Badger Pope, would bite the heads off live rats, or place a large piece of concrete on his chest and invite people to hit it with a sledge hammer.

Epidemics of diphtheria and scarlet fever were frequent. Louie would watch other children enviously as they were taken away in the hospital van and regret that she never became ill herself – something she believed that her three years on the breast explained. Eventually she had a severe attack of tonsillitis. Afterwards she would sit in the streets near the hospital, trying to catch the hospital smell of ether and be reminded of the bowls of bread and milk she had had there.

Her stepfather, meanwhile, was unable to keep a job and would drink away what money he did earn. He was forced to move them into a miserable cottage behind Great Corn Street, which would regularly flood. Once they were marooned on the upper floor. When the floods receded a flotsam of 'indescribable filth' and dead rats would be left behind. Even when later they moved to a slightly better cottage, Louie became accustomed to seeing its gas cooker under water.

One day when her father was short of beer money and sent her mother to pawn his boots she failed to return. Presently a policeman called to say that she had been arrested, certified insane and sent to a lunatic asylum. Here she died fifteen years later. For a while Louie kept house for her alcoholic stepfather, then she bought him a ticket to Birmingham and sent him there to his brother. So that he could not come back she left their home and went to live as a domestic at Pratt's Hotel.

Mrs Pratt became the best friend Louie ever had. Her work at Pratt's eventually enabled her to save £200 and to buy herself a small cottage. Here she lived in modest independence until it was requisitioned by the Bath Council and she was paid what she considered quite inadequate compensation.

Louie married and went to Ireland for fourteen years, but in 1972 after her husband had died she returned to Bath. It was when she saw new bungalows on the site of her cottage that anger made her begin her account of her childhood. In 1983 Graham Davis of Bath University was told that a former tea lady at the Camden Works Museum had written some memoirs. He discovered a coverless exercise book of some sixty handwritten pages, some in biro, some in pencil, with no paragraphs and few commas, but with scarcely a spelling mistake. As a small lonely girl, Louie had in part educated herself by reading Dickens and other Victorians. With Davis's help she edited her memoirs and they were eventually published as *Memories of a Street Urchin*. Her account of one stratum of Bath society is as vivid as any ever written.

George Saintsbury

In 1920 George Saintsbury (1845–1933), professor of English Literature at Edinburgh University for twenty years, took up residence at 1A Royal Crescent, the little two-storey house which joins 1 Royal Crescent to the first house in Upper Church Street. The same year he published *Notes on a Cellarbook*, the book for which he is best remembered. Saintsbury would say that he could tell the difference between an evening glass of sherry from a newly opened bottle and a glass from a bottle opened at lunch time. His love of wine was celebrated by the foundation of the Saintsbury Club, the aim of which was 'to bring together those literary men who, like Chesterton and Belloc, regarded wine as a more delectable beverage than beer'.

His *Cellarbook*, however, was only a tiny fragment of his

published work. The list of his books, J. B. Priestley said, 'makes the more indolent of us wonder what we do with our time'. At first they mainly concerned French literature, but gradually they covered the whole of English literature and much of European literature from the Greeks to the twentieth century. He also wrote huge amounts of journalism – enough to fill a hundred books, he calculated – for many magazines, from the *Manchester Guardian* to the *Saturday Review*. Mainly his articles were on literary or general subjects; politically he was a high Tory, deploring every great reform since the Reform Bill.

At Bath Saintsbury lived a private life, refusing for instance to be interviewed or to provide a Bath newspaper with a photograph on his eightieth birthday. But he was often to be seen in the streets of the city carrying a string bag of books, or standing in the Grand Parade looking at the view across the river which he admired. And he continued to read extensively and to publish regularly. When it became hard for him to get about, passersby in the Royal Crescent would see him at work in his study, with long white beard, wearing a black skull-cap. He died in his Bath house, but was buried at Southampton where he had been born.

Haile Selassie, Emperor of Abyssinia

In May 1936 Haile Selassie, Emperor of Abyssinia, fled to London as Italian troops approached his capital, Addis Ababa. But he was given no official welcome by the British government, which was trying to humour Mussolini, and was told to leave. He moved to Bath, in theory to take the waters. Here he bought Fairfield, a large Victorian villa in the suburbs, surrounded by dense shrubberies. He was virtually penniless, but was able to pay for the house with money lodged in London for a royal dinner service which he no longer needed.

To look after his children and grandchildren he hired local girls, but one of them remembers that she was never paid. His Abyssinian servants he housed in the furniture-less cellars. Also attending him was his butler, named Jesus, and a hermit lady who lived in a potting shed beside the back drive. Visitors who passed it would notice a terrible smell. For a chapel he used the greenhouse, its glass painted with whitewash on the inside. To this his three priests would process, chanting, dressed in splendidly ornate robes. On certain feast days the emperor would wash his servants' feet with a sprig of rosemary.

He became a familiar figure in the streets of Bath, a tiny man, wearing a black hat and black cape, carrying an umbrella whatever the weather, followed by his little black Pomeranian dog named Rosa. At a discreet distance behind came his two security men. In Bath he attended special showings at the local cinema of news films from the Abyssinian war, and in return invited the cinema manager's children to play at Fairfield.

Here certain royal proprieties were maintained. Meals were eaten in silence off golden plates beneath Venetian chandeliers. But he was still desperately poor, his troubles increased by having to support other Abyssinian exiles. When his electricity bill remained unpaid for many months the chairman of the local electricity board went to see him and found him sitting in his overcoat with a rug over his knees. He was sent no more bills, and an unknown donor had monthly lorryloads of coal delivered to him. Eventually a charitable trust gave him £2,000 a year – all subsequently repaid.

He never gave up hope of returning to Abyssinia, but this was not possible until Mussolini entered the war on the German side. British troops then invaded Abyssinia and, on 5 May 1941, he re-entered Addis Ababa, exactly five years after he had left it.

During his time at Bath he had become an enthusiast for the British way of life. One of his grandchildren had taught his budgerigar to sing 'God Save the King'. When the Emperor built himself a country palace in the African hills he called it 'Fairfield'. In 1954 he paid a final visit to Bath to receive the freedom of the city.

PART FOUR

The Second World War and After

The Bath air raids

Between nightfall on Saturday, 25 April 1942, and dawn on Monday the 27th, Bath suffered three air raids which killed 417 people, seriously wounded 350 more, destroyed or severely damaged nearly 1200 houses and did some damage to a total of 19,000. There were two raids on the Saturday–Sunday night, the first with high-explosive bombs, the second with incendiaries. The third raid, with heavier high-explosive bombs, was on the Sunday–Monday night.

The earliest bombers followed the River Avon into the city from the east, perhaps aiming for the station, but bombs fell all over the city. The most spectacular single hit was on a gasometer, which exploded. The most disastrous architecturally was on the new Assembly Rooms, which were gutted by fire. Opposite them, the Regina Hotel was totally destroyed. So was the west wing of Prior Park, one wing of the Bath General Hospital, and Lansdown Place East. In Queen's Square the Francis Hotel was seriously damaged. Buildings which escaped or were hit only by fire bombs were the abbey, the Pump Room complex, the rest of Queen's Square, the Circus and the Royal Crescent.

One young girl of eight has described being taken (with her deaf and blind grandmother) to an air-raid shelter on the first night.

It was like daylight outside. The sky seemed alight. It would suddenly light up with bright sheets of light. You could see the aircraft come over. They were machine-gunning as they came over Twerton Roundhill. You could see the red tracer bullets flying. I looked up and saw a plane machine-gunning along the back of the allotments. It seemed to confront us. The aircraft was glass-fronted and a face was visible. It was really pale in the light. They followed one behind the other, every half-minute or so. They seemed to skim the top of the Roundhill and then drop down towards the city centre.[1]

A despatch rider described how he hunted for Wally Angus, his missing deputy:

> On Sunday afternoon we still couldn't find him. I had to go round the mortuaries. I started at Old Bridge. I then tried St Peter's, but nothing. I picked up all the covers but there was nothing there. I reckon I turned at least 150 over. I tried Weston. Then I went to Walcot. About the third I turned over from the last was Wally Angus. I don't know how they got him out there. His helmet was brought back to the station. The bomb had gone right along the road and a piece of shrapnel had gone through the helmet. It killed him instantly.[2]

The Bath Preservation Trust

Early in 1909 the Rev. S. A. Boyd, Rector of Bath, with other citizens who were horrified by Bath Council's latest proposal for vandalising the city (the destruction of the fine colonnade which formed the north side of Bath Street so that the Pump Room Hotel could be extended), organised a petition of protest. On 1 March Boyd presented this with five hundred signatures to the Mayor, but the council ignored it and the proposal was passed.

Boyd and his friends – who included the Bath historian, William Tyte, then began a campaign in the local and national press, and at Bath, on 27 March, they held a public meeting of protest. Speaking to the meeting, Boyd said, 'As the corporation betrays such little regard for the architecture, associations, and traditions of Bath, the time seems to have come to form a "Bath Preservation and Defence Association"'. This was the origin of the body which named itself 'The Old Bath Preservation Society'.

The society won its battle, Bath Street was saved, and for seventy-seven years stood as evidence of Boyd's defence of Bath, before, in July 1986, it was gutted by fire. Though the City Council's Chief Executive has promised that the façade will be maintained when the buildings are restored, Boyd's successors wait anxiously to see whether or not Grosvenor Square Properties Ltd, the redeveloper, will keep this promise.

Boyd's battle to save a vital piece of eighteenth-century Bath was only one of scores which those who love the city have fought against a succession of Philistine councils and greedy private builders. Some they have won, but many lost. Nor was the Old Bath Preservation Society the first body to fight these battles. As early as the 1840s the Bath Protection Society had existed. There is no record of what provoked the formation of this society, but a silver tea set survives, which was presented in 1866 to Mr G. Lawrence by members of the society 'as a trifling acknowledgement' of his grandfather, George Lawrence's, 'kind and efficient services as their honorary secretary for upwards of twenty years'.

And in 1934 a third society, the Bath Preservation Trust, was formed. Its objects were, and still are, similar to those of the Old Bath Preservation Society, but for some eleven years both continued to exist, until in 1945 Miss Florence Tylee, the Old Bath Preservation Society's honorary secretary and a founder member, died, and it was amalgamated with the Bath Preservation Trust.

The Trust, like its predecessor, was founded to fight a more than typically destructive City Council proposal. This, known as the Bath Bill, involved moving the Mineral Water Hospital to a site near the Hot Spring – a good idea in itself – but in order to pay for the move, allowing the council to acquire some six hundred properties in the heart of the city, to destroy George Street, Alfred Street and the island site of Old Bond Street, and to extend the shopping area of Milsom Street to the north. The Bath Preservation Trust succeeded in getting the Bath Bill abandoned.

There is no space to detail the many battles which the Trust has subsequently fought – for example to save Green Park Station, and Ralph Allen's cottages, or to make it financially possible for owners to restore in their original style houses damaged in Bath's 1942 air raids by persuading the War Damage Commission to pay compensation on a 'cost of works' basis. Nor space to name more than one or two of the many who, voluntarily and without pay, have fought to save Bath with a skill and persistence which have defeated the salaried full-time efforts of bureaucrats, contemporary architects and so-called planners.

By about 1970, however, the campaign which the Trust was

fighting had become a desperate rearguard action, with the
council in full pursuit of the fashionable notions of development
which destroyed for ever the historic centres of so many English
towns. In June that year Sir Christopher Chancellor became
Chairman of the Trust. Also that year Peter Coard published
his influential book of drawings, *Vanishing Bath*. But it was not
until two years later, when Chancellor read the *Times* feature
on Bath which included Adam Fergusson's article, *Acres of
Georgian Rubble*, that he decided he had found the person who
might write the book which would fully expose Bath Council's
monstrous activities. The result was Fergusson's *The Sack of
Bath* (see page 229).

There is little doubt that the influence of *The Sack of Bath* on
opinion throughout the country caused the abandonment of the
'East/West relief road' scheme, to name only one of the most
blatantly destructive of the plans which were then being actively
considered. Less dramatic in itself as a victory, but in the end
more important, was that it led to the setting up of a body
known as the Joint Steering Committee, on which the Trust
was to play an equal part with the Department of the Environment, the Avon County Council and the Bath City Council.
This in turn led to the belated creation of a Conservation
Department in the city's planning office.

Meanwhile the Trust has continued to expand in all senses,
from a first membership of 81 and income of £218. 1s. 0d. to a
1986 membership of about 1100 and income of £100,000 In 1970,
after Bernard Cayzer had given it 1 Royal Crescent to turn into a
Georgian museum, it moved its offices there, then in 1984 to the
Countess of Huntingdon's Chapel when it undertook the chapel's restoration. Battles continue, and no doubt always will. The
very least that can be said for the Bath Preservation Trust is that,
had it not existed, Bath would by now have become a city with
a few isolated architectual set-pieces, instead of remaining what,
in spite of losses, it still is: the country's finest and most extensive
Georgian memorial.

The sack of Bath

The damage done by German bombs to Georgian Bath in April
1942 was minor and reparable compared to the damage done

after the Second World War by Bath City Council. The council allowed not just single buildings or small groups of them to be destroyed, but tore down street after street and acre after acre of the eighteenth-century city. Until 1950 Bath was one of two or three of the world's most complete period cities, its magnificent squares and crescents set against a background of lesser but invaluable terraces of artisan dwellings of the same period. With almost unbelievable lack of taste, if nothing worse, the council, during the next twenty-five years, let this essential background be destroyed, with the result that Bath's great buildings are now interspersed with twentieth-century horrors and surrounded by new buildings of an entirely alien character. Which of Bath's new buildings was the corporation really proud of, the chairman of Bath Council's Development Committee was asked in 1972. He answered, 'None.'

It was the following year that Adam Fergusson published *The Sack of Bath*, the short but devastating book which he had been encouraged to write by Christopher Chancellor, Chairman of the Bath Preservation Trust, and for which John Betjeman wrote some introductory rhymes. Betjeman's final couplet summed up the book's message:

> Goodbye to old Bath. We who love you are sorry
> They've carted you off by developer's lorry.

Fergusson needed to do nothing but record, crime by crime, without rhetoric or exaggeration, Bath Council's succession of acts of corporate vandalism, punctuating them with occasional examples of excuses of mischievous naivety. 'In few places', he wrote, 'has the notion of "urban renewal" been applied with such destructive vigour as here, or with such disregard for the finer subtleties of urban charm.'

His catalogue was supported by photographs of tumbling Georgian buildings (Calton Road, Lambridge Street, Philip Street, Beechen Cliff, Charles Street, Fielding's house at Twerton); of flattened acres of rubble where others had once stood (Southgate Street, Kingsmead Square, Ballance Street, Walcot Street); and of what had replaced them (Rosewell House, Kingsmead House, the Salvation Army Citadel, the Percy Club, the Harvey block, Lansdown View Estate, the Technical College – this last and most bleakly alien designed by a member of the Royal Fine Art Commission).

Three years earlier, Peter Coard's *Vanishing Bath*, a nostalgic collection of drawings of the buildings of Georgian Bath which had gone or were about to go, had already begun to alert the country to the pillage and destruction over which Bath Council was presiding. Together, the two books had a dramatic effect. It would be to indulge in a form of pathetic fallacy to write that a public body like Bath Council experienced shame, and optimistic to suggest that its individual members were embarrassed. But from this time onwards they began to change their behaviour. In 1973, as Fergusson saw it, there was still something left to hope for. 'Georgian Bath', he wrote, 'could yet be saved – enough of it, at any rate, for both visitor and citizen still to discover there some semblance of the atmosphere of the age of elegance.'

Fergusson's book is not exclusively a catalogue of disasters, but includes an analysis of how the sack of Bath was allowed to occur, suggesting that greed, intrigue and a total lack of taste were not the only causes. Laymen, even when their intentions are good, are ill-trained to interpret architects' plans or to question the financial estimates of planners. One of the saddest aspects of the destruction of so much of artisan Bath is that redevelopments which were excused on financial grounds were often just as costly as restoration of the old buildings would have been.

The Georgian Museum at 1, Royal Crescent

'Queen Anne in front, Mary Anne behind', is said to describe the work at Bath of the two John Woods, father and son. They would design the symmetrical and grandiose Palladian façades of their squares and crescents but leave it to other contractors to design and build the accommodation behind. Certainly the Royal Crescent was built in this way, as anyone can see who looks at its ragged outline from behind. So when the Bath Preservation Trust was given number 1 Royal Crescent – which might be considered Bath's premier address, the equivalent of No. 1, London, the Duke of Wellington's Apsley House – and set about turning it back into the house it had been when it was built in 1767, it had no easily verifiable pattern to follow.

For most of its life it had been a lodging house and its internal arrangements had been often changed. At one time, for example, it had shared a kitchen with 1A, then later had had a kitchen on its own first floor. But the Trust was certainly justified in turning it into the single house John Wood had intended his Royal Crescent houses to be, they were each for letting as superior accommodation to one tenant for the season, and rents as high as £140 were asked.

In the 1960s No. 1 was for a time occupied by squatters and became seriously dilapidated. It was this that enabled Bernard Cayzer to buy it at auction for £11,500. He saw it for sale when browsing through *Country Life*, he explained. Cayzer was a shipping tycoon, a director of the British and Commonwealth Line, particularly concerned with the passenger route to Cape Town. Seventeen years later, when he died, he left over £2 million, of which his gardener, John Smith, received £50,000 and a house. Smith had worked for Cayzer for thirty years in his fourteen-acre garden at Parish House, Timsbury.

'I have an insatiable curiosity to see how other people live,' Cayzer said, 'and I thought it would be wonderful if No. 1 could be seen again as it was when the first people lived there in 1767.' He took a major part in this transformation, paying most of the £77,000 which this cost and endowing the house generously.

Today the change is complete and the house's four main rooms are meticulously decorated and furnished in Georgian style. On the ground floor is a dining-room with table set for the dessert. Here are the expected decanter and glasses for port, together with pineapples and syllabubs, and less familiar but authentic period dishes of enlarged hundreds and thousands, and bilious green macaroons. An ornate screen of French design in one corner hid the chamber-pots.

Opposite is the study with card table, laid for a game in progress, scattered newspapers of the time and a desk with curiosities like a wax jack for melting sealing wax, and theatre tokens like large brown coins. Over the fireplace is a painting of four Bath characters of the previous generation: John Wood senior, John Gay (one of the landowners he dealt with), Ralph Allen, and Allen's builder, Richard Jones. In this room the chamber-pots were kept in wall cupboards.

Overhead is a bedroom with a curtained four-post bed. Laid

out on the dressing-table are period make-up and cosmetic devices like ceramic curlers. These were heated in boiling water and used for about twenty minutes – sufficient to melt the mixture of grease and flour which matted the hair of ladies at the time and allow it to set again in curls.

Opposite is the drawing-room, with table laid for the tea which the ladies took while the gentlemen continued to drink below, and a delicate pianoforte. This room has a magnificent view from its side-window of the full sweep of the Crescent.

Inevitably, the Bath Preservation Trust has been criticised for some of its changes at 1 Royal Crescent by those accustomed to previous nineteenth-century alterations, in particular for replacing its plate-glass windows with the original smaller panes. More seriously, the kitchen in the basement has too much of the flavour of a museum and too little of the sort of basement kitchen which the house must originally have had. On the ground and first floors, however, the conversion is admirable, and enables a Bath visitor to get a clear picture of the life led by the prosperous during its great period. The BBC used 1 Royal Crescent for its film of *Northanger Abbey*, and the consequent publicity helped to give the house its best season, with 60,000 visitors.

The yellow door in the Crescent

Late in 1970 Bath Council received complaints from residents of the Royal Crescent that the front door of No. 22 had been painted a bright yellow, entirely out of keeping with the white and brown doors of its neighbours. When questioned by Bath's *Evening Post*, one of them, Brigadier John Chippindall, said, 'If I told you what I think about the yellow front door, everything would fuse.'

The owner of No. 22, Miss Amabel Wellesley-Colley, was a descendant of the Duke of Wellington, and had lived in Bath since the 1920s. She claimed that she could paint her door what colour she liked, and that anyway it was a natural colour made by God. 'I mixed the paint myself,' she said, 'and matched it with a real primrose.'

Nevertheless the council took action against her under a 1968 regulation which forbade the alteration of the appearance of a

Grade I scheduled building without permission. They also ordered her to remove her primrose window blinds, and a wrought-iron window guard, described as resembling a barbecue grille. This, Miss Wellesley-Colley said, she needed for safety when sunbathing for her rheumatism.

Other citizens rallied to her cry that an Englishwoman's home is her castle, and she herself went to Westminster to lobby Conservative MPs. As a result, in April the following year Peter Walker, Minister of the Environment, ordered a public enquiry, after which he would personally make a final decision. The six-hour enquiry was held in February 1972. Among other things Miss Wellesley-Colley claimed that the council's order did not apply because the door had been last painted before the Act became law, a claim which the council tried to refute with colour slides. Miss Wellesley-Colley eventually won her case because the yellow paint of the door had faded, and because the blinds were inside, not outside the house and therefore not covered by the regulation.

This was not the end of the story, however. When the council refused to pay her £700 legal costs she repainted her door a bright primrose. She was now engaged in another battle for freedom, and had been summonsed at Bow Street for riding a bicycle down Rotten Row, Hyde Park. She would rather go to prison than pay a fine, she said. Instead she was conditionally discharged for a year. After the hearing, according to the *Evening Chronicle*, she 'cycled off wearing . . . a luminous orange golf cap'.

Meanwhile the council decided to hope that the door's new paint would once more fade, and took no further action. In 1977, however, it was told that the door had yet again been brightly painted yellow. 'I'm not admitting to anything,' Miss Wellesley-Colley said. 'They've got to prove it and produce evidence. There are a lot of nasty people about who are after my blood.' The council sent officials to interview Miss Wellesley-Colley, who were fortunately able to report that the door had merely been washed, and to recommend that no action need be taken since the 1972 paint had indeed faded.

In 1984 Miss Wellesley-Colley left Bath and gave her house to the Catholic Church. The Church resold it for £250,000. Whether or not, as rumour says, she made it a condition of her gift that the door should remain yellow, that is still its colour.

Today it rivals the Pump Room, the Roman Baths and the Georgian Museum at No. 1, Royal Crescent, as Bath's most visited tourist sight. The primrose blinds, however, have bleached to white, and the barbecue-like safety rail has gone.

The Pump Room today

In the 1970s and 1980s the Pump Room was extensively restored or redecorated a number of times, most recently in 1986 when the interior was repainted. The principal building officer of the city council admitted that the transformation was 'quite dramatic' and might not be to everyone's taste. It was not.

All colour and gilding was removed from the tall columns which are its principal internal feature, and they were painted plain white. Today the neighbouring dining-hall gives an idea of the highly ornate decoration which was swept away and which Bath's more conservative citizens preferred. The city council justified the change by claiming that it was a return to the original colour (or lack of colour) scheme. Under three layers of gilding and one of bronzing lay at least seven layers of white or off-white paint.

The council also erected curtains, though admitting that the Pump Room had not had them for its first forty-five years (1795–1840). They were 'a necessary modern addition for privacy and heat retention', it argued. The colours chosen were pink and green, and they cost £18,000. Unfortunately they puckered badly while being fire-proofed, and had to be put on the rack by the Shirley textile institute before, six and a half months late, they were eventually hung.

Despite complaints by traditionalists about the white paint, and by purists about the curtains, the Pump Room today is well patronised. Here citizens and visitors can still meet to take the waters, as their predecessors did in the eighteenth century, even if they bear little resemblance to the elegant drinkers shown on that early eighteenth-century fan, or to the grotesque later ones whom Rowlandson drew. Here they are still able to tell each other tales, some accurate, some less so, of the scandals of Bath.

NOTES
SOURCES
INDEX

NOTES

Part 1 (pages 13–29)

1. *Bath Abbey* guide, 1973, p. 9
2. Peirce, Robert, *Bath Memoirs . . .* , 1697, p. 259
3. Green, Emanuel, *Proceedings of the Bath Natural History and Field Club*, v. 4, pp. 105–20
4. James, P. Rowland, *The Baths of Bath in the 16th and 17th Centuries*, 1938, p. 98
5. Hamilton, Antoine, *Mémoires du Chevalier de Grammont*, 1713, 1958 ed. chap. 13
6. Wood, John, *An Essay Towards a Description of Bath*, 2nd ed. 1749, p. 437
7. Clarendon, Edward Earl of, *The History of the Rebellion*, 1819 ed. bk. 7 p. 376
8. *Ibid*, bk. 7 p. 380
9. *Ibid*, bk. 7 p. 378
10. *Ibid*, bk. 7 p. 380
11. *Ibid*, bk. 7 p. 379
12. *Ibid*, bk. 7 p. 380
13. Wood, *ed. cit.* p. 221

Part 2 (pages 31–185)

1. Goldsmith, Oliver, *The Life of Richard Nash*, 1762, pp. 7–8
2. *Ibid* p. 10
3. *Ibid* p. 12
4. *Ibid* p. 14
5. *Ibid* p. 8
6. *Ibid* p. 18
7. *Ibid* p. 20
8. *Ibid* pp. 40 and 36
9. *Ibid* p. 34
10. *Ibid* p. 37
11. *Ibid* p. 54
12. *Ibid* p. 74
13. *Ibid* pp. 73, 74 and 75
14. *Ibid* p. 178
15. *Notes and Queries*, 2nd series, No. 79, 4 July 1857, pp. 1–2 and 41–3
16. Graves, Richard, *The Triflers*, 1806, pp. 62 and 63
17. Allen, Ralph, *Ralph Allen's own Narrative, 1720–1761*, 1960, p. 25
18. *An Eighteenth Century Correspondence*, ed. Dickens and Stanton, 1910, p. 255
19. *Bath Journal*, 10 February 1746
20. Bath Corporation minutes, quoted *Bath and County Graphic*, February 1899, p. 113
21. *Bath and County Graphic*, March 1899, p. 125
22. Roberts, Cecil, *And so to Bath*, 1940, p. 164
23. Historical Manuscripts Commission, Bath, Papers at Longleat
24. *Town and Country Magazine*, 16 May 1773
25. *Dictionary of National Biography*
26. Chantreau, *Voyage dans le tres Royaumes d'Angleterre, d'Ecosse et d'Irlande, fait en 1788 et 1789*, 1792, p. 232
27. Kielmansegge, Count, quoted Williams, Marjorie, *Lady Luxborough Goes to Bath*, 1946, p. 18
28. Fiennes, Celia, *Through England on a Saddle . . .* , 1888, p. 13

29. Wood, *ed. cit.* p. 438
30. *Ibid* p. 439
31. Goldsmith, *op. cit*
32. *Ibid* p. 50
33. *Farley's Bristol News-Paper*, 11 November 1727
34. Perkins, Hutton, to Lord Chancellor Hardwicke, 17 September 1752
35. Hervey, Lord John, *Memoirs of the Reign of George II*, ed. Sidgewick, 1931, p. 195
36. Williams, Charles Hanbury, *Works*, 1822, v. 1, p. 134
37. Coxe, William, *Memoirs of Robert Walpole*, 1798, v. 3, pp. 88–9
38. Dodd, Dudley, *Bath Assembly Rooms*, 1979, p. 18
39. *Ibid* pp. 24–5
40. Wood, *ed. cit.* p. 222
41. *Ibid* p. 223
42. Quoted, Bulloch, John Malcolm, *An Aberdeen Falstaff*, 1930, p. 17
43. *Bath Argus*, 24 June 1899
44. *Dictionary of National Biography*
45. Wood, *ed. cit.* p. 388
46. *Ibid* p. 389
47. Cotton, Charles, *The Compleat Gamester*, 1674, 1930 ed. p. 82
48. Wood, *ed. cit.* p. 390
49. Tyte, William, *Bath in the Eighteenth Century*, 1903, p. 55
50. *Bath and County Graphic*, October 1897, p. 66
51. Cibber, Theophilus, *Lives of the Poets*, 1753, p. 351
52. Peach, R. E. M., *Life and Times of Ralph Allen*, 1895, pp. 73–4
53. Newton, Bishop Thomas, *Works*, 1787 v. 1, p. 116
54. Stukeley, Rev. William, *Family Memoirs of the Rev. William Stukeley*, v. 1, p. 129
55. Harris, George, *Life of Lord Chancellor Hardwicke*, 1847, v. 1, p. 477

56. *Letters to and from the Rev. Philip Doddridge*, ed. Stedman, 1790, pp. 184–5
57. *Dictionary of National Biography*
58. *Life of Mr James Quin*, 1766, 1887 ed. p. 57
59. *Ibid* p. 69
60. *Dictionary of National Biography*
61. *Times Literary Supplement*, 11 May 1922
62. Quoted, Gadd, David, *Georgian Summer*, 1971, p. 171
63. Britton, John, *The History and Antiquities of Bath Abbey Church*, 1825, p. 103
64. Quoted Gosse, Philip, *Doctor Viper*, 1952, p. 81
65. *Dictionary of National Biography*
66. *Ibid*
67. *Monthly Review*, 1777, p. 146
68. *Notes and Queries*, 5th series, v. 6, p. 545
69. *Gentleman's Magazine*, 1791, v. 1, p. 618
70. Moore, Thomas, *Memoirs of the Life of the Right Honourable Richard Brinsley Sheridan*, 1825, p. 67
71. *Ibid* p. 73
72. Rae, W. Fraser, *Sheridan*, 1896, v. 1, p. 173
73. Moore, *op. cit.* p. 74
74. *Ibid* p. 98
75. *Ibid* pp. 112–13
76. *Dictionary of National Biography*
77. *Ibid*
78. Roberts, *op. cit.* p. 218
79. *Dictionary of National Biography*
80. Egan, Pierce, *Walks through Bath*, 1819, pp. 304–5
81. *Notes and Queries*, 4th series, v. 4, p. 347
82. Ruffhead, Owen, *Life of Alexander Pope*, 1769, p. 546
83. Eaves, T. C. Duncan, and Kimpel, Ben D., *Samuel Richardson*, 1971, pp. 63–4

84. *Ibid* p. 202
85. Peach, R. E. M., *Historic Houses in Bath*, 1883, v. 1, p. 154
86. *Bath Advertiser*, 27 October 1759
87. Foster, J. K., *Life and Times of the Countess of Huntingdon*, 1839, v. 1, p. 443
88. *Ibid* v. 1, p. 445
89. Tyte, *op. cit.* p. 114
90. *Ibid*
91. *Ibid*
92. *Memoirs of Dr Whalley*, 1863, v. 2, p. 441
93. *Dictionary of National Biography*
94. Clifford, James L., *Hester Lynch Piozzi*, 1941, p. 450

Part 3 (pages 187–221)

1. Kersley, George D., *The Three Rs*, 1980, p. 25

2. Ison, Walter, *The Georgian Buildings of Bath*, 1980, p. 73
3. Phillips, John, *Memoirs of William Smith*, 1844, p. 28
4. *Ibid* p. 64
5. *Ibid* p. 78
6. *Dictionary of National Biography*
7. Redding, Cyrus, *Memoirs of William Beckford of Fonthill*, 1859, v. 2, p. 363
8. Forthegill, Brian, *William Beckford*, 1979, p. 326
9. *Ibid* p. 330
10. Peach, *Historic Houses*, v. 1, p. 122

Part 4 (pages 223–234)

1. Rothnie, Niall, *The Bombing of Bath*, pp. 39–40
2. *Ibid* p. 76

SOURCES

Bath is well documented. In the mid-eighteenth century John Wood, the elder, the man who did most to set its architectural tone, wrote his own account: *Essay Towards a Description of Bath*. Much of what we know about the city in the first half of that century comes from Wood, in particular from his expanded 1749 edition. Twenty-two years later Oliver Goldsmith borrowed heavily from Wood when he published his biography of Richard Nash, but added material of his own.

These two important sources are by no means alone. Many of Bath's doctors wrote about the city or its waters: Thomas Guidott, *A Discourse of the Bath*, 1676; Robert Peirce, *Bath Memoirs; . . .*, 1697; William Oliver, the elder, *Practical Dissertation on Bath Waters*, 1707; William Oliver, his younger cousin, *A Practical Essay on the Use and Abuse of Warm Water Baths in Gouty Cases*, 1757; George Cheyne, *Observations Concerning the Nature and the Method of Treatment of Gout*, 1720, and several other titles; and Charles Lucas, *Essay on Waters*. So, above all, did Tobias Smollett, both in his *An Essay on the External Use of Water*, 1752, and in his novels. It may be no irony that the last of these, *Humphrey Clinker*, 1771, brings the city and its society to life more successfully than any non-fiction account. The same could be said about Henry Fielding's fictionalised Ralph Allen in *Tom Jones*, and of course about Jane Austen's *Northanger Abbey* and *Persuasion*, for their accounts of Bath life.

Though Philip Thicknesse was a quack rather than a doctor and less to be trusted than Smollett, he was as persistently angry, and there is much of interest in his *Memoirs and Anecdotes*, 1788–91, his *The Valetudinarian's Bath Guide*, 1780, and his *New Prose Bath Guide for the Year 1778*. Also in *The Triflers* and other anecdotal writing of the Rev. Richard Graves, rector of nearby Claverton for fifty-five years throughout the second half of the eighteenth century.

Bath's two eighteenth-century poets, the seamstress, Mary Chandler (*A Description of Bath*, 1734), and the gentleman of leisure, Christopher Anstey (*The New Bath Guide*, 1766), are valuable for the information they provide – if not as poets; there are also several anonymous accounts in prose and verse of much interest, including *A Step to the Bath*, 1700, *The Disease of Bath*, 1737, and *A Journey to Bath and Bristol*, undated but probably published at about the same time.

Beyond these, many of the well-known people who visited Bath commented on it in their letters or journals, from Pepys and Pope to James Boswell, Sarah Siddons, Mrs Thrale and Fanny Burney. And for general comments on Bath characters or visitors, Horace Walpole and Lord Hervey are, as usual, delightfully frank.

Among periodicals, the *Gentleman's Magazine*, and *Notes and Queries* are full of curious information about Bath characters during the city's great years. Much can also be gleaned by a careful reading of Bath's newspapers.

Nineteenth-century writers who drew on these sources and often added new material of their own included Richard Warner, *The History of Bath*, 1801; John Britton, *The History and Antiquities of Bath Abbey Church*, 1825; R. E. M. Peach, *Historic Houses in Bath and their Associations*, 1883, and *Life and Times of Ralph Allen*, 1885; and Charles G. Harper, *The Bath Road*, 1899.

In the twentieth century, A Barbeau's *Life and Letters at Bath in the Eighteenth Century*, 1904, is outstanding. Also useful are William Tyte's *Bath in the Eighteenth Century*, 1903; Lewis Melville's *Bath Under Beau Nash*, 1907; P. Rowland James's *The Baths of Bath in the 16th and Early 17th Centuries*, 1938; Cecil Roberts's *And so to Bath*, 1940; Benjamin Boyce's excellent life of Ralph Allen, *The Benevolent Man*, 1967; Walter Ison's *The Georgian Buildings of Bath*, 1969; David Gadd's *Georgian Summer*, 1971; and R. S. Neal's *Bath 1680–1850, A Social History*, an economic historian's investigation into the city's usually ignored working population.

NOTE: Quotations are given with their original spellings and punctuation. In *prose* quotations, however, modern practice has been adopted for capital letters.

Index

INDEX